Pleasures of the

VIETNAMESE TABLE

ALSO BY MAI PHAM

The Best of Vietnamese and Thai Cooking

Pleasures of the
VIETNAMESE TABLE

 Recipes and Reminiscences from Vietnam's Best

Market Kitchens, Street Cafés, and Home Cooks

MAI PHAM

HarperCollins*Publishers*

PLEASURES OF THE VIETNAMESE TABLE. Copyright © 2001 by Mai Pham. All rights reserved. Printed in the United States of America. No part of this book may be used or reproduced in any manner whatsoever without written permission except in the case of brief quotations embodied in critical articles and reviews. For information, address HarperCollins Publishers Inc., 10 East 53rd Street, New York, NY 10022.

HarperCollins books may be purchased for educational, business or sales promotional use. For information please write: Special Markets Department, HarperCollins Publishers Inc., 10 East 53rd Street, New York, NY 10022.

FIRST EDITION

Designed by Cassandra J. Pappas

Illustrations by Nancy Andre

Photography by Mai Pham

Library of Congress Cataloging-in-Publication Data
Pham, Mai.
Pleasures of the Vietnamese table: recipes and reminiscences from Vietnam's best market kitchens, street cafés, and home cooks/ Mai Pham.—1st ed.
p.   cm.
Includes index.
ISBN 0-06-019258-5
1. Cookery, Vietnamese.   I. Title.
TX724.5.V5 M35   2001
641.59597—dc21   00.066369

01 02 03 02 03 04 05 ❖/RRD 10 9 8 7 6 5 4 3 2 1

To my grandmother
HUYNH THI KIEN
for teaching me that food is love

And to
TRONG NGUYEN
for this and much more

Acknowledgments

In the Vietnamese tradition, all success results from the work, guidance and blessings of *many* people, including those who have passed on. So with the successful completion of this book, I first wish to thank my *ong ba,* or ancestors, for helping me to create and share this book, and my parents, Pham Van Xuan and Vo Thi Thom, for instilling in me a passion for food and cooking.

At Lemon Grass Restaurant—the source of much of my joy for the past twelve years— I thank my manager Kate Griffin, along with William Bernard, Thaddeus Winter, David Young, Quyen Ha, Tang Nguyen, Kiet Nguyen, Albert Castorena, Su Hoang, Hoang Ngo, Tuyet Lieu Ngo, Juan Camargo, Andre Douglas, and all the wonderful service staff for making our restaurant consistently the best year after year. To our great customers—your laughter, your applause and your loyalty make it all worthwhile.

My deepest gratitude goes to my business partner, Trong Nguyen, whose energy, talent, and sharp mind never cease to amaze and inpire me, and to our dynamic management team at World of Good Tastes and La Bou Bakery and Cafés. I'm proud to be working alongside such caring people as Marlene Underwood, Lisa Limcaco, Michael Kyalwazi, Suzanne Ferris, Angie Barrett, Alfonso Ozuna, Bette Chauvin, Trista Harman, Que Tran, Thuyen Nguyen, Huong Nguyen, Caryl Hearn, Maria Lurie and many others.

At HarperCollins, my thanks go to Susan Friedland, who first embraced the concept for this book after reading an article I'd written on *pho,* the Vietnamese beef noodle soup, and to Vanessa Stich, Roberto de Vicq de Cumptich, Betty Lew, David Koral and others for their very excellent work on the manuscript; to Carrie Weinberg and Gypsy Lovett for their publicity efforts; to my talented agent, Jane Dystel; to Cassandra Pappas for enhancing the recipes and stories with her artistic designs; and to our own staff graphic artists Michelle Khazaeepoul, for her creative contributions, and Nancy Andre for her lovely watercolors and pencil illustrations.

In the media, my thanks go to Laurie Ochoa, formerly of the *Los Angeles Times;* Susan Spungen of *Martha Stewart Living;* Michael Bauer, Miriam Morgan and former staff member Mary Ann Mariner of the *San Francisco Chronicle;* and to Martha Holmberg, Joanne Smart and Susie Middleton of *Fine Cooking,* for their keen interest in Vietnamese cuisine and for encouraging me to share my passion with a national audience.

I'm grateful to Tom and Ae Glasheen for both their friendship and generous help with recipe development; to Minh Xuan Ngo, Lan Ngo, Mai Hoang, Nickolay Kachagin, Tuy Nguyen, Jeff Drescher and Bridget Feighan for their invaluable help with recipe testing; to Nguyen Dinh Xuong for his help with Vietnamese language and translations; to Helen Burns and Janet Fletcher for their editorial input; to Quoc K. Tran for his meticulous research and to my siblings Phred Pham, Loc Pham and Denise Pham Healy for sharing and tasting recipes as well as answering food and computer questions.

In Vietnam, my gratitude goes to more street food vendors and cooks than I can possibly name here, folks who've showered me with great good and others who've supported my research over the years.

In Saigon, my sincere *cam on* goes to Pham Thi Ngoc Tinh, Nguyen Doan Cam Van, Nguyen Huu Hoang Trang, Dieu Ho and the Caravelle, New World, Omni and Huong Sen Hotels; in Hue, Nguyen Thi Hanh, Lai Thi Minh Huong of the Huong Giang Hotel and the Morin Hotel; in Hanoi, U.S. Ambassador Pete Peterson and his wife, Vi; U.S. Agricultural Trade Officer Ross Kreamer and his wife, Chris; cultural expert and journalist Huu Ngoc of The Gioi Publishing; Minh Tam, Dam Thanh, Pham Ba Khanh Thinh of Seasons of Hanoi Restaurant; the Nikko, Heritage, Metropole and Golden Key Hotels; in Can Tho and Sapa, the Victoria Hotel; in Danang, the Furama Hotel and in Nha Trang, the Ana Mandara Resort; and in Bangkok, the Amari Watergate, Shangri-La and Indra Regent Hotels.

I'm grateful to Marcia Selva and her staff at Global Spectrum in Washington, D.C., and her associates in Vietnam, including Tran Dinh Song, and Hoang Tran Anh and at Trails of IndoChina, Linh Nguyen and John Tue Nguyen, for their help with in-country travel arrangements and for their commitment to making the best of Vietnamese culture more accessible to Westerners.

Thanks to my favorite suppliers and purveyors, including Suong and Nho Pham, and Can and Oanh Pham, who grow the most beautiful Vietnamese herbs this side of the Pacific Ocean. To Jerry and Sidney Mahoney, for finding and bringing to us the best seafood; and to

Hemingway Fish, General Produce, Del Monte Meat, Saigon Market, Vinh Phat Market and Wing Wa Market, and to our friends at the Sacramento farmers' markets. When I think about what it all takes to bring the best to the Vietnamese table, I feel extremely grateful to these folks.

At The Culinary of Institute of America, my warmest thanks go to Ferdinand Metz, Tim Ryan and Mark Erickson for their support over the years in bringing Vietnamese culinary traditions to a wider professional audience. To the late Catherine Brandel, Toni Sakaguchi, Robert and Cathy Jorin, Ken Woytisek, Lars Kronmark, Robert Danhi, and Bill and Holly Briwa for their friendship and support, and for their dedication to teaching authentic Asian flavors. And last but not least, to Greg Drescher, whose insights, passion and long-standing commitment to the preservation of traditional cultures and cuisines around the world have greatly inspired my work. I share his vision and cherish his love and support.

Contents

✳

Pleasures of the

VIETNAMESE TABLE

Introduction

Heaven
Please make the rain fall
So I may have water to drink
So I may plow my rice field
So I may have my bowl of rice
And my fish in great slices
—A Vietnamese farmer's verse

RETURN TO VIETNAM

Vietnam today is a land of peace and action, of old and new. In the lush, emerald green countryside, women wearing traditional conical hats work diligently to transplant rice seedlings. At a floating market in the Mekong Delta, a couple maneuvers their boat past competing vendors, hoping to sell out their juicy crab apples. At pagodas surrounded by lotus-blooming ponds, elderly monks say their prayers as incense smoke swirls above the altar.

On the streets, where freshly painted billboards touting cellular phones stand next to soaring buildings, a driver with a live pig strapped on his motorcycle weaves in and out of traffic, heading to the slaughterhouse.

In recent years, since the opening of Vietnam to the Western world, there's a new sense of excitement. I can feel it each time I return. The streets are more crowded and the rooftops get higher. The market stalls are bursting with new merchandise, from yet more types of rice paper to the latest tennis shoe designs. Clothes are brighter and

Couple takes fruits to floating market in Can Tho.

more colorful, and the smiles seem wider. I love what I see, what I hear, and most of all, what I eat.

It's very different from the country that my family and I left more than twenty-five years ago, just days before Saigon fell to Communist rule on April 30, 1975. We'd left with the clothes on our backs, fighting our way through the pandemonium at the airport before climbing aboard a plane that would fly us to safety. In the distance I could see the artillery smoke surrounding the city. I remembered my frail grandmother back at the house. She stood at the front gate as we said good-bye, crying as I had never seen anyone cry before. She was fearful that we would never see one another again.

Six years ago, I ventured back to Vietnam for the first time. I had two dreams to fulfill—to reunite with my then ninety-six-year-old grandmother and to eat *pho* (rice noodle soup with beef and aromatic herbs), my favorite food on earth, on Vietnamese soil. What unfolded was something much more encompassing, something that would later deeply affect my life. I reconnected with my extended family for the first time in more than two decades. I made peace with my homeland, a country that had seen nothing but war and suffering for almost a century.

During my first trip back I spent most of my time in the Mekong Delta, in my ancestral village of Quoi Son, just being by my grandmother's side, making up for lost time. When I touched her silvery white hair, kissed her pinkish skin and tightly held her bony hands for the first time in more than twenty

Fresh herbs are eaten like vegetables.

My first reunion with my grandmother.

years, I felt such joy and relief. Not only had she survived, but she thrived. Granted she'd become older and weaker, but there were things about her that hadn't changed, like the wrinkles in her nose when she smiled, the way she laughed and her inquisitive demeanor.

As I walked around her home, the same house where several generations of my family had lived, I noticed that all the furniture, including the family altar, was still there. The picture of my grandfather—that handsome man with shoulder-length hair—still graced the altar, along with burning incense and offerings of fruit. And the kitchen, it still looked exactly the same. No walls, just a thatched roof supported by large beams. There were two clay stoves and a barbecue pit, all fueled by the coconut husks gathered from the plantation. It was in this modest kitchen that my grandmother prepared many splendid meals, and it was here that she instilled in me a passion for cooking.

EXPLORING THE LAND AND FOOD

Thanks to that nurturing reconnection, I became more at ease about being back. I started roaming the country, traveling the back roads, from the northern mountainous terrain of Sapa to the southern tip of Ha Tien. It was the first time since the war that I had ventured far outside of my hometown of Saigon.

But it wasn't until I savored my first bowl of *pho* that I finally came to terms with being back. I was so excited as I walked down the narrow alley near our home to find the little soup shop that my sister Denise and I once frequented. It was still there, still packed with hungry diners. For a moment I was taken aback by the noise, the slurping, the

An incense urn at a pagoda in Cholon, Saigon.

yelling of orders, the banging of dishes. The noodle man was there, bare chested, working in front of the steaming soup pot, swinging his copper wire basket of noodles, dipping them in and out of the hot water.

When my bowl arrived, I felt ecstatic. The noodles were so soft they practically melted. The broth had the buttery beefy flavor I remembered so fondly. Even the chili sauce tasted like real chili sauce. I looked up, hoping to see if anyone else around felt the same way, but all I heard was slurping.

In the weeks following, after many bowls of *pho,* I felt very much at home. I could see that the sins of war had been forgiven, that the animosity had dissipated, and that in peacetime, the Vietnamese—both southerners like myself and northerners—were actually friends, not foes.

I spent endless hours at places where I used to eat as a youngster—not at fancy restaurants, but at market stalls, street cafés and wherever I could catch up with home cooks. No

A member of the Hmong ethnic tribe and I in Sapa.

Father and son go to market in northern Vietnam.

matter where I traveled, I found myself lingering in front of stoves, watching the cooks chop and stir. I scrutinized their movements and facial expressions and chronicled as much as I could, both on paper and on film.

I ate and chatted with these cooks, sometimes at the very same market stall day after day. Sometimes I even followed them home for more secrets on how to prepare all the dishes that I love, from the best steamed rice rolls to the most fragrant warm soy milk with pandanus leaves.

THE WORLD OF PHO AND NOODLES

Since that first trip, I've gone back to Vietnam every year, to see my grandmother and to further explore the world of Vietnamese noodles and street foods. Each time I returned I ate endless versions of *pho* and immersed myself in all kinds of street and market foods. I also spent a lot of time with my aunts and uncles, learning about our favorite family recipes, dishes my mom used to make for us when we were still living in Saigon.

Pleasures of the Vietnamese Table is a collection of these recipes—dishes that I think are the best that Vietnam has to offer. They include noodles—noodle soups, noodle salads and noodle stir-fries—as well as other favorites. Although many are traditionally cooked and served at market stalls and street corners, they're easily replicated in a

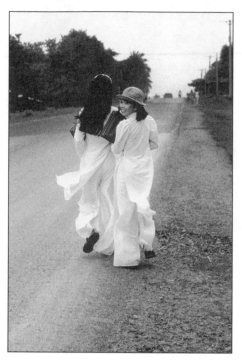

Schoolgirls dressed in the traditional ao dai.

home kitchen. In Vietnam, street foods are highly regarded and the people who cook them are considered master chefs. Many have spent a lifetime perfecting one, or at most a few, specialty recipes that are typically packed with flavors. Instead of relying on many courses to create a spectrum of tastes, they must deftly achieve this with just one bowl or plate. It makes sense, then, that if one wants to truly learn great Vietnamese cooking, one would focus on these dishes.

In developing the recipes, I've made every effort to retain and preserve the authenticity of each dish. Where modifications were necessary and appropriate, I've made sure the flavors remain true. Most recipes were given to me by the street vendors whom I was fortunate to work with over the course of my travels. Many have even become new additions to our menu at Lemon Grass Restaurant, much to the delight of our customers. Other recipes came from my mother and aunts and other home cooks. But regardless of the source, all have been tested and can be easily re-created in an American home kitchen.

Let me then take you to the parts of Vietnam that I love and share with you all the delectable flavors that I have been so fortunate to experience. Along the way, I'll share glimpses of the local culture and introduce you to the cooks who've enchanted me with the idea that love, life and food—when woven together against the backdrop of family and tradition—is the most beautiful form of human expression.

MAI PHAM

Vietnamese Cuisine: An Overview

FROM THE BEGINNING

I once asked my grandmother where she thought Vietnamese cuisine came from. After thinking about it for a few seconds, she started laughing, her hands waving in the air. "Where else but from our *ong ba* (our ancestors)?" she asked. That's my grandmother for you.

There's no question that Vietnamese cuisine is deeply rooted in the cooking of neighboring China. A quick look at our history shows that our ancestors came from China, part of a tribal group who migrated south and settled in the northern part of Vietnam about 1500 B.C. Over the centuries, empires rose and fell. By the second century B.C., the Chinese annexed the country and rigorously imposed their system of government and religion. They introduced ancestor worship and Confucianism and Buddhism, established schools to spread the Chinese script and levied taxes to support a system of mandarin rule. Over time, the Vietnamese began to adopt the food traditions of southern China, including the custom of eating with chopsticks, cooking by stir-frying and steaming and using ingredients such as noodles, soy sauce, ginger and tofu.

Being at a major crossroads of Southeast Asia, Vietnam was continually prone to other foreign influences as well. In the sixteenth century, European explorers started arriving, bringing foods from the New World, such as tomatoes and peanuts. During

the French rule, which lasted a hundred years from the mid-1800s to the mid-1900s, the Vietnamese learned to eat butter, yogurt, the baguette, coffee and vegetables like asparagus and artichokes. In addition, trading and migration between neighboring Thailand, Cambodia and Laos—all greatly influenced by India—led to the adoption of curries and spices into the local cooking.

But as much as Vietnamese cuisine has borrowed from or been influenced by foreign cultures, it has always managed to retain its unique character. When you look at it closely, what really sets it apart boils down to three main factors: the extensive use of *nuoc mam* (fish sauce) to season almost every dish, the high consumption of *rau thom* (aromatic herbs) and the distinctive style of eating small pieces of meat or seafood wrapped in lettuce or rice paper and dipped in sauce.

These characteristics apply to all three culinary regions of Vietnam, although each has a slightly different approach to cooking. In the rich, fertile south—the rice bowl of the country—the food is particularly vibrant and robust and makes liberal use of garlic, shallots and spices. Southern cooks are partial to sweet and sour flavors and eat more fresh herbs than in any other part of the country. Historically southerners have always been more open to foreign influences and cultures, as evidenced by the popularity of Indian- and French-inspired foods in Saigon. In the former imperial capital of Hue and in the central region where the climate is cooler, the food tends to be spicier and heavier. The preferred noodles are thicker and broths are tinged with bright red chilies. The seat of the Nguyen dynasty from the early 1800s to the mid-1900s, Hue is known for its refined royal cuisine. Royal banquets are said to have included more than fifty dishes, all elaborately and artfully prepared by hand, many in miniature sizes. Today, Hue dishes are often prepared in a similar fashion.

In the harsh, mountainous terrain of the north, the cooking is simple and straightforward, in large part because the region suffered more deprivation from the war than any other region. Dipping sauces are made saltier so they can be eaten with lots of rice. Soups are mostly clear broths with vegetables and only a little meat. Sticky rice is served without the rich mung bean paste and the shredded coconut toppings common in the south.

Despite that, the north has its own great culinary traditions as well. Some of the best dishes originated in this area, including *pho* (rice noodle soup with beef), *cha ca* (grilled fish seasoned with dill) and *bun cha* (grilled pork with rice noodles). In fact, it is these great dishes that have placed Hanoi back on the culinary map in recent years.

FUNDAMENTALS OF VIETNAMESE FLAVORS

As you read and experiment with the recipes in this book, you'll come away with the impression that Vietnamese cooking isn't about complicated techniques. Rather, it's about securing the freshest possible ingredients and, with minimal handling, combining them in a way that showcases their simple, natural goodness.

Unlike the European approach of blending and harmonizing ingredients as one sees in slow braises or sauce reductions, the Vietnamese prefer to cook by layering flavors, textures and temperatures so that the ingredients remain separate and distinct. Take *pho bo,* for example. The noodles and broth provide substance and by themselves the flavors are rather delicate. However, when eaten with fresh herbs, chilies and limes, the flavors are immediately transformed, becoming spicy, aromatic and tangy all at the same time.

Picture another scenario at a typical multiple-course family meal: simmered Ginger Chicken, which is fairly well seasoned, is served with a delicately flavored soup, a steamed vegetable dish, a stir-fry and some steamed unsalted rice. But the meal isn't quite complete without a platter of fresh herbs and a bowl of spicy salty fish dipping sauce to tie together all the flavors. For the cook, the ultimate aim is to present the diner with a feast of contrasts across the entire meal, as well as with each bite.

THE VIETNAMESE PANTRY

To create delicious and authentic Vietnamese food, it's important that you have a firm grasp on the essential ingredients listed below. The building blocks of Vietnamese flavors, they're used to make dipping sauces and season foods. You can use this list as a shopping guide for stocking your Vietnamese pantry. Fish sauce, fresh herbs and rice noodles are so integral to our cuisine that I've provided additional information under separate sections.

You can buy all the ingredients at Asian markets and possibly in well-stocked supermarkets and specialty stores. If you have access to an Asian market but don't live near one, consider buying extra to save for later use. Many items (such as fish sauce and dried rice noodles) are shelf-stable and will last for some time. Fresh ingredients such as vegetables, aromatic roots, meats and seafood should be bought as close to cooking time as possible. In some instances where I think it might be helpful, I've included my favorite brands. However, these preferences will probably change as new products continue to enter the marketplace each year.

Sauces and Spices

Fish sauce *nuoc mam* (Viet Huong, Flying Lion Phu Quoc, Saigon)

Almost every Vietnamese dish is seasoned with this quintessential sauce. A liquid extraction made from fermented fish and salt, *nuoc mam* is used to salt and enhance foods and to make dipping sauces. When cooking, start with a small amount and increase as necessary. Wipe the opening of the bottle clean after each use and store on the counter or in the refrigerator. Fish sauce will last almost indefinitely. (For more information, see page 24.)

Bean sauce *tuong hot* (La Bo De, Dragonfly)

Made from whole or crushed fermented soybeans, this sharp-tasting sauce is used to season stir-fries and to make sauces. When used in a dipping sauce (such as one served with salad rolls), it's generally cooked with vinegar, puréed onions and sometimes sticky rice, then garnished with chilies and ground peanuts. In recent years, a ready-to-serve dipping sauce called *tuong goi cuon* (salad rolls sauce) has become available under the brand La Bo De.

Hoisin sauce *sot tuong* (Koon Chun)

Made from soybean purée and five-spice powder, this condiment is used in dipping sauces, marinades and stir-fries. When used as a dipping sauce, hoisin is prepared the same way as the bean sauce above. Many Vietnamese restaurants use this sauce for salad rolls and for serving with *pho*.

Ground chili paste *tuong ot toi* (Rooster)

An important condiment, this fiery sauce is made with coarsely ground red chilies, garlic and vinegar. It's used to garnish sauces and noodle and rice dishes.

Chilies and dipping sauces are key to Vietnamese cuisine.

Oyster sauce *dau hao* (Hop Sing Lung, Ng Yup or any higher-priced brands)

A thick brown sauce made from oyster extract, salt, sugar and spices, this seasoning ingredient is used to add savoriness to Chinese-style dishes. It does a wonderful job of coating meats and seafood, giving them a shiny, succulent look. When using this sauce, reduce the amount of salt or fish sauce in the dish, as it can be salty. For a vegetarian version, try vegetarian mushroom oyster sauce.

Soy sauce *nuoc tuong* (Pearl River Bridge, Kikkoman)

Although not used as extensively as fish sauce, soy sauce is a common seasoning in vegetarian and stir-fried dishes. Vietnamese cooks make delicious dipping sauces by combining it with lime juice, garlic and chilies. (For Soy-Lime Dipping Sauce, see page 29.)

Rice and Noodles

Rice *gao*

The Vietnamese prefer *gao thom,* the long-grain jasmine variety, and use the absorption method to cook rice. For best flavor, serve the rice promptly after it's finished cooking. Asian markets carry dozens of brands and the best way to select rice is to just try several and stick to those you like. (For more information on cooking rice, see page 136.)

Rice, glutinous or sweet *gao nep* (Elephant, Erawan)

Sticky rice is used extensively in desserts and breakfast items. More dense and starchy than regular rice, it's typically used to make puddings and fillings for banana leaf–wrapped cakes. Sticky rice is usually soaked in water overnight, then steamed.

Rice flour *bot gao* (Elephant, Erawan)

Not to be confused with sweet sticky (glutinous) rice flour, this is the most common starch in Vietnamese cooking. It's made from short-grain rice and used to make sweet and savory noodles, crepes, dumplings and cakes. When shopping for this item, make sure it's rice flour from Thailand, not the generic rice flour used in baking.

Rice paper *banh trang* (Kim Tar, Elephant, Erawan)

Rice papers are thin wrappers made from rice flour (sometimes in combination with tapioca starch), salt and water and are sun-dried on bamboo trays, which give them their distinctive pattern. They're available in round, square and triangular shapes. When purchasing rice paper, look for packages with thin, translucent sheets. Avoid the thick, opaque ones. Before using, you must reconstitute dried rice papers in warm water until pliable. They're used to wrap salad rolls and spring rolls. (See page 97.)

Rice vermicelli *bun* (Thap Chua, GGG)

Sold as rice sticks, these dried small, wiry noodles are used extensively in Vietnamese cuisine to make noodle salads and soups. More fragile than pasta,

The most common noodles are rice sticks (left), rice vermicelli and bean threads.

they need less cooking time. Rinse well in water after cooking and let the noodles become dry and sticky before serving. In Vietnam, these noodles are sold fresh, but in the United States (except in a few Asian markets) they're only available dried. (See page 112.)

Rice sticks *banh pho* (Elephant, Two Ladies, Kim Tar)

These flat, thin dried noodles resemble linguine and are available in several widths—small, medium and large. Also made from rice flour, salt and water, they're used in noodle soups and stir-fries. To expedite the cooking time, these noodles are first soaked in water, then boiled. (For information on cooking rice noodles for *pho* and other dishes, see page 53.)

Other Ingredients

Coconut milk *nuoc cot dua* (Mae Ploy, Chao Koh, Taste of Thai)

Coconut milk is used to enrich curries and desserts. In Vietnam, cooks either make it by squeezing grated coconut with hot water or buy it freshly made at the market. In the United States, the canned products are easily available although not quite as good. When buying this product, make sure it is unsweetened (see page 140).

Fragrant herbs *rau thom*

The Vietnamese eat an enormous amount of herbs. A family meal often consists of a table salad, which includes lettuce and different varieties of mint and basil. To eat, diners just snip off the sprigs and add to their bowls or plates, creating little salads as they go. Fresh herbs are also used as garnishes and accompaniments to soups, salads, and noodle dishes. For a more detailed list of Vietnamese herbs, please see page 40.

Peanuts *dau phong*

An important ingredient in Vietnamese cuisine, peanuts are used in a great variety of dishes. They're typically roasted, then chopped and used to add richness and texture to many noodle salad and rice dishes.

Tamarind pulp *me*

Made from the flesh of tamarind pods, this thick paste is used to add tartness to soups and stir-fried dishes. The seedless pulp is sold as blocks (a liquid concentrate is also available but not as good) and needs to be softened in warm water before it is strained and the juice is added to food. Look for this product in the dried food section of Asian markets.

TECHNIQUES AND APPROACHES

Before proceeding to the kitchen, read through the first chapter to gain a good grasp of how Vietnamese flavors are combined and how a meal comes together. Having this crucial information will be very helpful once you dive into your first recipe. Also read the recipe thoroughly before cooking and try to visualize the techniques and imagine how the flavors may taste. I've often found that this process can help you become better prepared for the actual cooking.

Fortunately, Vietnamese cuisine isn't, for the most part, complicated. Because it relies so much on dipping sauces and the contrasting of flavors and textures, the cooking techniques are basic—boiling or simmering, stir-frying or frying, steaming and grilling. There is less to do at the stove since much of the creation of flavor happens at the table, where the diner dips this food into that sauce, and eats this with that.

Perhaps one of the most important steps in the kitchen is the pounding of spices in a mortar and pestle to make dipping sauces. This pounding action creates more intense flavors than, say, the blending motion of a food processor. This is particularly important when making salad dressings and dipping sauces because the flavors need to be intense enough to balance other delicate-tasting foods such as steamed rice or steamed vegetables.

Another technique that deserves special attention is the layering of ingredients, especially in noodle dishes and rice dishes with raw herbs and vegetables. As discussed in the previous chapter, the Vietnamese cook strives to create flavors by layering different yet complementary ingredients and by presenting them in such a way that they remain separate. For this reason, vegetables and meat are often cut into thin slices or strips and are handled with great care so they don't break down during cooking and become too blended and homogeneous.

SPECIAL EQUIPMENT AND TOOLS

Most Vietnamese dishes can be easily prepared with regular pots and pans. However, the following tools will make the job easier and the food will come out tasting and looking better.

For dishes that require frying and stir-frying, a 14- or 16-inch wok is the most practical for everyday cooking. It's big enough so you can cook quickly without crowding the pan. Plus you can always cook a small amount in a large wok but not vice versa. (You can also use a wok as a steamer by placing a steamer on a rack over boiling water.) You might also consider buying a couple of sizes of nonstick pans and skillets, especially if you want to make Vietnamese crepes and pan-seared tofu. For simmering, you can use any medium-sized pot or saucepan.

Claypots are wonderful cooking vessels for preparing deeply flavored braised dishes. I always have a few different kinds and sizes in my kitchen, and I also use them as serving dishes. (For more information on handling and cooking with claypots, see page 144.)

A Chinese two-tier aluminum steamer is a great tool to have if you do a lot of steaming. I have a 16-inch steamer that I use all the time to steam whole fish and chicken, sticky rice and various rice cakes. (For more information on Chinese steamers, see page 172.)

The Japanese mandoline is another valuable tool. It can cut vegetables into delicate, attractive slices and strips (see page 84). You can achieve these cuts with a knife, but it requires more patience and practice. If you like eating salads as much as I do, consider investing in a mandoline.

For noodle soup recipes, buy a long-handled wire strainer for dunking noodles in boiling water and some large, deep Chinese- or Japanese-style bowls in which to serve them.

However, if you buy only one thing for the Vietnamese kitchen, make it a mortar and pestle (see page 31). A useful tool for making dipping sauces and marinades, the mortar is great for pounding chilies, garlic and herbs.

CREATING A MEAL FROM THIS BOOK

From a menu-planning standpoint, keep in mind that this book consists of two kinds of recipes—street or market foods and home-style dishes. In Vietnam, when you're hungry for a certain street food, you'd go to your favorite vendor and order that specialty. Then, if you want something else, you'd move to another vendor and eat another specialty and so on, until you're full. What's especially rewarding about hopping from one street café or market kitchen to another is that you get to eat foods prepared by true masters, people who've worked with the same small set of recipes for years, often decades.

To create a similar experience at home, you can offer several dishes at the same time. For example, Sizzling Saigon Crepes (page 117) and Vietnamese Spring Rolls (page 92) make a fun roll-your-own meal since both call for wrapping foods with lettuce and herbs. If you're still hungry you can serve Hue Chicken Salad (page 79) or one of the many other salads in this book. Recipes in chapters 2, 3 and 4 are particularly appropriate for such casual menus. To a Westerner, these meals are reminiscent of a "grazing" menu, made up of several appetizer-type dishes as opposed to a more predictable first and second course affair.

Grilled meat with fresh herbs and rice paper as served in Hoi An.

If you're interested in serving *pho* or one of the other meal-in-a-bowl soups in chapter 2, you won't need to worry about offering many other dishes. With a generous portion of noodles and the towering plate of herbs that should accompany the dish, *pho* certainly has enough carbohydrates, proteins and vegetables to make a satisfying meal in itself. And in the *pho* tradition, one can always finish the meal with delicious Vietnamese Coffee (page 222) or one of the many sweet drinks, such as Iced Red Bean Pudding with Coconut Milk (page 212).

For a more home-style meal, refer to recipes in chapters 5, 6 and 7. A typical Vietnamese family meal consists of two meat or seafood dishes, a vegetable side dish and a soup. Since the foundation of such meals is rice, it's important that it be properly cooked and served steaming hot in generous quantities. For tips on cooking rice, please refer to page 136. Some menu suggestions are also included in the back of this book. Additional information also can be obtained by visiting http://www.lemongrassrestaurant.com.

chapter one

Layer after Layer

Essential Sauces, Condiments and Aromatic Herbs

Vietnamese Dipping Sauce

Light Vietnamese Dipping Sauce

Ginger-Lime Dipping Sauce

Vietnamese Bean Dipping Sauce

Soy-Lime Dipping Sauce

Sweet Soy Sauce with Chilies and Ginger

Chili-Lime Dipping Sauce

Scallion Oil

Fried Shallots

Caramel Sauce

Roasted Peanuts

Shallot-Garlic Marinade

Marinated Daikon and Carrots

Marinated Chilies

Chicken Stock

Jars of condiments at a street vendor's stand. The marinated daikon and carrots are used to garnish and flavor sauces.

Baskets of bird chilies, favored for their flavor and heat.

E ach day at the crack of dawn, Chi Tuyet (Sister Tuyet) and her cousin arrive at the Ben Thanh Market in Saigon with baskets of rice noodles and crates of herbs and vegetables. For the past fifteen years, they've been coming here to sell their famed *bun thit nuong* (rice noodles with grilled pork). It's the only dish they offer, but it's a dish that unveils the secrets of Vietnamese cooking.

After she unloads her ingredients and starts the charcoal brazier for the meat, Chi Tuyet begins to uncork her jars of dipping sauces, wiping and lining them up in the front row of the stall. The largest jar contains *nuoc cham* (Vietnamese dipping sauce). The others are filled to the rim with crispy shallots, pickled garlic and cucumbers, fresh chilies, chili paste, ground peanuts, scallion oil and dried shrimp. "This is what drives my business," boasts Chi Tuyet, pointing to the beautiful array of sauces and condiments.

While we speak, Chi Tuyet places the pork skewers on the grill. As the meat sizzles and the charcoals flare, a delicious aroma ascends. It is now mid-morning and the entire food section hums with activity. Cooks are busy ladling soups, grilling meats and filling orders. A group of hungry shoppers stops to inspect a steaming pot of soup with crab dumplings. A man carrying a block of ice twice his size tries to squeeze through. Chi Tuyet slips the smoky pork off the skewers and places it on a bed of soft, cool noodles and crunchy herbs and greens. She garnishes the bowl with marinated daikon and carrots, scallion oil and chopped peanuts.

To eat, I add a generous amount of *nuoc cham* before tossing the noodles a few times. After one bite, I can understand immediately what Chi Tuyet had meant when she said earlier that the success of her food—and her business—depends on these very sauces and toppings. Even though the noodle dish is made with all kinds of ingredients, the flavors don't begin to come together until the final sauce and condiments are added. The sweet and spicy sauce immediately enhances the dish while the scallion oil gives it savoriness. A sprinkling of roasted peanuts adds richness and nuttiness and a dab of chili paste gives the dish a fiery finish. Without these toppings, *bun thit nuong* wouldn't be the fabulous dish that it is.

In fact, as I look around at the food stalls around Chi Tuyet, every vendor has the same attractive display of condiments. It seems clear that no matter what is being served, these accompaniments are every bit as important as the main dishes themselves.

This chapter contains the essential dipping sauces and condiments that accompany many of the recipes in this book. Together they make up the most basic component of Vietnamese cuisine. Most are simple and quick to make and can be easily prepared in advance and stored in the refrigerator.

One thing to keep in mind as you're preparing them is the critical role that they play in balancing the flavors of other dishes or the meal as a whole. For example, if a noodle or rice dish calls for scallion oil or fried shallots, make sure you serve it that way. Otherwise, the dish will lack flavors and not be balanced. To a novice cook, some of the dipping sauces may seem overly seasoned and salty, or too sour, or even bland (like the Light Vietnamese Dipping Sauce, which is supposed to be delicate, so it won't overpower the accompanying rice cake with shrimp dish). Reserve judgment until you have tasted them with other components of the dish.

These principles underscore a recurring theme that makes Vietnamese cooking particularly distinct from other Asian cuisines. Flavors are built on several levels—by layering meat or seafood with starch and fresh herbs, by contrasting the hot with the cool, the soft with the crunchy, and by using dipping sauces and condiments to blend them all together on a plate or in a bowl.

VIETNAMESE DIPPING SAUCE

nuoc cham

Nuoc cham is a must at every Vietnamese table, no matter what is served. You can use this condiment for dipping meat, seafood and vegetables, and for drizzling on rice. When serving it with steamed meats (such as steamed chicken), I often reduce the water by half so the sauce is more concentrated.

You can often determine a family's roots just by looking at and tasting their *nuoc cham*. If it's clear and dotted with chopped chilies, the cook is probably from the central or northern regions, where a simple and straightforward version is preferred. But if it's diluted with water and lime juice and sweetened with sugar, one can surmise that the cook is from the verdant south.

Although it will keep up to two weeks in the refrigerator, *nuoc cham* is best when freshly made. I prefer the intense flavor of the tiny Thai bird chilies, but any hot chilies will do.

1. Cut the chilies into thin rings. Remove one-third of the chilies and set aside for garnish. Place the remaining chilies, garlic and sugar in a mortar and pound into a coarse, wet paste. (If you don't have a mortar, just chop with a knife.) Transfer to a small bowl and add the water, lime juice and fish sauce. Stir well to dissolve. Add the reserved chilies and carrots. Set aside for 10 minutes before serving.

NOTE: *Nuoc cham* is very amenable to variations and adaptations. In Vietnam, cooks like to use various vegetables to flavor the sauce, such as thinly sliced marinated daikon and carrots, ginger, scallion oil or peanuts and even slices of kohlrabi and the core of a white cabbage. Each impart a distinctive savoriness.

3 Thai bird chilies or
   1 serrano chili, or to taste
1 clove garlic, sliced
3 tablespoons sugar
⅔ cup warm water
1½ tablespoons fresh lime juice
5 tablespoons fish sauce
2 tablespoons finely shredded
   carrots for garnish
   (optional)

Bottles of nuoc mam, the quintessential seasoning sauce.

Nuoc Mam, the Quintessential Sauce

Without good fish sauce, the father's daughter will not shine
—Vietnamese proverb

I have always been struck by the above saying. On one level, it points to the Vietnamese view of the universe and how everything is seen from the family's perspective. The implied pronoun—in this case "she"—is replaced with the "father's daughter." On another level, it suggests that without good fish sauce, the quintessential sauce of Vietnamese cuisine, food can never taste good, no matter how talented the cook.

While the saying about the fish sauce may sound a bit exaggerated, it really isn't. At our own home in Saigon we used fish sauce at every meal in two different ways—for making dipping sauce and for seasoning food. Whenever we sat down to the table, there was a bowl of *nuoc cham,* which is the diluted dipping sauce made from *nuoc mam,* the concentrated fish sauce. It wasn't particularly impressive, just a clear, amber-tinted sauce with bits of garlic and chilies, but somehow it often ended up being the highlight of the meal. If one dish was deemed wonderful, the *nuoc cham* would take credit. If an entire meal was spectacular, well, it was the sauce that tied the flavors together.

In our family, my sister Denise was the only person entrusted with the task of making the sauce. Her version was always consistent, a guarantee of a perfect meal. To this day, whenever we get together she's still the *nuoc cham* master.

She usually begins the ritual by smashing garlic cloves. Using a stone mortar and pestle, she pounds them with chilies and sugar until they become a paste. (The sugar eases the process and keeps the chilies from splashing into the eyes.) Then she juices a lime, gently scraping off the pulp, making sure the inner white flesh doesn't get too bruised and make the sauce bitter. The lime juice is then combined with the fish sauce and chili mixture for an interesting balance of sweet and sour. The prized concoction is now ready to be placed in the middle of the family table.

In Vietnam, the best fish sauce comes from *ca com* or *ca linh,* both of the anchovy family, and are made by small producers like Tran Thien and his wife Kim Sa, whom I met on a trip to Ha Tien, not too far from the fish sauce capital of Phu Quoc Island off the southern coast of Vietnam. Thien grew up helping his father make *nuoc mam*—first for family consumption and later for sale at the local market. In recent years he's decided to expand the family business, hoping to get in on the international market. "The country is rebounding after all the war years. *Nuoc mam* is now very popular throughout the world and my dream is to make the best product and export it," he says.

To stay on schedule, Tran contracts with a local fisherman who brings him fresh *ca com*, highly favored for its flavor and oil content. Since his house sits right on the river, the boat unloads it at the back door. After rinsing the fish, he transfers them to a tank where they're layered with one-third of the fish weight in salt. The fish are left to ferment in the brine for four months, after which a liquid is collected, drip by drip, and then pumped back into the tank. This simultaneous percolation and fermentation process continues for about eight months, after which it is siphoned and bottled.

The first extraction contains 35 to 38 percent protein and is sold as *nuoc mam nhi* (premium grade), which commands a considerable price tag. The second and third pressings are made by adding more brine to the same batch of fish and allowing it to ferment for a much shorter cycle. They're sold as *nuoc mam thuong* (regular fish sauce) and *nuoc mam kho* (cooking fish sauce). The latter pressings have less flavor and are generally used for cooking as opposed to making dipping sauces.

In the United States, it's difficult to distinguish premium grades from lesser ones because they're not bound by any labeling standards. In general, the higher-priced bottles containing a lighter-colored sauce tend to be better. In Vietnam, the premium product is slightly viscous and lighter in color than the dark brown liquid common in the West. It's best to try several brands and stick with those that you like. I find that Viet Huong, Flying Lion Phu Quoc and Golden Boy (all made in Thailand) are best for dipping sauces and the more pungent products such as Squid, Tiparos and Saigon are better for cooking. But in recent years there's been a deluge of new brands entering the marketplace. With the improved trade relations between the U.S. and Vietnam, I suspect we'll see even more in the near future.

LIGHT VIETNAMESE DIPPING SAUCE

 nuoc cham lat

MAKES 1¼ CUPS

1 cup raw shrimp shells

2 cups water

3½ tablespoons fish sauce

4 tablespoons sugar

1 teaspoon rice vinegar

1 to 2 Thai bird chilies or
½ serrano chili, cut into
thin rings

One of the greatest rewards of working in the food business is meeting other great cooks. Pham Thi Ngoc Tinh is one of them. Passionate about the cooking of her native Hue, she's made it her charge to preserve it. At her small, family-run Thuong Chi Restaurant in Saigon, she specializes in central regional cooking, reviving recipes that have been forgotten or are no longer cooked.

This is the dipping sauce Tinh prepares to accompany many Hue specialties, such as *banh beo* (Steamed Rice Cakes with Shrimp, page 105). Unlike the all-purpose Vietnamese Dipping Sauce, which is southern in influence, this recipe is delicately flavored with shrimp broth. If you don't have shrimp shells, use whole shrimp.

1. Combine the shrimp shells and water in a small pan. Bring to a boil, then reduce the heat and simmer for 5 minutes. Strain and set aside to cool.
2. Measure 1 cup shrimp broth and place in a bowl. Add the fish sauce, sugar, vinegar and chilies, and stir well. This sauce will keep up to 2 weeks if refrigerated in a covered jar.

GINGER-LIME DIPPING SAUCE

nuoc mam gung

MAKES ABOUT ¾ CUP

This is probably one of my favorite standby sauces. Intensely gingery and spicy, it goes well with foods that have been simply prepared, such as steamed or grilled chicken, meat or seafood. Although this sauce will keep for up to two weeks, I prefer to make it fresh because the ginger tends to lose its sharp flavors when held overnight.

1 teaspoon chopped garlic
2 to 3 Thai bird chilies or
   1 serrano chili, chopped
3 tablespoons sugar
3 tablespoons minced ginger
¼ cup fish sauce
2 tablespoons fresh lime juice
3 tablespoons water

1. Place the garlic, chilies, sugar and ginger in a mortar and pound into a paste. (You can also chop by hand.) Transfer to a small bowl and add the fish sauce, lime juice and water. Stir well to combine. Set aside for 15 minutes before serving.

VIETNAMESE BEAN DIPPING SAUCE

 tuong goi cuon

MAKES 1½ CUPS

¼ cup fermented whole soybeans
    (page 225)

½ cup water

⅓ cup unsweetened coconut
    milk (page 140)

2 tablespoons rice vinegar

3 tablespoons chopped yellow
    onion

2 tablespoons sugar

GARNISHES

1 tablespoon ground chili paste,
    or to taste (page 225)

1 tablespoon chopped Roasted
    Peanuts (page 35)

Unlike the clear *nuoc cham,* this dipping sauce is quite thick and used with dishes such as Rice Paper–Wrapped Salad Rolls and Grilled Shrimp on Sugarcane (pages 95 and 125). There are many versions of this recipe, including one that my mother likes to make with sticky rice as a thickener. In Hue, the sauce often includes ground pork and liver.

This recipe is very simple to make and delicious, especially if you can find fermented whole soybeans. You can also embellish it with garlic, chilies and ginger and serve it on grilled fish, chicken and beef. If you can't find soybeans, substitute ⅓ cup hoisin sauce and omit the sugar.

1. Place the soybeans, water, coconut milk, vinegar, onion and sugar in a blender or food processor and process just until smooth. Transfer the mixture to a saucepan and bring to a boil over moderate heat. (If you don't have a food processor, cook the soybean mixture first, then beat with a whisk.) Reduce the heat and simmer until the sauce thickens enough to coat a spoon, about 5 minutes. Add a little water if it's too thick. Set aside to cool.

2. To serve, transfer to individual sauce bowls and garnish each with chili paste and chopped peanuts. This sauce will keep up to 2 weeks if refrigerated in a tight-lidded jar.

SOY-LIME DIPPING SAUCE

nuoc tuong pha

MAKES ABOUT 1 CUP

This vegetarian dipping sauce can be made with any soy sauce, including the Japanese-style Kikkoman, although the Vietnamese prefer the lighter-bodied Chinese-style products marketed under the brands Kim Lan, Bo De and Pearl River Bridge. Like dipping sauces made with fish sauce, you can embellish this with different aromatics such as ginger and cilantro.

1. Place the garlic, chilies and sugar in a mortar and pound into a paste. (You can also chop the garlic and chilies by hand.) Transfer to a small bowl and add the soy sauce, lime juice and water. Stir until well blended. This sauce will keep up to 3 weeks if stored in the refrigerator in a tight-lidded jar.

1 clove garlic

2 fresh Thai bird chilies

2½ tablespoons sugar

⅓ cup soy sauce, preferably Chinese style

2½ tablespoons fresh lime juice with pulp

¼ cup water, or to taste

Shallots and chilies form the aromatic base of many dishes.

SWEET SOY SAUCE WITH CHILIES AND GINGER

 nuoc tuong den ot

MAKES ½ CUP

3 tablespoons sweet soy sauce
   (page 31)

2 tablespoons water

1 tablespoon minced ginger,
   preferably young ginger

1 teaspoon ground chili paste
   (page 225)

2 to 3 Thai bird chilies or
   1 serrano chili, cut into
   thin rings

Whenever I'm in Saigon, I can't resist going to the Chinatown section of Cholon to look for Hainan chicken, a steamed chicken dish served with rice cooked in chicken broth. What makes it particularly wonderful is this sweet soy dipping sauce filled with chopped ginger and chili paste. I've found that it's good on anything steamed, including steamed vegetables and dumplings, as well as boiled noodles.

1. Combine all the ingredients in a small bowl and set aside for 10 minutes before serving so the flavors are well blended. This sauce will keep for 2 weeks if stored in the refrigerator in a tight-lidded jar.

CHILI-LIME DIPPING SAUCE

 nuoc mam chanh

MAKES ABOUT ½ CUP

1 or 2 cloves garlic

3 Thai bird chilies, chopped,
   or to taste

3 tablespoons sugar

3 tablespoons fish sauce

3 tablespoons freshly squeezed
   lime juice with some pulp
   and segments

3 tablespoons water

This spicy and limey dipping sauce is guaranteed to add zip to steamed and grilled foods and even salads. If you have a mortar and pestle, put it to work. This is one dish that benefits greatly from the pounding of the fresh chilies.

Make sure to use fresh lime and gently scrape the segments and pulp into the sauce. For a real authentic touch, add about a cup of thinly cut strips (about 1/16 inch wide) of cucumber to the sauce. Serve the sauce with fried or grilled fish or rice.

1. Place the garlic, chilies and sugar in a mortar and pound into a paste. (You can also chop the chilies and garlic by hand.) Transfer to a small bowl and add the fish sauce and lime juice and pulp. Set aside for 15 minutes for the flavors to develop. This sauce will keep for up to 2 weeks stored the refrigerator in a tight-lidded jar.

The Mortar and Pestle

In the Vietnamese kitchen, the mortar and pestle is an important tool for pulverizing herbs, spices and other ingredients. The pounding imparts a more intense flavor than chopping and mincing. I use a mortar and pestle to make dipping sauces and marinades and to grind roasted peanuts and toasted rice paper. Meatballs and shrimp and fish pastes can also be prepared with one. Although a small food processor can also do the job, it isn't quite the same. Instead of pounding and mashing the ingredients into irregular pieces (which is desired in a Vietnamese dipping sauce), the machine chops and minces in a more uniform fashion.

When using the pestle, pound it freely in an up-and-down motion. Many novices make the mistake of pressing (as opposed to pounding) the pestle into the mortar, which tends to make the job harder and longer. Once in a while, run the pestle in a circular motion against the sides of the mortar to push the ingredients back into the center.

For grinding spices and herbs, buy a stone—not wooden—mortar and pestle and one that's six inches or wider at the rim so the ingredients don't spill out so easily. The stone version, with its rough surfaces, does a better job of pulverizing spices and herbs while the wooden one is more appropriate for pounding soft, fleshy ingredients, such as green papayas.

SCALLION OIL

 mo hanh

MAKES ½ CUP

¼ cup vegetable oil
5 scallions, green parts only, cut
   into thin rings

I always have a small jar of this simple and versatile condiment in my kitchen. It can be used to garnish everything from rice, noodles, soups and salads to grilled meats and is particularly useful for enhancing the savory flavor of vegetarian dishes. If you refrigerate scallion oil, bring it to room temperature before serving.

1. Heat the oil in a small pan over moderate heat. Add the scallions and stir 10 seconds. Immediately remove from the heat and transfer the oil with the scallions to a small bowl. Place in the refrigerator to cool for 10 minutes. (This helps the scallions stay green.) Remove and set aside at room temperature until ready to serve. This sauce will keep up to 2 weeks stored in the refrigerator in a tight-lidded jar.

Scallion oil provides a wonderful savory flavor.

FRIED SHALLOTS

hanh phi

Like scallion oil, fried shallots add a new dimension to savory dishes. Use this important garnish on noodle dishes and foods that have been simply prepared, like steamed dishes.

When frying the shallots, keep a close eye on them as they can turn from golden to brown in seconds. I remove the shallots from the oil about 10 seconds before I think they're ready because they'll continue to cook from their own heat.

5 shallots, cut crosswise into ⅛-inch-thick slices (about ½ cup)

1 cup vegetable oil

1. Spread the shallots out on paper towels and set aside to air-dry for 30 minutes.
2. Combine the shallots and oil in a skillet and bring to a slow boil. Reduce the heat to low and cook until the shallots are golden, about 15 minutes. Stir so the shallots brown evenly.
3. Remove with a slotted spoon or strain the oil through a wire-mesh sieve. Transfer the shallots to a plate or tray lined with paper towels. (Discard the oil or save it to use as a cooking oil in stir-fries.) Once cool, the shallots are ready to use. If stored in a jar with a tight lid at room temperature, the shallots will keep up to 1 week.

CARAMEL SAUCE

 nuoc mau

MAKES ½ CUP

½ cup sugar
⅓ cup boiling water

This is one of the most important sauces for grilled meats, claypot specialties and other simmered dishes. It adds body and color to foods while imparting a sweet, smoky flavor. Be very careful when making this because burnt sugar is extremely hot. To avoid overcooking the sugar, bring the water to a boil before starting the recipe.

1. Place the sugar in a small, heavy-bottomed saucepan over moderate heat. The sugar will melt and start to caramelize in about 2 to 3 minutes. Stir a few times (the edges will start to brown fast) and let the mixture bubble until it turns dark brown, about another minute or so. Quickly but carefully remove the pan from the heat and slowly stir in the boiling water. Stand back as the mixture might splatter. Set aside to cool. If stored in a tight-lidded jar at room temperature, this sauce will keep up to 1 month.

ROASTED PEANUTS

dau phong ran

MAKES 1 CUP

The Vietnamese love peanuts and eat them in many different ways. They boil them and eat them as snacks and add them to soups and desserts. But the most popular way of preparing peanuts is to roast them and use them as a garnish for noodles, salads and sticky rice. Store-bought peanuts are a substitute, but freshly roasted peanuts are much more flavorful.

1 cup raw, shelled peanuts, skins removed

1. Place the peanuts on a cookie tray and bake in a preheated 325-degree oven until golden, about 20 minutes. Halfway into the baking, gently shake the tray so the peanuts roast evenly. (You can also roast the peanuts in a dry pan over low heat.) Remove and set aside. Use the peanuts whole or coarsely chop them with a mortar and pestle, a food processor or a knife.

SHALLOT-GARLIC MARINADE

 nuoc uop

MAKES ABOUT ⅔ CUP

¼ cup coarsely chopped shallots

½ tablespoon coarsely chopped
garlic

1 tablespoon fish sauce

1½ teaspoons Caramel Sauce
(page 34) or ½ tablespoon
brown sugar

½ tablespoon soy sauce

½ teaspoon salt

1 teaspoon sugar

¼ cup vegetable oil

Every Vietnamese cook has his or her favorite version of this
marinade. It's used to create the distinctive sweet, smoky flavor of the grilled pork commonly served with noodles. It's
also great on lamb, chicken, shrimp, and tofu.

1. Place the shallots, garlic, fish sauce, Caramel Sauce, soy
   sauce, salt, sugar and oil in a food processor and process
   until well blended, about 15 seconds. (You can also chop
   the shallots and garlic very finely by hand, then mix them
   with the remaining ingredients.) Although you can refrigerate this marinade for several days, it's best when freshly
   made.

Soy Sauce

Like fish sauce, soy sauce is an essential ingredient in our cooking, especially in dishes of Chinese origin. One of the world's oldest condiments, soy sauce is made with cooked soybeans, roasted wheat and a mold starter that have been mixed in a briny solution and allowed to ferment. After a period of six months to a year, the liquid is drained and bottled.

The Southeast Asian kitchen is usually stocked with several different kinds of soy sauce, but they generally fit into two main categories—light and dark. Light soy sauce is thinner, saltier and more appropriate for dipping sauces. In this category, you can use the Chinese soy sauce brands such as Pearl River Bridge or Kikkoman. Always taste the sauce before using because each brand differs in saltiness and flavor. Avoid brands such as La Choy, which are made from hydrolized vegetable protein and are not true soy sauces. If you shake the bottle, you'll see that the sauce is thinner than the naturally brewed soy sauce.

In the second category, there are two (but similar) kinds—*dark soy* (also called black soy sauce), which contains molasses and is thick and full bodied, and *sweet soy sauce*, which is even thicker and sweeter. Both blacken food and are typically used only in small amounts, especially in cooked noodles and braised dishes. For example, *pho xao tieu chau*, a Chinese-style noodle dish, gets its delicious caramelized flavor from drizzling the sweet soy sauce into the hot pan.

MARINATED DAIKON AND CARROTS

 cu cai ca rot chua

MAKES ABOUT I QUART

1 cup rice or distilled white
    vinegar

5 tablespoons sugar

2 pounds small daikon, peeled,
    halved lengthwise and cut
    across into ½-inch-thick slices

2 carrots, peeled and cut into
    matchstick strips

1½ teaspoons salt

A favorite condiment in our home around Tet (Vietnamese New Year), this is served in much the same way as a vegetable, often accompanying a simmering dish like *thit heo kho* (Aunt Tam's Pork in Claypot, page 150). Sweet and sour, these crunchy vegetables also make a great garnish for dipping sauces.

1. Combine the vinegar and sugar and bring to a boil. Remove from the heat and set aside to cool.
2. Place the radishes, carrots and salt in a bowl and toss several times. Set aside for 20 minutes, then rinse thoroughly. Using your hands, squeeze the vegetables to remove the excess water. Pat dry with paper towels and place in a bowl.
3. Add the vinegar mixture and let the vegetables marinate at least 1 hour before serving. To store, transfer to a tight-lidded jar and refrigerate. The vegetables will keep for up to 3 weeks.

MARINATED CHILIES

 ot ngam giam

MAKES ABOUT I¼ CUPS

¾ cup rice or distilled white
    vinegar

⅓ cup sugar

2 teaspoons sea salt

Simple to make, these chilies greatly enhance noodle soups and rice dishes. If you like spicy foods, I'd suggest making extras to have on hand at all times. The blanching keeps the chilies green, and the garlic—even if you don't eat it—adds to the flavor and presentation.

1. Combine the vinegar, sugar and salt in a glass jar large enough to hold all the ingredients. Stir well to dissolve. Set aside.
2. Bring a small pot of water to a boil. Using a sieve, dip the chilies and garlic into the boiling water for 5 seconds. Drain completely, then put in the vinegar mixture, pushing the chilies and garlic down so they are fully submerged. Cover and refrigerate for at least 1 day before serving.

10 serrano or jalapeño chilies, cut into ¼-inch rings

10 small cloves garlic (optional)

CHICKEN STOCK

nuoc dung ga

MAKES ABOUT 2 QUARTS

In Vietnamese cooking, a good chicken stock is rich but clear, with no salt or seasonings added. A neutral-tasting stock makes it easier for the cook to season and balance the flavors of the final dish.

4 pounds chicken backs and bones, excess skin and fat removed, rinsed

2½ quarts water

1. Place the chicken backs and bones in a large stockpot and add the water. Bring to a boil, then reduce the heat to low. Simmer for at least 2 hours, skimming the surface often to remove any foam or impurities that rise to the top.
2. Remove the stock from the heat. Let cool, then strain before using. You can refrigerate the stock for up to 1 week, or freeze it for future use.

Asian Herbs: For Flavor and for Health

For centuries, cultures and cuisines around the world have embraced herbs, not only for their flavors and aromas but also for their medicinal qualities. In Thailand, cooks love to throw cupfuls of basil into their salads, stir-fries and soups, treating them no differently than vegetables. In Laos and Cambodia, herbs are used to garnish and perfume noodle soups, broth soups and salads.

But nowhere do fresh herbs play as important a role as they do in Vietnam, where a typical meal often includes, among other things, a huge platter of table salad piled high with *rau thom,* or aromatic herbs. The selection varies according to the meal. If the table salad accompanies *pho* (rice noodles with beef soup), it will include saw-leaf and Asian basil. If it goes with grilled meats, it will have a generous amount of green and red perilla and different kinds of mint. To eat, we either tear the greens into small pieces and add them to our bowls, or use them to wrap little pieces of meat or seafood and dip in sauce.

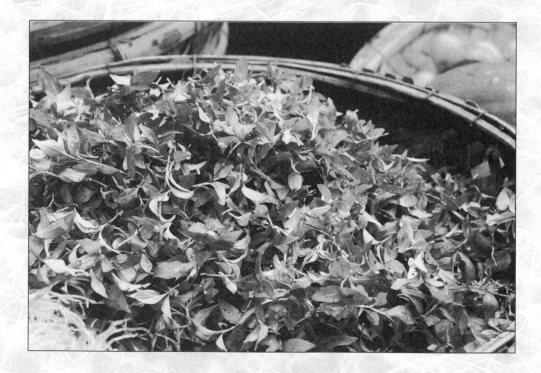

There is no question that fresh herbs play a critical role at the Vietnamese table.

The high consumption of herbs fulfills both practical and culinary purposes. The traditional Vietnamese diet relies mostly on a huge amount of rice, so herbs (as well as fish sauce) are necessary to make that staple food more palatable. Herbs are also easily available and affordable. Many grow wild, thriving along the edges and banks of wet rice fields. Unlike the Western notion of using herbs in small amounts to season food, the Vietnamese use them as greens. For example, when savoring Grilled Shrimp on Sugarcane (page 125), a single diner can easily consume two to three bunches of fresh herbs, picking the leaves off the sprigs as the meal progresses.

Rau thom is also considered a valuable yin food. Like the Chinese, the Vietnamese believe in the necessary balance of the yin and yang energies. Foods are classified as either *nong* (hot, or yang) or *mat* (cool, or yin). Most starches and proteins constitute the hot energy and as a rule, must be paired with the cool herbs and vegetables. But beyond this, herbs are also eaten to prevent or cure specific illnesses. For example, the various types of mint and basil are believed to aid digestion and blood circulation and to promote general wellness.

When purchasing herbs, choose the freshest-looking sprigs you can, free of blemishes. Don't wash them until you're ready to use them. Store them in a plastic bag in the refrigerator. (The Vietnamese like to blow air into the bags to prevent the herbs from getting bruised.) Before using, trim to the desired length, then refresh by submerging the whole sprigs in cool water, soaking them for 30 minutes, draining or spinning them dry in a salad spinner.

The following are the most commonly used Vietnamese herbs. Unfortunately, the nomenclature is a bit confusing, since some herbs have more than one English name. To be most accurate, it's best to use their botanical or Vietnamese names. Many are available at Asian markets in larger cities and at specialty stores and farmer's markets during the summer. If can't find them in your area, try mail order from the nurseries listed on page 237. Mint and *rau ram* are very easy to grow and if you're serious about Vietnamese cuisine, consider planting them. For the best-tasting tender herbs, plant them in bright shade or filtered light and in areas where they can be protected from frost. For more information on growing Asian herbs, Carole Saville's *Exotic Herbs* is one of the best sources I've seen on the topic.

Asian basil/Thai basil/anise basil—*Ocimum basilicum*—*rau que*

To me, this is one of the most seductive herbs in Vietnamese cuisine. Every time I smell a bunch, either at the produce section of an Asian market or at a farmer's market stall, my immediate inclination is to go get a bowl of *pho*. With pointed oval green leaves and purplish stems and flowers, this beautiful herb is a must when it comes to noodle soups. Delicately scented with licorice, this popular variety of the Asian basil family is used all over Southeast Asia. The Thais love to toss cupfuls into their stir-fries, soups and curries. They also deep-fry the leaves for garnishes. The Vietnamese prefer them raw, using them in pho (*chapter 2*) and in any dishes in which meats are wrapped in lettuce. Don't substitute sweet basil because it's too strong. Use mint instead.

Crab claw herb—*rau cang cua*

Spicy and tart, this rare but delicious herb is commonly used in salads in Vietnam. Delicate and a bit spongy, *rau cang cua* has small green oval leaves that are shiny on the top and pale on the bottom. Oftentimes they're sold with heavy flowering tops (hence the name crab claw.) This unusual herb can sometimes be found at farmer's markets during the summer.

Fish mint/fishscale mint—*Houthuynia cordata*—*rau diep ca*

You will either love or hate this herb. Unlike other herbs, *rau diep ca* doesn't have much of an aroma, but it does have a strong taste. It is sour, almost like sorrel, with fishy undertones. It has dark-green, arrowhead-shaped leaves with light brown, leggy stems. (This green herb is a cousin of the same *houthuynia* that is used as a decorative ground cover.) In Vietnam, fish mint is served in table salads that accompany grilled meats and fish. It's particularly refreshing and flavorful in Lemongrass Beef on Cool Noodles (page 120). Substitute mint or Asian basil.

Lemongrass—*Cymbopogon citratus*—*xa*

This is the main herb used to make marinades for grilled meats. A woody, fibrous pale green stalk, lemongrass imparts a sublime citrusy flavor to foods. It's used in two main ways—finely chopped or pounded into a paste and added to marinades or stir-fries, such as Stir-Fried Chicken with Lemongrass and Chilies (page 145); or cut into 2- to 3-inch pieces and used to infuse broths and curries. Peel the 2 to 3 tough outer layers of the stalk and use only the bottom bulb (about 3 to 4 inches from the base), discarding the fibrous tops.

Mint/spearmint—*Mentha arvensis*—*rau hung lui*

The most versatile and widely used herb is probably mint, especially the mild-tasting, fuzzy-leafed variety. In Vietnam, mint is harvested when the leaves are tiny, smaller than the size of a penny, and have a slightly more coriander-like than a sharp mint flavor. It's the main herb in table salads and in dishes wrapped in rice paper like Rice Paper–Wrapped Salad Rolls (page 95). Mint is a natural accompaniment to rich foods like pork.

The Vietnamese also eat another type of mint called *rau hung cay*, although not as extensively as *rau hung lui*. Unlike the spearmint variety, *rau hung cay* has thin, paper-like oval leaves with serrated edges. Its mild peppermint taste is preferred in noodle dishes. Substitute spearmint.

Rice paddy herb—*Limnophila aromatica*—*ngo om*

If you bundle up and chop these darling little herbs, your hands will smell like cumin perfume. Both the long, thin stems and the tiny green leaves about ¼ inch long are used extensively to flavor soups, like Sweet-and-Sour Shrimp Soup with Fresh Herbs (page 71). To experience this fragrant herb at its finest, chop and add it to your soup just before serving. *Ngo om* also makes an elegant garnish. Substitute cilantro.

Red perilla/shiso/beefsteak—*Perilla frutescens*—*rau tia to*

A bit lemony and anise-like, *rau tia to* has purple stems with wide, oval leaves that are deep purple on the bottom and dark green on top. Its fuzzy texture gives a faintly scratchy feel in the throat. The Vietnamese like to shred the leaves and add them to noodles or use in table salads and as wrappers. It is one of the preferred herbs in Sizzling Saigon Crepes (page 117) because the strong anise flavor helps to season the mild-tasting rice-flour crepe. Substitute Asian basil.

Saw-leaf herb/saw-tooth herb/cilantro—*Eryngium foetidum*—*ngo gai*

If you saw this saw-leaf herb as a whole plant, you might think twice about eating it. A member of the coriander family, this stiff, thistle-like herb grows in clusters with leaves spreading close to the ground. The dark-green leaves are 3 to 4 inches long with serrated edges (hence the name). They are chewy when raw but quickly soften in hot soups. *Ngo gai* has a refreshing floral and cilantro-like aroma. The Vietnamese love to garnish their *pho* with this herb. Substitute cilantro or Asian basil.

Pepper leaf, wild betel leaf—*Piper sarmentosum*—*la lot*

This is a relative of the betel leaf used for chewing betel nuts. In Vietnam, *la lot* is used as a wrapper for grilled meats and as an aromatic leaf for flavoring soups and stir-fries. When used to season food, it's shredded and added toward the end of the cooking, as in the Spicy Lemongrass Tofu (page 193). For wrapping, you can substitute large red perilla leaves or grape leaves. For flavoring foods, substitute Asian basil.

Vietnamese balm/green perilla—*Elsholtzia ciliata*—*rau kinh gioi*

This lesser-known herb also happens to be one of the most flavorful. Also referred to as green perilla because of its resemblance to red perilla, *rau kinh gioi* is a relative of lemon balm, but has a more pronounced lemongrass flavor. *Rau kinh gioi* is a shrubby plant similar to red perilla and has light-green oval leaves with serrated edges. It is used with noodles and in soups but is particularly delicious in Hanoi Rice Noodles with Grilled Pork (page 121). Substitute red perilla or Asian basil.

Vietnamese coriander—*Polygonum odoratum*—*rau ram*

I love *rau ram,* especially the small tender sprigs that our farmer grows for the restaurant. They're spicy, sharp and flavorful, with the hint of coriander. *Rau ram* has small pointed green leaves, about 1 to 1½ inches long, with brown veins and slightly knobby brown stems. These aromatic leaves are usually eaten raw, in salads such as Hue Chicken Salad (page 79), and in noodle soups such as Hue Beef Vermicelli Soup (page 61). *Rau ram* can be easily propagated by placing some stems in water and letting them root. Plant in shade or filtered sun and keep snipping the tops to encourage new growth. Small young leaves have the best flavor. *Rau ram* also makes a great houseplant or hanging plant. Substitute mint or Asian basil.

chapter two

A Bowl of Pho

Irresistible Noodle Soups and Broth Soups

Vietnamese "Pho" Rice Noodle Soup with Beef

Quick Pho

Vietnamese Rice Noodle Soup with Chicken

Hue Beef Vermicelli Soup

Rice Noodle with Shrimp Dumpling Soup

My Tho Noodle Soup

Noodle Broth

Rice Soup with Chicken and Ginger

Curry Noodle Soup with Chicken

Roast Duck and Egg Noodle Soup

Noodle Soup with Meatballs

Chicken and Cellophane Noodle Soup

Sweet-and-Sour Shrimp Soup with Fresh Herbs

Napa Cabbage Soup with Shrimp Dumplings

Tofu, Tomato and Chive Soup

Serving pho *at a busy soup shop in Saigon.*

Oh my beloved
life without you is like
pho without its broth
—Vietnamese song

The traffic noise gets louder by the minute as motorists and cyclists pour into Hang Giay Street. On the sidewalk, shoppers are browsing through the neighborhood fruit stands, looking for the best picks. But the people sitting next to me at this low table are oblivious to all the commotion. Instead, they're anxiously wiping their chopsticks, fiddling with their little dishes of lime and chopped chilies. It's morning in Hanoi, and morning means *pho*, the country's beloved rice noodle soup with beef.

Up until a few years ago, the thought of coming to Hanoi seemed so remote. How could I ever visit a place that brought tragic memories of the war all over again, a city where my father's enemies once ruled?

But after one bite of my noodles, I immediately knew. I had come to taste my favorite food in the city that created it. This particular bowl of *pho* was as soothing and delicious as I had imagined it would be. Unlike the darker broth and the more chewy noodles served in other parts of Vietnam and in the United States, the rice noodles here are almost sheer, and the broth is clear, like spring water, yet intensely aromatic of beef marrow bones.

As I slurp my steaming soup, I can't help but flash back to Saigon in the sixties, when my parents used to take my siblings and me to Pho 79. It was a noodle shop like this one, small and run-down, with wobbly tables and squeaky stools. Yet no one ever judged Pho 79 by its looks, only by the enticing beefy aroma that wafted through the air and the crowds that squeezed through the front door each day. Every time we arrived, the place was packed. As soon as we found a party about to leave, we would dash over, waiting inconspicuously for the right moment to seize our table.

Once seated, we felt relieved. My parents would then place their usual order: *pho* with the rare and cooked beef topping and *ca phe sua da*—a delicious coffee drink served with condensed milk and ice. While waiting, we would grab the chopsticks and spoons from an aluminum container and dust them off. Moments later, our soup would arrive. We would bend down and inhale the aroma, as if to verify its authenticity. Invariably, the broth smelled utterly beefy, laced with just-roasted spices. The rice noodles looked velvety and fresh, the edges of the rare beef curled up expectantly in the hot broth. All was well.

Then, our arms and hands would fly across the table, all reaching for the lime, basil, saw-leaf herbs and fresh chilies to garnish our bowls.

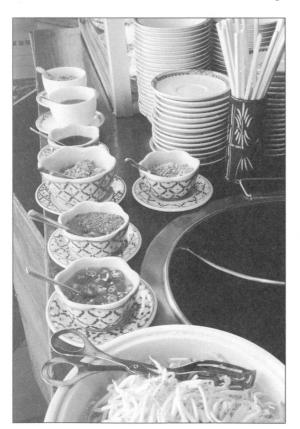

Toppings such as chilies, onions and cilantro are used to flavor soups.

Even though our family first discovered *pho* in Saigon, the dish actually originated in Hanoi, following the French occupation in the latter part of the 1800s. The Vietnamese, who valued cows and buffaloes as indispensable beasts of burden, didn't eat red meat, preferring instead pork, chicken and seafood. When the French arrived, however, many Vietnamese, especially those belonging to the upper classes, began to share the French affection for beef. Dishes made with *boeuf* began appearing at the markets and in restaurants, and in time, red meat became part of the Vietnamese diet.

How this actually led to the creation of *pho* remains a debate. Some scholars believe the dish parallels the history of Vietnam, harboring both a Chinese and a French connection. It was the French, they theorize, who introduced the idea of using bones and lesser cuts of beef to make the broth. (After all, in a society that wasted nothing, what was one to do with all the bones carved from *biftecks*?) In fact, they believe the dish was first created when Vietnamese cooks learned to make *pot-au-feu* for their French masters. The name *pho*—pronounced *fuh*—might have even come from the French word *feu*, for fire.

Others argue that while the French popularized beef, it was actually the Chinese who created *pho*, as evidenced by its use of noodles and ginger. According to Huu Ngoc, a Hanoi-based scholar who's written extensively about the local culture and cuisine for more than five decades, historical records suggest that the soup is related to an ancient dish called *chao pho* and *luc pho*, which translates into soup with *pho* and beef with *pho*. The word *pho*, he says, was probably a mispronunciation of *phan*, as in the Chinese phrase *nguu nguc phan*, which means rice paste soup with beef.

Regardless of the origin, the Vietnamese were quick to interject their own ideas. Using ingredients inspired by their foreign rulers, they customized *pho* by adding *nuoc mam* (fish sauce), the defining ingredient.

In the 1930s, in part spurred by nationalistic sentiments, some Hanoi scholars wrote passionately about *pho*, crediting it not only as a food that provided the necessary nutrients in one convenient bowl, but a food that symbolically freed the people who created and ate it. At last, the Vietnamese were free to express themselves, if only through their *pho*.

The infectious enthusiasm for the dish spread south in 1954, when the country was partitioned in two. The north fell under Communist control and almost a million northerners fled, taking with them a dream of a new life in the democratic south and a love of *pho*.

Pho took the south by storm. My mother, a southerner who had just moved from her village to Saigon, had never seen or heard of the soup until the late fifties. At the time my mother and her contemporaries slurped on *hu tieu*, a Chinese-style rice noodle soup made with pork. But when she first tasted *pho*, she became an instant convert. From then on, whenever she and my father could afford it, which was about once a month, they would treat themselves to this new delicacy.

When *pho* migrated south, it was embellished. Reflecting the abundance of its new surroundings, it was served with more meat, more noodles, more broth. Southerners demanded richer and livelier flavors and discernible textures. They started adding bean sprouts and herbs, such as saw-leaf and basil. But it didn't stop there. Garnishes such as lime wedges, fresh chilies, chili sauce and *tuong*, or bean sauce, were added, giving the dish a new character. As in the north, it quickly became a favorite, but only after it had been modified to reflect southern taste and mentality.

In 1975, when my family and I first arrived in the United States, following the fall of Saigon, one of the foods we missed most desperately was *pho*. We ate *pho* whenever we could, even though the versions of the soup we found here lacked the distinctive herbs and complex flavor of real *pho*. To us, a steaming bowl of *pho* was a welcome thought. A taste of home, it warmed our spirit and gave us the comfort and solace needed during our first difficult years in America.

Fortunately, over the years, immigrant families such as ourselves have readjusted and rebuilt our lives. And somehow, in the midst of all this transformation, *pho*—which followed us through tumultuous times and journeys—has become a big part of our everyday life. Authentic recipes have been dusted off, preserved and cooked with great fervor.

And so, as I'm slurping my bowl of *pho* in Hanoi, I can't help but ponder the parallels of this great soup and my own life. It's comforting to know that wherever I happen to be, whether it's in Vietnam or California, *pho* will always lurk in the background, ready to nourish and sustain me.

There are several key things to keep in mind as you prepare *pho* and other noodle soups. First, *pho* takes time to prepare and it's best that you don't get distracted by trying to cook too many other dishes when making this special soup. It's really best eaten by itself.

Second, focus on the noodles. Unlike pasta, rice noodles are very delicate and require special attention to come out right. Follow the instructions on preparing the noodles and make sure they're absolutely hot before ladling the broth on top.

For the recipes in this chapter, it helps to have the proper kitchen tools and the correct size bowls. If you love noodle soups as I do, invest in a good, heavy-bottomed soup pot, a long-handled wire strainer for cooking noodles and some big, deep 32-ounce soup bowls. It's absolutely critical to have bowls large enough to accommodate a generous amount of broth to keep the noodles hot throughout the meal. Nothing is worse than lukewarm noodle soup.

And lastly, pay attention to the garnishes. What gives *pho* its distinctive qualities are the last-minute additions of the paper-thin onions, the fresh herbs, the lime wedges and the chilies.

Preparing Noodles for Pho

For *pho,* use dried rice noodles, the white, translucent linguine-type noodles sold as *banh pho,* or rice sticks. They come in 14- or 16-ounce bags and are available in small, medium and wide widths. For *pho,* buy the small, $1/16$-inch-width noodles.

To use, first soak the noodles in cold water for 30 minutes, then drain. Bring a big pot of water to a rolling boil. When you're ready to serve (not before), place the noodles, one portion at a time, into a sieve and lower it into the boiling water. Using chopsticks or a long spoon, stir so the noodles untangle and cook evenly. Blanch just until they're soft but still chewy, about 10 to 20 seconds depending on the thickness. Drain completely, then transfer to a preheated bowl. Cook the remaining noodles the same way. The bowls are now ready to be assembled. (If you're cooking for several people, you may also cook the noodles all at once by adding them directly to the pot of boiling water. Just make sure to serve them immediately.)

If you're able to buy fresh *pho* noodles, which are now becoming increasingly available, omit the soaking but blanch them in boiling water.

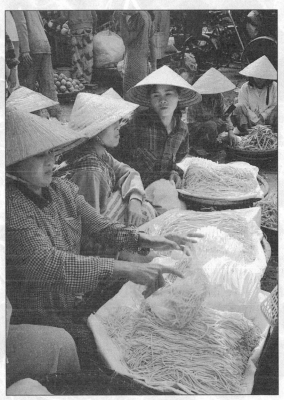

Vendors sell fresh pho *noodles at an outdoor market.*

VIETNAMESE "PHO" RICE NOODLE SOUP WITH BEEF

 pho bo

BROTH

5 pounds beef marrow or
    knuckle bones

2 pounds beef chuck, cut into
    2 pieces

2 (3-inch) pieces ginger, cut in
    half lengthwise and lightly
    bruised with the flat side of
    a knife, lightly charred
    (page 55)

2 yellow onions, peeled and
    charred (page 55)

¼ cup fish sauce

3 ounces rock sugar, or
    3 tablespoons sugar

10 whole star anise, lightly
    toasted in a dry pan

6 whole cloves, lightly toasted
    in a dry pan

1 tablespoon sea salt

NOODLE ASSEMBLY

1 pound dried $1/16$-inch-wide
    rice sticks, soaked, cooked
    and drained (page 53)

⅓ pound beef sirloin, slightly
    frozen, then sliced paper-
    thin across the grain

This beloved noodle soup is a complete meal in itself and is best served for breakfast or lunch on a weekend. Because the simmering takes at least two hours, I like to prepare the broth a day ahead of time and keep it in the refrigerator, where it will last for three days. Many cookbooks call for it to be made with oxtail bones, but I prefer marrow bones and beef chuck, which is what *pho* cooks in Vietnam use. A good *pho* broth needs to be clear, not muddy and dark, and certainly fragrant of beef, anise and ginger.

You can serve this soup with several toppings, but the easiest ones to prepare at home are cooked and raw beef. If you're pressed for time, refer to the next recipe for a quick version that uses store-bought stock.

To use broth that has been made in advance, bring it to a boil, then add fresh ginger to refresh it. Come serving time, get friends or family to help cook the noodles and assemble the bowls. Make sure that the broth is boiling hot and the bowls preheated. Allow about 1 part noodles to 3 parts broth for each bowl.

1. In a large stockpot, bring 6 quarts water to a boil. Place the bones and beef chuck in a second pot and add water to cover. Bring to a boil and boil vigorously for 5 minutes. Using tongs, carefully transfer the bones and beef to the first pot of boiling water. Discard the water in which the meat cooked. (This cleans the bones and meat and reduces the impurities that can cloud the broth.) When the water returns to a boil, reduce the heat to a simmer. Skim the surface often to remove any foam and fat. Add the charred ginger and onions, fish sauce and sugar. Simmer until the

beef chuck is tender, about 40 minutes. Remove one piece and submerge in cool water for 10 minutes to prevent the meat from darkening and drying out. Drain, then cut into thin slices and set aside. Let the other piece of beef chuck continue to cook in the simmering broth.

2. When the broth has been simmering for about 1½ hours total, wrap the star anise and cloves in a spice bag (or piece of cheesecloth) and add to the broth. Let infuse until the broth is fragrant, about 30 minutes. Remove and discard both the spice bag and onions. Add the salt and continue to simmer, skimming as necessary, until you're ready to assemble the dish. The broth needs to cook for at least 2 hours. (The broth will taste salty but will be balanced once the noodles and accompaniments are added.) Leave the remaining chuck and bones to simmer in the pot while you assemble the bowls.

3. To serve, place the cooked noodles in preheated bowls. (If the noodles are not hot, reheat them in a microwave or dip them briefly in boiling water to prevent them from cooling down the soup.) Place a few slices of the beef chuck and the raw sirloin on the noodles. Bring the broth to a rolling boil; ladle about 2 to 3 cups into each bowl. The broth will cook the raw beef instantly. Garnish with yellow onions, scallions and cilantro. Serve immediately, inviting guests to garnish the bowls with bean sprouts, herbs, chilies, lime juice and black pepper.

GARNISHES

½ yellow onion, sliced paper-thin

3 scallions, cut into thin rings

⅓ cup chopped cilantro

1 pound bean sprouts

10 sprigs Asian basil

1 dozen saw-leaf herb leaves (optional)

6 Thai bird chilies or 1 serrano chili, cut into thin rings

1 lime, cut into 6 thin wedges

Freshly ground black pepper

How to Char Ginger and Onions

To char ginger, hold the piece with tongs directly over an open flame or place it directly on a medium-hot electric burner. While turning, char until the edges are slightly blackened and the ginger is fragrant, about 3 to 4 minutes. Char the onions in the same way. Peel and discard the blackened skins of the ginger and onions, then rinse and add to the broth.

How to Enjoy Pho at a Restaurant

In Vietnam, *pho* is mostly restaurant food. Although it can be prepared at home, most people prefer the ritual of going out to a noisy soup shop, where they can slurp their favorite soup while chitchatting and gossiping. Fortunately, *pho* shops are mushrooming across the U.S. Many are quite successful, especially in cities with larger Vietnamese communities. The best way to choose a *pho* shop is to find one that is busy (higher turnover usually means fresher ingredients) and one that serves all the proper garnishes. Personally, I would not patronize a soup shop that does not, at the very least, offer fresh Asian basil (and preferably saw-leaf herb).

Eating *pho* is an art in itself and the following guidelines are designed to help you better appreciate this wonderful dish.

1. When ordering *pho,* beware. It comes in many sizes, from small to *xe lua* or "train" size, which can feed two or three. Unless you're super-hungry, go for the medium bowl.

2. You can choose individual or combination toppings, from rare to well-done beef, to briskets and meatballs, even tripe, tendon, and so on. If you're not sure, try the *pho tai nam,* the rare and well-done combination, as in the accompanying recipe.

3. Eat *pho* while it's piping hot. If you wait for it to cool down, the noodles will expand and become soggy, and the dish will taste bland. (Some connoisseurs don't even talk while they eat their *pho,* preferring to save serious chatting for later.)

4. Begin by adding bean sprouts, fresh chilies, and a little squeeze of lime. Using your fingers, pluck the Asian basil leaves from their sprigs and, if available, shred the saw-leaf herbs and add them to the soup. Add them little by little, eating as you go. (If you put them in all at once, the broth will cool too fast and the herbs will overcook and lose their bright flavors.) Chili sauce and hoisin sauce are traditional condiments, but I avoid them because, to my taste, they mask the flavor of *pho.*

5. Push the garnishings into the hot broth and gently turn the noodles.

6. With spoon in one hand and chopsticks in the other, pull the noodles out of the broth and eat, alternatively slurping the broth. It's perfectly acceptable to be seen with clumps of noodles dangling from your mouth, eyes squinting from the steam.

7. The broth is served in large amounts to keep the noodles warm and to help season the dish. It's not meant to be consumed in its entirety. But if you're in the mood, it's not considered rude to tip the bowl and slurp down every last drop.

Consider finishing the meal with Vietnamese Coffee (page 222) with condensed milk and ice. Brewed in individual filters at the table, it's sweet, delicious and very strong. If you're planning a busy day, get one. It will keep you buzzing for a while.

QUICK PHO

 pho nhanh

SERVES 6 AS A MAIN DISH

BROTH

6 whole star anise, lightly toasted
in a dry pan for 2 minutes

6 whole cloves, lightly toasted in
a dry pan for 2 minutes

1 teaspoon whole black
peppercorns

2 quarts store-bought low-
sodium chicken broth

2 cups water

1 (3-inch) piece ginger, cut in
half lengthwise, lightly
bruised with the flat side of a
knife and charred (page 55)

1 small yellow onion, charred
(page 55)

3 tablespoons fish sauce

1 tablespoon sugar

¼ teaspoon salt

2 chicken thighs or breasts
(about 1¼ pounds)

NOODLE ASSEMBLY

1 pound dried 1/16-inch-wide
rice sticks, cooked (page 53)

⅓ yellow onion, sliced paper-
thin (about ⅓ cup)

2 scallions, cut into thin rings

3 tablespoons finely chopped
cilantro

Whenever I need a quick fix for a *pho* craving, I resort to this recipe. Although nothing can compare to the made-from-scratch version, this is also very good. The key is to come up with a flavorful broth, scented with the prerequisite charred ginger and star anise, and then to serve the dish with all the necessary herbs and garnishings. The only commercial broth that I've found at the supermarket that would work is chicken, not beef, broth since the latter is too dark for this recipe. If you have access to an Asian market, you might want to look for canned *pho* stock. It's quite good, although it contains MSG. Even though this recipe is made with chicken broth, you can serve either a chicken or beef topping with it.

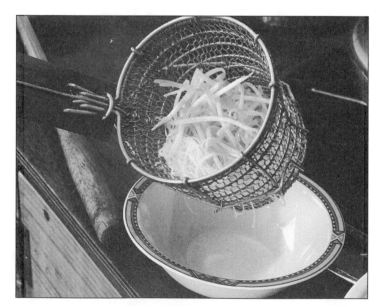

Blanching bean sprouts for noodle soup.

1. Place the star anise, cloves and peppercorns in a spice bag (or a piece of cheesecloth); set aside.

2. Place the chicken broth, water, charred ginger and onion, fish sauce, sugar, salt and spice bag in a large pot and bring to a boil. Add the chicken and cook for 5 minutes. Reduce the heat and simmer until the chicken is done, about 15 minutes. Remove the chicken and set aside to cool. Let the broth continue to simmer. When the chicken is cool enough to handle, hand-shred into ½-inch-thick strips. Set aside until ready to serve.

3. To serve, place the cooked noodles in preheated bowls. (If the noodles are not hot, reheat in a microwave or dip briefly in boiling water.) Garnish each bowl with a few slices of yellow onions and some shredded chicken. Ladle a generous amount of boiling broth on top. Garnish with scallions and cilantro. Invite guests to garnish their bowls with bean sprouts, fresh herbs, chilies, squeezes of lime juice and black pepper.

GARNISHES

½ pound bean sprouts

10 sprigs Asian basil

1 dozen saw-leaf herb leaves
   (optional)

3 Thai bird chilies or
   1 serrano chili, cut into
   thin rings

1 lime, cut into 6 wedges

Freshly ground black pepper

VIETNAMESE RICE NOODLE SOUP WITH CHICKEN

pho ga

SERVES 6

Whenever I'm in Saigon, I love going to the noodle shops on Pasteur Street and getting my fill of chicken *pho*. The choice of toppings is almost endless—breast meat, leg meat, thigh meat, wings and giblets, and all with or without the skin. And, if you get there early, you can order a side of immature (unlaid) chicken eggs.

This recipe is also delicious without any exotic parts of the chicken. Use a good-quality bird and take care to not let the broth boil too vigorously or it will get cloudy.

BROTH

6 whole star anise, lightly toasted
   in a dry pan for 2 minutes

6 whole cloves, lighted toasted in
   a dry pan for 2 minutes

1 teaspoon whole black
   peppercorns

3 pounds chicken backs,
   skin removed

1 whole chicken (about
  3½ pounds), split in half
1 (4-inch) piece ginger, cut in
  half lengthwise, lightly
  bruised with the flat side of
  a knife, charred (page 55)
2 yellow onions, peeled and
  charred (page 55)
¼ cup fish sauce
2 tablespoons sugar
1 tablespoon sea salt

NOODLE ASSEMBLY
1 pound dried 1/16-inch-wide
  rice sticks, cooked (page 112)
½ yellow onion, sliced
  paper-thin
3 scallions, cut into thin rings
⅓ cup chopped cilantro

GARNISHES
1 pound bean sprouts
20 sprigs Asian basil
1 dozen saw-leaf herb leaves
  (optional)
3 Thai bird chilies or
  1 serrano chili, thinly sliced
1 lime, cut into 6 wedges
Freshly ground black pepper

1. Place the star anise, cloves and peppercorns in a spice bag; set aside.

2. In a large stockpot, bring 5 quarts water to a rolling boil. Add the chicken backs and chicken halves. Boil vigorously for 3 minutes, then reduce the heat to a simmer. Skim the surface as necessary to remove any fat or foam. Add the charred ginger, onions, fish sauce, sugar and salt. Cook until the chicken is just done, about ½ hour. Remove the chicken (but not the chicken backs) and set aside to cool.

3. Add the spice bag to the pot and cook the broth for a total of 1½ hours. Remove and discard the spice bag. Reduce the heat to very low.

4. Remove the skin from the chicken and discard. Hand-shred half of it into bite-sized strips. (Save the other half for another use, like chicken salad. You don't need much to garnish *pho*, but you do need a whole chicken to make a good broth.)

5. To serve, place the cooked noodles in preheated bowls. (If the noodles are not hot, reheat in a microwave or dip briefly in boiling water.) Place some yellow onions and shredded chicken on top. Bring the broth back to a rolling boil, then ladle 2 cups into each bowl. Top with scallions and cilantro. Invite guests to garnish their bowls with bean sprouts, fresh herbs, chilies, squeezes of lime juice and black pepper.

HUE BEEF VERMICELLI SOUP

bun bo Hue

MAKES 6 SERVINGS

In Hue, there's no question that this dish—not *pho*—is the most popular noodle soup. It is heartier, made with both pork and beef and lots of chilies and lemongrass. For best flavor, prepare the aromatics and float them in the broth right at the end. The preferred noodles for this dish are not the rice sticks used in *pho*, but a fat, round rice vermicelli similar to spaghetti. Recent brands from China actually label them as noodles for *bun bo Hue*. If you can't find them, use the smaller noodles called *bun* (rice vermicelli, page 112).

1. Peel the tough outer layers of the lemongrass and discard. Finely chop enough for 2 tablespoons and set aside. Using the flat side of a knife, lightly bruise the remaining stalks. Cut into 3-inch pieces; set aside.

2. Place the pork bones, pork leg and beef shank in a large pot. Add water to cover, bring to a boil, then drain. Return the bones, pork and beef to the pot and add 3 quarts fresh water. Add the lemongrass stalks. Bring to a boil, then reduce the heat to a simmer. Cook until the meat is tender but still firm, about 1 hour. Skim the surface to remove any foam or fat that rises to the top.

3. With a slotted spoon, remove 1 piece of the pork leg and 1 piece of the beef shank and submerge in cool water for 10 minutes to keep them from turning dark. Remove from the water and trim any excess fat or chewy parts from the shank and pork. Slice both meats into thin bite-sized strips; set aside. Allow the remaining meat to simmer in the broth.

4. Add the fish sauce, salt, sugar and shrimp sauce to the broth and continue to simmer.

BROTH

3 lemongrass stalks, bottom
   white parts only
3 pounds pork bones
1½ pounds boneless pork leg,
   cut in 2 pieces
1½ pounds beef shank,
   cut in 2 pieces
3 tablespoons fish sauce
1 teaspoon salt
2 tablespoons sugar
1 teaspoon shrimp sauce
   (page 229)
2 tablespoons vegetable oil
2 teaspoons annatto seeds
   (optional, page 223)
1 teaspoon minced shallot
1 teaspoon dried chili flakes

NOODLE ASSEMBLY

1 pound dried fat rice
   vermicelli (like spaghetti),
   cooked until soft, about
   10 minutes, drained and
   rinsed (page 112)
½ yellow onion, sliced
   paper-thin
¼ cup chopped cilantro
2 scallions, cut into
   thin rings

1 cup *rau ram* (Vietnamese
   coriander leaves), coarsely
   chopped

2 cups very thinly shredded
   cabbage, soaked in cold water
   and drained (optional)

1 lime, cut into 6 wedges

4 Thai bird chilies, chopped

5. Heat the oil in a small saucepan over moderate heat. Remove the pan from the heat and add the annatto seeds, if using. Let them foam for 30 seconds, then strain the oil into another pan (or remove the seeds with a slotted spoon). Heat the annatto oil over moderate heat and add the shallot, chili flakes and reserved chopped lemongrass. Stir until fragrant, about 10 seconds. Remove from heat immediately and add to the broth.

6. To serve, divide the cooked noodles evenly among preheated bowls. (If the noodles are not hot, reheat in a microwave oven or blanch in boiling water.) Top with a few strips of pork and beef shank. Ladle a generous amount of hot broth on top and garnish with sliced onion, cilantro and scallions. Serve with *rau ram,* cabbage, if desired, lime wedges and chilies on the side.

RICE NOODLE WITH SHRIMP DUMPLING SOUP

 bun rieu

SERVES 6

DUMPLINGS

¼ pound raw shrimp, peeled,
   deveined and patted dry

¼ pound ground pork or
   ground chicken

½ teaspoon white pepper

½ teaspoon salt

2 teaspoons fish sauce

1 egg

3 tablespoons finely chopped
   yellow onion

A specialty of the north, this soup is traditionally made with *cua dong* (rice field crabs), which are prized for their delicate sweet flavor. Vietnamese cooks use a mortar and pestle to pound them lightly before making dumplings. This version calls for shrimp, although cooked crabmeat would be lovely, too. I like to make this soup when tomatoes are at their peak.

1. To make the dumplings, place the shrimp, pork, white pepper, salt, fish sauce, egg and onion in a food processor and pulse until the mixture becomes a lumpy paste, about

15 seconds. (Do not overmix or the dumplings will be tough.) You can also mince all the ingredients by hand. Transfer to a bowl until ready to use.

2. To make the broth, heat the oil in a pot over moderate heat. Add the shallot and garlic and stir until fragrant, about 20 seconds. Add the chilies, fish sauce and tomatoes and stir for 1 minute. Add the chicken broth, water, shrimp paste, salt and lime juice and bring to a boil. Reduce the heat to a simmer.

3. Scoop a heaping tablespoon of the shrimp mixture and slip it into the broth. Make all the dumplings this way. Cook until the dumplings rise to the surface and are cooked, about 10 minutes.

4. To serve, place the cooked noodles in preheated bowls. Ladle a generous amount of boiling stock into each bowl and top with several dumplings. Garnish with scallions and cilantro. Serve immediately with cabbage, bean sprouts, basil, chilies and lime wedges on the side.

A pot of shrimp dumpling and noodle soup.

BROTH

1 tablespoon vegetable oil

1 tablespoon minced shallot

1 teaspoon chopped garlic

1 teaspoon ground dried chilies

3 tablespoons fish sauce

4 ripe tomatoes, quartered
   (about 2¼ cups)

5 cups fresh Chicken Stock
   (page 39) or store-bought
   low-sodium chicken broth

2 cups water

1 teaspoon *ruoc* (shrimp paste),
   page 229

¼ teaspoon sea salt

1 teaspoon fresh lime juice

NOODLE ASSEMBLY

1 pound dried *bun* (rice
   vermicelli or rice sticks),
   cooked 3 to 4 minutes,
   drained and rinsed (page 112)

2 scallions, cut into thin rings

¼ cup chopped cilantro

GARNISHES

2 cups thinly shredded white
   cabbage, soaked in cold water
   30 minutes and drained

½ pound bean sprouts

½ cup Asian basil or
   rau ram leaves

2 Thai bird chilies or
   1 serrano chili, chopped

1 lime, cut into 6 thin wedges

MY THO NOODLE SOUP

 hu tieu My Tho

SERVES 6

1 recipe Noodle Broth (page 65)

1 pound pork shoulder or
    pork butt

1 tablespoon vegetable oil

1 shallot, minced

1 clove garlic, minced

⅓ pound ground pork

1 teaspoon fish sauce

NOODLE ASSEMBLY

1 pound dried large ⅛-inch-wide
    rice sticks, cooked (page 53),
    drained and rinsed

12 medium raw shrimp, peeled,
    deveined and cooked

¼ yellow onion, sliced paper-thin

2 tablespoons Chinese-style
    preserved cabbage
    (optional, page 228)

2 scallions, cut into thin rings

¼ cup chopped cilantro

GARNISHES

1 pound bean sprouts

3 Thai bird chilies, sliced

1 lime, cut into 6 wedges

Whenever I visit my grandmother in the Mekong Delta, I always stop at one of the noodle shops near the ferry station for a bowl of *hu tieu My Tho*. Named after the capital of Tien Giang province, this dish is a cousin of Chinese egg noodle soup but is made with rice noodles and poached, rather than barbecued, pork.

1. Bring the broth to a simmer in a large pot, then add the pork shoulder and cook until done, 30 to 40 minutes. (The meat should still be firm for better slicing.) Remove the pork and submerge in cool water to keep the meat from turning dark, about 15 minutes. Remove, cut into thin slices and set aside. Continue to simmer the broth until ready to serve.

2. In a skillet, heat the oil over moderate heat. Add the shallot and garlic and stir until fragrant, about 20 seconds. Add the ground pork and fish sauce and stir well. Set aside until ready to use.

3. To assemble, bring the broth back to a vigorous boil. Place some of the cooked noodles in each preheated soup bowl. Top with 1 tablespoon of the ground pork mixture, a few slices of the pork shoulder and 2 shrimp. Ladle a generous amount of hot broth into each bowl. Top with sliced onion, a teaspoon of the preserved cabbage, if desired, and some scallions and cilantro. Invite guests to garnish their bowls with bean sprouts, chilies and a squeeze of lime.

NOODLE BROTH

nuoc leo 拼

To a Vietnamese cook, the most important thing about making broth is that it must be clear. So when making this, simmer the broth uncovered and do not let it boil vigorously. You can use this all-purpose stock for any noodle soup, be it with egg noodles or rice noodles. The dried toasted squid imparts a distinctive savoriness.

1. Place the water in a soup pot and bring to a rolling boil. Add the bones and squid. Reduce the heat to low and simmer for at least 2 hours, skimming often to remove any foam and impurities that rise to the top. Thirty minutes before the end of the cooking time, stir in the soy sauce and salt. Strain the broth before using.

4 quarts water

5 pounds pork and/or chicken bones

1 small dried squid (page 229), lightly toasted on a grill or in a dry pan

⅓ cup soy sauce, preferably light

salt to taste

RICE SOUP WITH CHICKEN AND GINGER

chao ga 粥

Rice soup is one of the simplest and most satisfying dishes you can make. It can be served plain, with just a scattering of scallions, or it can be more sumptuous as in this recipe. If you're pressed for time, use store-bought chicken broth and cooked chicken to garnish it. For an authentic meal, serve this with Hue Chicken Salad (page 79). While it may sound strange to pair hot soup with cold salad, the combination actually works.

2 quarts water

½ whole chicken, excess fat trimmed

¼ teaspoon sea salt

2 teaspoons vegetable oil

1 clove garlic, sliced

½ cup rice, preferably long-grain jasmine, rinsed and drained

1 tablespoon fish sauce

1 tablespoon minced ginger

2 scallions, cut into thin rings

4 sprigs cilantro, thinly sliced

2 tablespoons Fried Shallots
(optional, page 34)

Freshly ground white or
black pepper

You can use any rice, but long-grain jasmine variety is best for this recipe. The toasting of the rice prior to cooking it in the broth gives the soup its nutty flavor. This is also great with minced beef, pork or tofu.

1. Bring the water to a rolling boil in a large soup pot. Add the chicken and salt. Reduce the heat and simmer the liquid. Skim any foam or fat that rises to the surface.

2. Place the oil, garlic and rice in a skillet over moderate heat. Stir gently until the grains start to turn opaque, 3 to 4 minutes.

3. Add the rice to the soup pot. Cook until the chicken is just done, about 25 minutes total. Remove the chicken and set aside to cool. Add the fish sauce and ginger to the soup. Let the rice continue to cook until the kernels open and are tender, about 30 minutes total.

4. Remove the skin from the chicken and shred the meat into bite-sized strips.

5. When ready to serve, ladle the soup into preheated soup bowls and garnish each with chicken, scallions, cilantro, shallots, and pepper. Serve immediately.

CURRY NOODLE SOUP WITH CHICKEN

 bun cari

SERVES 4

1 tablespoon vegetable oil

2 cloves garlic, minced

1 teaspoon ground chili paste
(page 225)

3 tablespoons curry powder,
perferably the Vietnamese
Three Golden Bells brand

My mother often prepared this dish during Tet, or Vietnamese Lunar New Year, as part of a banquet offering to our ancestors. It's basically a curry made with extra broth, which is then poured over rice noodles and vegetables. When serving, make sure the curry is piping hot so the noodles and vegetables, which are served at room temperature, won't turn the whole dish tepid.

1. Heat the oil in a medium pot over moderate heat. Add the garlic and stir until fragrant, about 10 seconds. Add the chili paste, curry powder and chicken and stir-fry for 1 minute. Add the coconut milk, chicken broth, turmeric, fish sauce and sugar. Bring to a boil, then reduce the heat to a simmer.

2. Divide the *rau ram*, lettuce and bean sprouts among 4 preheated soup bowls. Divide the cooked noodles among the bowls. Bring the curry to a rolling boil, then ladle a generous amount of stock with some of the chicken over the noodles. Garnish each bowl with cilantro and scallions. Serve immediately with the lime wedges and the optional chilies on the side.

½ pound boneless, skinless chicken thighs, sliced into bite-sized strips

1½ cups unsweetened coconut milk

4 cups homemade Chicken Stock (page 39) or store-bought low-sodium chicken broth

¼ teaspoon ground turmeric

3 tablespoons fish sauce

1 tablespoon sugar

½ cup *rau ram* (Vietnamese coriander), leaves only

1 cup shredded romaine lettuce

1 cup bean sprouts

1 pound dried *bun* (small rice vermicelli or rice sticks), cooked 4 to 5 minutes, rinsed and drained (page 112)

3 tablespoons chopped cilantro

2 scallions, cut into thin rings

GARNISHES

1 lime, cut into 4 wedges

4 Thai bird chilies or 2 serrano chilies, cut into thin rings (optional)

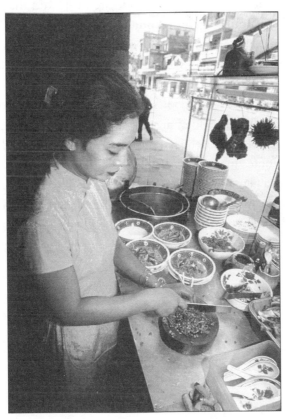

A woman makes mi, *or egg noodle soup, in Nha Trang.*

ROAST DUCK AND EGG NOODLE SOUP

 mi vit tim

SERVES 4

1 tablespoon vegetable oil

1 shallot, thinly sliced

1 quart Noodle Broth (page 65)
or store-bought low-sodium
chicken broth

1 cup water

1 tablespoon soy sauce

½ teaspoon five-spice powder

2 teaspoons sugar

1 (1-inch) piece ginger, peeled
and cut in half lengthwise

½ teaspoon salt, or to taste

1 pound fresh egg noodles,
cooked until soft but still
firm, 3 to 4 minutes

⅓ pound baby bok choy or any
Asian mustard greens, cut
diagonally into 2-inch pieces
and blanched in boiling water
for 20 seconds

½ Chinese-style roast duck,
boned and sliced into
bite-sized pieces

2 tablespoons chopped cilantro

2 scallions, cut into thin rings

⅓ cup Marinated Chilies
(page 38) or 2 to 3 Thai bird
chilies or ½ serrano chili,
chopped

This hearty soup is one of my favorite winter meals, especially on Sundays, when often all I want is something simple and comforting. If you have access to good Chinese barbecued duck this is very quick to prepare. If you don't, any roast duck or chicken will work. I've called for fresh Chinese-style egg noodles, but you can use any kind, including instant ramen noodles.

1. Heat the oil in a pot over moderate heat. Add the shallot and stir until fragrant, about 20 seconds. Add the broth, water, soy sauce, five-spice powder, sugar, ginger and salt and bring to a boil. Reduce the heat and simmer the mixture for 10 minutes.

2. Divide the cooked noodles evenly among 4 preheated soup bowls. (If the noodles are not hot, reheat in a microwave oven or blanch briefly in boiling water.) Top with bok choy and some duck slices. Bring the broth to a rolling boil. Ladle a generous amount into each bowl and garnish with cilantro and scallions. Serve with the Marinated Chilies or fresh chilies on the side.

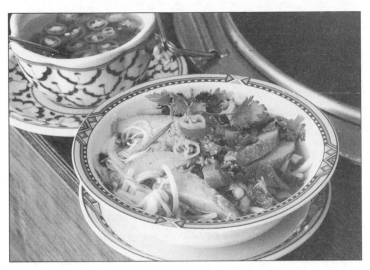

Hu tieu, *the southern-style noodle soup, can be topped with any meat including sausage and pork.*

NOODLE SOUP WITH MEATBALLS

hu tieu bo vien

SERVES 4

Something of a Chinese version of *pho*, this soup is a popular dish in our neighborhood and in the Chinatown section of Saigon. The broth is made by simmering pork and beef bones along with meatballs, tripe, brisket and other cuts of beef. The meatballs and meat are served as a topping and are often dipped in hoisin sauce and chili sauce. However, I prefer the delicate flavors of the toppings and do not serve any sauce with this dish.

The best noodles for this soup are the thin, wiry rice vermicelli (also sold under the Thai name *sen mee*), but you can also use the more common rice sticks used for *pho*.

1. Combine the beef with the shallot and fish sauce. Place in a food processor and process into a smooth paste. Remove

MEATBALLS

⅔ pound beef chuck, cubed

1 tablespoon chopped shallot

1 tablespoon fish sauce

BROTH

1 quart store-bought beef broth

4 cups water

1½ teaspoons five-spice powder

1 (2-inch) piece ginger, peeled and bruised with the flat side of a knife

2 tablespoons soy sauce

1 tablespoon sugar

½ pound bean sprouts, blanched

⅔ pound dried small rice sticks,
  cooked, drained and rinsed
  (page 53)

5 romaine lettuce leaves, each cut
  into thirds

⅓ pound beef sirloin,
  thinly sliced

2 scallions, cut into thin rings

¼ cup chopped cilantro

3 tablespoons Fried Shallots,
  page 34 (optional)

GARNISHES

10 sprigs Asian basil

4 lime wedges

4 Thai bird chilies or another
  fresh chili, chopped

and mold into meatballs, each about ⅔ inch in diameter.
Set aside.

2. In a pot, combine the beef broth, water, five-spice powder,
   ginger, soy sauce and sugar and bring to a boil. Add the
   meatballs and reduce the heat. Skim the top to remove any
   foam or impurities. Simmer until the meatballs are cooked
   through, about 10 minutes. Remove and set aside until
   ready to serve.

3. To serve, bring the broth to a rolling boil. Divide the bean
   sprouts and cooked rice noodles among 4 preheated soup
   bowls. (If the noodles are not hot, reheat in a microwave
   oven or blanch briefly in boiling water.) Place a few pieces
   of romaine, a few slices of sirloin and meatballs on top of
   the noodles. Pour the hot broth over the noodles and garnish with scallions, cilantro and Fried Shallots, if desired.
   Invite guests to add basil leaves, squeezes of lime juice and
   chilies to their bowls before eating.

CHICKEN AND CELLOPHANE NOODLE SOUP

 mien ga

SERVES 4

1 tablespoon vegetable oil

1 clove garlic, thinly sliced

1 shallot, thinly sliced

5 cups fresh Chicken Stock (page
  39) or store-bought low-
  sodium chicken broth

2 cups water

½ pound boneless, skinless
  chicken breast

As a kid, I loved just sucking on these soft, transparent noodles, also known as bean threads or glass noodles. Even
though they come dried and wiry, they cook up plump and
succulent and can easily double in size. Eat the soup soon
after it's cooked because the noodles can absorb nearly all the
broth if left in the bowl too long.

1. Heat the oil in a large pot over moderate heat. Add the garlic and shallot and stir until fragrant, about 20 seconds.

Add the chicken broth and water and bring to a boil. Add the chicken breast and cook until just done, 8 to 10 minutes. Remove and set aside to cool.

2. Add the cellophane noodles, mushrooms, fish sauce and sugar. Reduce the heat to a simmer and cook for 5 minutes. Stir in the boy choy.

3. Hand-shred the chicken into bite-sized strips. Using chopsticks or tongs, divide the noodles among 4 preheated bowls and ladle broth over them. Place some chicken on top, then garnish with the scallions, cilantro and black pepper. Serve immediately.

2 ounces cellophane noodles, soaked in water for 30 minutes, drained and cut into 12-inch strands

4 dried wood-ear mushrooms, soaked in hot water 30 minutes, woody stems discarded and cut into 2 or 3 pieces, if large

1½ tablespoons fish sauce

2 teaspoons sugar

1 cup chopped baby bok choy or spinach

2 scallions, cut into thin rings

3 tablespoons chopped cilantro

Freshly ground black pepper

SWEET-AND-SOUR SHRIMP SOUP WITH FRESH HERBS

canh chua tom

SERVES 4

Unlike noodle soups, this *canh,* or clear broth soup, is meant to be eaten with other foods. At our home, my mom often served this with a savory dish like Aunt Tam's Pork in Claypot (page 150). Traditionally this is made with catfish, but any seafood works nicely, as does chicken or tofu. Make sure to add the herbs right before serving to get the most flavor and aroma. Taro stem, prized for its sponge-like texture, gives this soup an interesting dimension, but it's equally delicious without it. For this recipe, I prefer to use Costa Rican pineapple, which is similar to the sweet and crunchy Vietnamese variety.

1 tablespoon vegetable oil

1 teaspoon minced garlic

½ teaspoon ground chili paste (page 225)

1 quart fresh Chicken Stock (page 39) or store-bought low-sodium chicken broth

1 cup water

1 tablespoon fish sauce, or to taste

1 tablespoon sugar

2 tablespoons tamarind pulp,
    soaked in ⅓ cup water for
    30 minutes, then pushed
    through a sieve, solids
    discarded
1 (8-inch) piece taro stem,
    peeled and cut diagonally
    into ½-inch slices
    (optional, page 231)
2 Roma tomatoes, cut into
    1-inch cubes
2 tablespoons fresh lime juice
⅓ pound raw shrimp, peeled
    and deveined
¼ fresh pineapple, cut into
    thin bite-sized chunks
    (about ½ cup)
2 tablespoons Fried Shallots
    (page 34)
1 cup bean sprouts
2 tablespoons rice paddy herb
    (page 43) or cilantro, chopped
2 tablespoons Asian basil leaves,
    chopped
2 Thai bird chilies, chopped,
    or to taste

1. Heat the oil in a large saucepan over moderate heat. Add the garlic and chili paste and stir until fragrant, about 10 seconds. Add the chicken stock, water, fish sauce, sugar, tamarind, taro slices, if using, tomatoes and lime juice and bring to a boil. Reduce the heat and simmer for 5 minutes. Add the shrimp and pineapple and cook until the shrimp are just done, about 2 minutes. Remove from the heat.

2. Stir in the Fried Shallots, bean sprouts, rice paddy herb, basil and chilies. Transfer the soup to a tureen and serve immediately.

NAPA CABBAGE SOUP WITH SHRIMP DUMPLINGS

canh cai

SERVES 6

The Vietnamese have an affinity for making dumplings out of all kinds of meat and seafood, molding them into different shapes and sizes and adding them to soups, stews and even sandwiches. As a child, I loved helping my mother make this soup and watching the dumplings rise to the top as they cooked. This soup and a well-seasoned seafood dish like Caramelized Garlic Shrimp (page 174) make a satisfying meal.

1. Combine the shrimp, mushrooms, onion, 2 teaspoons of the fish sauce and all of the black pepper in a bowl. Mash with a fork until well blended and sticky. Set aside.
2. Heat the oil in a medium pot over moderate heat. Add the shallot and garlic and stir until fragrant, about 10 seconds. Add the chicken stock, water and the remaining 2 teaspoons fish sauce. Bring to a boil, then reduce the heat slightly to maintain a simmer.
3. Scoop a heaping tablespoon of the shrimp mixture and drop it into the soup. Make more dumplings this way and add to the liquid. Cook, skimming the surface as needed, until the dumplings float to the top and are cooked through, about 10 minutes. Add the cabbage and cook for 2 minutes. Season with salt and pepper, garnish with scallion and cilantro and serve immediately.

¼ pound raw shrimp, peeled, deveined and minced

3 dried black mushrooms, soaked in water for 30 minutes, stemmed and chopped

⅓ cup finely chopped yellow onion

4 teaspoons fish sauce

¼ teaspoon freshly ground black pepper

½ tablespoon vegetable oil

1 shallot, minced

1 clove garlic, minced

4 cups fresh Chicken Stock (page 39) or store-bought low-sodium chicken broth

1 cup water

½ Napa cabbage, cut crosswise into ¼-inch-wide slices (about 3 cups)

Salt and freshly ground black pepper to taste

1 scallion, cut into thin rings

3 sprigs cilantro, thinly sliced

TOFU, TOMATO AND CHIVE SOUP

 canh dau hu he

SERVES 4

1 tablespoon vegetable oil

2 shallots, sliced

5 cups fresh Chicken Stock
   (page 39) or store-bought
   low-sodium chicken broth

1 tablespoon fish sauce

6 ounces soft or medium tofu,
   drained and cut into
   1-inch cubes

2 ripe tomatoes, cut into
   thin wedges

2 small bunches chives, ends
   trimmed and cut into 3-inch
   lengths (about 1 cup)

8 sprigs cilantro, cut into
   2-inch lengths

This northern soup is typical of how *canh* (clear broth soup)
is prepared in Vietnam. It calls for chicken stock and simple
ingredients. You can use any vegetables you like, from root
vegetables to leafy greens. By itself, the soup may taste bland,
but at the Vietnamese table, a clear broth soup is designed to
balance the entire meal. You will want to serve this with other
main dishes, such as Caramelized Garlic Shrimp (page 174)
or Ginger Chicken (page 143).

1. Heat the oil in a soup pot over moderate heat. Add the
   shallots and stir until fragrant, about 10 seconds. Add the
   chicken stock, fish sauce, tofu and tomatoes bring to a boil.
   Reduce the heat to a simmer and cook for about 5 minutes. Add the chives and cilantro and simmer for 1 minute.
   Remove the pan from the heat, transfer to a soup tureen or
   bowl and serve immediately.

chapter three

Sweet and Sour and the Yellow Moon

Salads and Savory Snacks

Hue Chicken Salad

Table Salad

Cucumber Salad

Roasted Eggplant with Scallion Oil

Banana Blossom Salad with Chicken

Pomelo and Grilled Shrimp Salad

Hanoi Calamari Salad

Lotus Stem Salad

Cabbage Salad with Shrimp and Pork

Green Mango Salad with Grilled Beef

Beef Wrapped in Pepper Leaves

Vietnamese Spring Rolls

Vietnamese Sandwich

Rice Paper–Wrapped Salad Rolls

Mustard Leaf–Wrapped Salad Rolls

Hanoi Shrimp Cakes

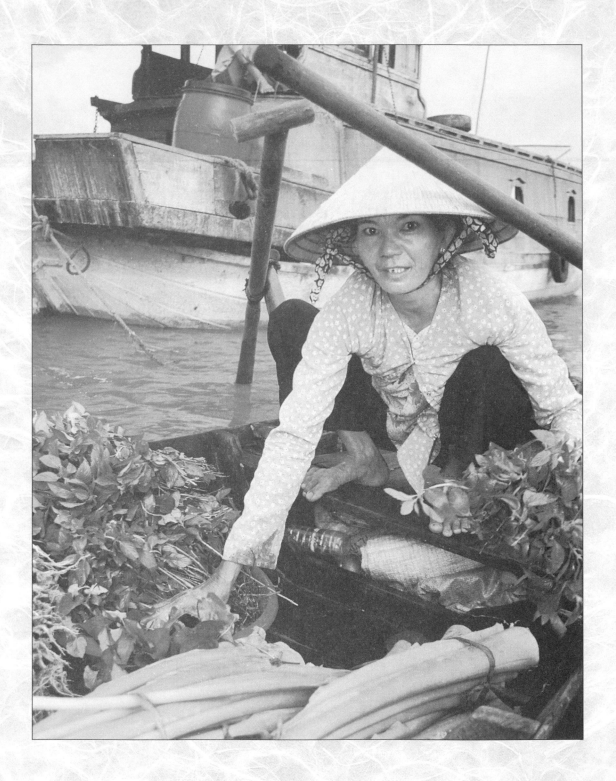

Come back to Hue if you so yearn
Back to the Perfume River
For her water runs deep
For she loves you still
Back to the Ngu Mountains
For the birds have flown home
Waiting for you still
—Vietnamese song

By nightfall, the banks of the Perfume River are like steamed rice cakes—soft, wet and puffy, and under the yellow moon they reflect a shimmering glow. In the distance, I see small boats drifting, the silhouettes of thin women standing at one end pushing their long oars back and forth.

As in other parts of Vietnam, December is unpredictable. Sun and heat easily succumb to rain and cold. Tonight, though, it's somewhere in between—a blessing, I suppose—as it allows me to sit on the terrace listening to the waves lapping up against the edge of the bank.

"When it's cold, it's so cold that your bones shrink," says Nguyen Thi Hanh, chef of the Huong Giang, a historic hotel with the most captivating view of the river. Tonight she'll personally cook me a traditional Hue dinner including *ga bop* (the local version of chicken salad) which is very characteristic of Vietnamese salads in general. "I want to make sure you're getting correctly prepared Hue food," says Chi Hanh, or Sister Hanh, while gently folding the *rau ram* (Vietnamese coriander) into the salad. "Most people just throw the ingredients together and that's wrong."

The first step, she explains, is to hand-shred the chicken while it's still warm and massage it with lime juice and paper-thin slices of onions. The meat should be about the size of an index finger or it may dry out, and the onions must be harvested young so they're more sweet than pungent. Chi Hanh says that adding one aromatic at a time keeps the flavors separate, as opposed to having them all blended in the dressing.

Chi Hanh's meticulous and perfectionist demeanor is typical of cooks from the central region. Known for their strong will and passion, they're particularly proud of the royal cuisine, which flourished during the reign of the Nguyen Dynasty from the early 1800s to the mid-1900s.

Take the case of the chicken salad: In the south, it contains cabbage, but Hue cooks wouldn't even think of adding it, for fear it would dilute the flavors and ruin the dish. As a result, *ga bop* is made with just chicken, onions and a generous amount of herbs. In the true royal cuisine tradition, many salads are not tossed in the kitchen, but arranged in attractive piles so their colors and textures can be appreciated before they're mixed at the table.

Chi Hanh learned to cook from an aunt who had worked at a palace kitchen, and prefers to serve her salads the traditional way. "I'm afraid that if we don't preserve *com vua* [royal cuisine] the young generation will never know it and that would be sad," she says. In an effort to uphold the Hue traditions, Chi Hanh joins a handful of local chefs in staging events like royal dinners and cooking classes and working with visiting chefs and food writers like me.

Her *ga bop* is succulent, the herbs are tender and fragrant and the dressing is so tart it puckers my entire mouth. The dish is simple, yet so complex. In many ways, it's like the people of Hue themselves. Despite the devastating war years and the economic hardships, the people here remain proud and hopeful. Many have so little in terms of material comfort, yet they speak with such conviction and passion—about their music, their poetry and about something as simple as their *ga bop.*

This chapter includes both salad and appetizer-type recipes. In Vietnam, they're served either as part of a meal or, more often, as a snack. The salads share one thing in common: They are tossed in a dressing with no or very little oil, making them low in fat. Limey and highly seasoned, these salads are often served as a savory dish and eaten with rice. In fact, you can make a whole light meal by serving several of these salads and appetizers together.

HUE CHICKEN SALAD

ga bop

SERVES 4

The two most critical ingredients in this recipe are the chicken, which must be juicy and cooked just right, and the *rau ram,* which must be used liberally. The technique for cooking the chicken is based on the Chinese method of submerging a whole bird in boiling water. This simple method produces moist, succulent chicken every single time. In Hue, *ga bop* is served as a snack with beer or as a side to *chao ga* (chicken rice soup). To me it's delicious served any way, even with just a bowl of steamed rice!

1. Fill a large pot with 2 quarts water, add 1 teaspoon sea salt and bring to vigorous boil. Add the chicken and bring the water back to a boil. Reduce the heat and simmer for 10 minutes. Turn off the heat, cover the pot and let the chicken sit in the covered pot for 20 minutes. Remove the chicken and set aside to cool.
2. Remove and discard the skin and bones from the chicken. Hand-shred the meat into ¼-inch-thick strips and place in a bowl.
3. Add the black pepper, 1 teaspoon salt and sugar and gently massage into the chicken. Add the lime juice, sliced onion, chilies, *rau ram* and oil and toss gently.
4. To serve, line a serving plate with the lettuce leaves and place the chicken salad on top.

Sea salt

½ whole chicken, thigh and leg scored for faster cooking

½ teaspoon black peppercorns, lightly toasted in a pan and ground, or ½ teaspoon freshly ground black pepper

2 teaspoons sugar

2½ tablespoons fresh lime juice

1 small yellow onion, sliced paper-thin and rinsed (about ½ cup)

2 Thai bird chilies or 1 serrano chili, chopped, or to taste (optional)

1 cup loosely packed *rau ram* (Vietnamese coriander) leaves or mint leaves

½ tablespoon vegetable oil

4 butter lettuce leaves, preferably inner leaves

TABLE SALAD

 rau song

1 red- or green-leaf lettuce,
  leaves separated, washed and
  drained
½ cucumber, thinly sliced
2 cups bean sprouts
5 or 6 sprigs each of mint, Asian
  basil, *rau ram* and red and
  green perilla or any herb
  combination

In Vietnam, a table salad is used in two main ways—as an accompaniment to meals in which little pieces of meat and seafood are wrapped in the lettuce and eaten out of hand and as an all-purpose salad. When eaten as a salad, diners tear off a piece of lettuce with some herbs and add to their bowls of rice or noodles, or fold the leaves and herbs into little packets to dip into a sauce. A nice table salad can include any combination of *rau ram,* Asian basil, red and green perilla and slices of starfruit or green bananas. For detailed descriptions of favored Vietnamese herbs, see page 40.

1. Arrange the greens in an attractive manner on one side of a large platter. Place the cucumber, bean sprouts and herbs on the other side. Place the platter in the center of the table and serve.

NOTE: If a table salad accompanies a grilled meat dish, you can also serve presoaked rice papers on the side. Just layer some lettuce in between the rice sheets so they don't stick. Or let the guests wet the rice sheets themselves by soaking them in a bowl of warm water at the table.

CUCUMBER SALAD

dua leo ngam giam

SERVES 4

The Vietnamese love cucumber and use it as an all-purpose vegetable. Sometimes the cucumbers are just cut into thin rounds and served plain; other times they're dressed in a sweet-and-sour dressing like this one. This refreshing salad goes well with grilled and steamed meats and seafood. It's even great with a bowl of fried rice. The preferred cucumber to use here is the baby version of the English cucumber, but any pickling variety will do. For interesting variations, sprinkle different herbs on top.

1. Combine the vinegar, lime juice, sugar and salt in a bowl. Stir well and add the cucumbers, shallots, chili, if using, and cilantro. Set aside to stand for 15 minutes, then transfer to a bowl to serve.

¼ cup rice or distilled white vinegar

1 tablespoon fresh lime juice

3 tablespoons sugar

½ teaspoon salt

6 pickling cucumbers, halved and cut into ⅛-inch-thick slices (about 2½ cups)

2 shallots, thinly sliced

½ serrano or other fresh chili, sliced (optional)

6 sprigs cilantro, chopped

ROASTED EGGPLANT WITH SCALLION OIL

ca tim nuong

SERVES 4

In Saigon, where there are literally thousands of small family-run restaurants, it's very hard for one to stand out from the rest. Yet Ba Ca Doi manages to do just that. Owner Hoang Thi Tuc, who has been cooking for more than forty years, and her daughter Dinh Thi Huong offer a changing menu each day. This dish is one of their best. For the most authentic flavor, roast the eggplants over charcoals. If you can get small, slender eggplant (about six inches or shorter), serve them whole, with the stems and caps intact.

1 pound slender, dark purple Asian eggplant

2 tablespoons vegetable oil

2 scallions, sliced into thin rings

2 Thai bird chilies, chopped, or to taste

1 tablespoon fish sauce

Pinch salt

1. Using tongs, place the eggplant on a hot charcoal barbecue or gas burner. (You can also place it directly on an electric stovetop over moderate heat.) Roast the eggplant, turning for even charring, until soft on the outside but still firm on the inside, about 3 to 4 minutes. Remove and let cool.

2. When cool enough to handle, hold the eggplant by the cap under slow running water and peel from top to bottom. Pat dry. Place in a wide bowl. If using larger eggplant, cut each crosswise into 3-inch-long pieces. Pull each piece into two strips. If using very small eggplants, leave them whole.

3. Heat the oil in a skillet over moderate heat. Add the scallions and stir quickly, about 20 seconds. They should foam upon contact and become fragrant. Remove the pan from the heat and add the chilies, fish sauce and salt. Stir, then pour the scallion oil over the eggplant. Toss gently, and transfer to a serving plate. Serve warm or at room temperature.

Banana blossoms.

BANANA BLOSSOM SALAD WITH CHICKEN

goi bap chuoi ga

SERVES 4

My rediscovery of the banana blossom happened in a peculiar way. I was meandering through an orchard behind a house on stilts, where I was staying in Vinh Long—a magical place perched over a small tributary in the Mekong Delta. It was dusk, but appeared much darker because of the big shady trees. All of a sudden, I nearly bumped into a football-looking thing with red flaps and what looked like teeth. I was terrified until I realized that it was just a banana blossom hanging from a large stem, the tiny bananas peeking between the bracts. Since that day, I have been enamored of this fruit.

Banana blossoms are enjoyed throughout Asia, from Burma to Laos to the Philippines. In Vietnam, *bap chuoi* is used primarily in salads and as a soup garnish. It doesn't taste anything like a banana, but does create a tannic sensation in the mouth similar to the feel or the taste of unripe persimmons, which somehow nicely complements the flavors of fish sauce, chilies and lime. In this recipe, only the petals, or bracts, are used. (Some recipes call for the small fruits to be boiled before being tossed into a salad.)

If you don't have banana blossom, substitute white cabbage. You can also turn this into a delicious vegetarian dish by substituting tofu for the chicken and soy sauce for the fish sauce.

1 clove garlic

2 to 3 Thai bird chilies or
    1 serrano chili

2 tablespoons sugar

3½ tablespoons fresh lime juice

2 tablespoons water

2 tablespoons fish sauce

1 medium banana blossom
    (about ⅔ pound)

8 ounces cooked chicken,
    shredded into bite-sized pieces

½ cucumber, seeded and cut into
    thin strips (about ⅔ cup)

¼ yellow onion, sliced
    paper-thin lengthwise

1 cup loosely packed *rau ram*
    (Vietnamese coriander) or
    Asian basil leaves, cut in half

2 tablespoons Fried Shallots
    (page 34)

2 tablespoons chopped Roasted
    Peanuts (page 35)

1. Place the garlic, chilies and sugar in a mortar and pound into a paste. Transfer to a small bowl and combine with 3 tablespoons of the lime juice, the water and fish sauce. Stir well and set the dressing aside.

2. Peel the two or three tougher outer layers of the banana blossom and discard. Remove the bottom core. Using a Japanese mandoline or a sharp knife, slice the blossom crosswise into 1/16-inch-thick pieces. Rinse well and place in a bowl. Add cold water to cover and stir in the remaining ½ tablespoon lime juice. Let stand for 15 minutes. Remove the shredded blossom (but leave the banana pieces that have sunk to the bottom) and drain in a colander. Pat dry with paper towels.

3. Place the chicken in a bowl and add half the dressing. Set aside to marinate for 10 minutes. Add the banana blossom, cucumber, onion, *rau ram,* shallots and half the peanuts. Add the remaining dressing and toss gently. Transfer the salad to a serving plate, garnish with the remaining peanuts and serve.

The Japanese Mandoline

In the Vietnamese kitchen, the *dao bao* is an indispensable tool. Similar to a large peeler, this knife is used to thinly slice banana blossom, carrots, cabbage, cucumber and other vegetables and is especially useful for making salads. In the United States I've found that the Japanese mandoline, which is available at Asian markets and specialty kitchenware stores, can do basically the same job and is perhaps easier to handle. If you like Asian salads, it is a valuable kitchen tool to have.

POMELO AND GRILLED SHRIMP SALAD

goi buoi

SERVES 4

In this salad, the pomelo—which is more fragrant and sweeter than its cousin the grapefruit—greatly enhances the smokiness of grilled shrimp. If you can't find pomelo, substitute grapefruit, and if the one you have is especially tart, use a little less than is called for below.

1. Combine the shrimp, shallot, fish sauce, soy sauce, sugar and oil in a bowl. Set aside to marinate for 20 minutes.
2. Thread 4 shrimp on each skewer. Grill or broil until the shrimp are just done, about 2 to 3 minutes. Set aside.
3. Place the carrots, cucumbers, pomelo, dipping sauce, basil, cilantro, chili and peanuts in a large bowl and toss gently. Remove the shrimp from the skewers, add them to the salad and gently toss a few times. Transfer to a serving plate and serve.

16 medium shrimp, peeled and deveined

1 teaspoon minced shallot

1 teaspoon fish sauce

1 teaspoon soy sauce

½ teaspoon sugar

2 tablespoons vegetable oil

4 (8-inch) bamboo skewers, soaked in hot water for 30 minutes and drained

⅓ cup matchstick carrot strips, soaked in ice water for 30 minutes and drained

⅓ cup matchstick cucumber strips, soaked in ice water for 30 minutes and drained

1 cup pomelo segments, separated into bite-sized pieces

¼ cup Vietnamese Dipping Sauce (page 23)

20 Asian basil leaves, coarsely chopped

1 tablespoon chopped cilantro

1 Thai bird chili, chopped

2 tablespoons chopped Roasted Peanuts (page 35)

A roadside pomelo stand in the Mekong Delta.

HANOI CALAMARI SALAD

 goi muc Hanoi

SERVES 4

1 pound fresh or frozen cleaned
   or whole calamari, preferably
   small
1 (1-inch) piece ginger, peeled
   and cut into thin slivers
   (about 1 tablespoon)
⅓ cup Chili-Lime Dipping Sauce
   (page 30)
1 shallot, thinly sliced
1 Thai bird chili or ½ serrano
   chili, or to taste, chopped
1 or 2 bunches Asian celery,
   chewy bottom discarded,
   stalks cut into thin matchsticks, soaked in cold water
   for 30 minutes and drained
   (about 2½ cups)
½ hothouse cucumber, cut into
   thin matchsticks, soaked in
   cold water for 30 minutes and
   drained
⅓ cup Asian basil leaves,
   cut in half

When I first tasted this delightful dish at the Seasons of Hanoi Restaurant, I knew I had found my favorite calamari salad. One of the first upscale restaurants to open after the economic and trade reform policies in the early 1990s, Seasons is known for its efforts in reviving the cooking traditions of the north.

In this recipe, the Asian celery—which is more aromatic than the regular variety—adds a distinctive flavor and crunch. If you can't find it, use regular celery or fennel, but slice it thin.

1. To clean a whole calamari, pull the tentacles from the tube section. Trim off the tentacles by carefully cutting them right above the eyes. Save the tentacles and discard the bottom part. Pull the thin backbone from the body and discard. Cut the tube into rings about ½ inch thick. Rinse well, making sure the inside of the calamari rings are clean.

2. Bring a pot of water to a rolling boil. Place the calamari in a sieve and dip it into the hot water just until the calamari plump up, about 5 seconds, depending on the thickness. Drain completely and place in a bowl. Add the ginger and the sauce and set aside for 5 minutes. Add the shallot, chili, celery, cucumber and basil leaves and toss gently. Transfer to a serving plate.

LOTUS STEM SALAD

goi ngo sen

SERVES 4

Lotus stems look like long, thin spears of asparagus but don't taste anything like them. In Vietnam, they're prized for their crunchy texture and for their ability to absorb sauces. In the United States, you can find lotus stems (labeled lotus rootlets) packed in brine in jars. It you can't find the stems, try lotus roots, which are readily available fresh at Asian markets. They're like *jícama,* crunchy and white, with a beautiful lace-like pattern on the inside. Peel and thinly slice the tuber, then soak in cold water with a little lemon juice.

1 clove garlic, minced

1 Thai bird chili or
    ½ serrano chili, chopped

1½ tablespoons fish sauce

2 tablespoons fresh lime juice

1½ tablespoons sugar

1 (8-ounce) jar lotus stems,
    drained, or 1 cup thinly sliced
    lotus root

½ cucumber (preferably
    hothouse), seeded, cut into
    thin strips, soaked in cold
    water for 30 minutes and
    drained

¼ pound deveined shrimp,
    cooked, peeled and cut in
    half lengthwise

⅓ cup *rau ram* (Vietnamese
    coriander) or Asian basil
    leaves

2 tablespoons Fried Shallots
    (optional, page 33)

3 tablespoons chopped Roasted
    Peanuts (page 35)

3 sprigs cilantro, cut into
    2-inch lengths

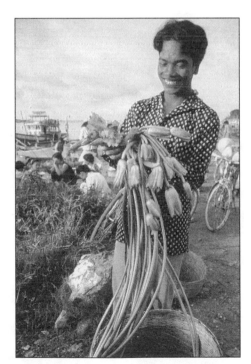

Like lotus stems, lily stems add textures to salads and soups.

1. Combine the garlic, chili, fish sauce, lime juice and sugar in a bowl and stir well. Set the dressing aside.
2. Cut the lotus stems diagonally into 2-inch pieces. Place in a bowl and cover generously with water. Using bamboo chopsticks (like the disposable ones at Chinese restaurants), stir the water continuously for 2 to 3 minutes. (The rough surface of the chopsticks will catch the fibers.) Remove the fibers that are wrapped around the chopsticks and discard. Drain the lotus stems and add to the dressing. Toss several times and set aside to marinate for 10 minutes.
3. Add the cucumber, shrimp, *rau ram,* shallots, if using, and peanuts and toss gently. Transfer the salad to a serving plate, garnish with the cilantro and serve.

The Lotus

The lotus is a beloved plant in Asia, symbolizing purity, perfection and beauty. Every part of the plant is eaten or used. The beautiful white and pink flowers grace temple shrines and family altars. The stamens are made into an aromatic tea, which some believe works like a mild sleep enhancer. The seeds are dried, then boiled and made into candies or added to puddings and cakes. The large round leaves are used to wrap sticky rice and other foods for steaming.

The lotus has long stems connecting the main plant to its many leaves and flowers. In Vietnam, these stems are peeled, sliced and added to soups and salads. At the base of the plant are clusters of bulbous roots that taste like *jícama* or water chestnuts. When the tubers are sliced crosswise, you can see the beautiful lacy patterns within. Lotus roots are believed to help purify the blood. The Vietnamese and Chinese love them in braised dishes and soups.

CABBAGE SALAD WITH SHRIMP AND PORK

goi tom thit

SERVES 4

In Vietnam, the most popular salad happens to be one of the easiest to make. In this traditional version, the pork and shrimp are simply poached, then added to paper-thin slices of cabbage, carrots, cucumbers and *rau ram* and tossed in a lime-based dressing. You can make this with any meat combination (chicken would be great, too), or you can omit the meat and serve it as a side salad. For best results, use a Japanese mandoline for slicing the vegetables.

1. Combine the onion, chilies, if using, fish sauce, lime juice, salt, sugar and water in a large bowl. Set the dressing aside until ready to use.
2. Using a Japanese mandoline, shred the cabbage into 1/16-inch-thick pieces. (You can also cut it by hand.) Place the cabbage in a large bowl and cover with cold water. Cut the carrot into long matchsticks and add to the bowl to soak for 30 minutes. Cut the cucumber on the diagonal into 1/8-inch-thick slices and set aside.
3. Add the shrimp and pork to the dressing and marinate for 5 minutes. Remove the cabbage and carrot from the water and spin dry. Add to the bowl of shrimp and pork, along with the cucumber, *rau ram,* cilantro, shallots, if using, and half of the peanuts. Toss gently and transfer to a serving plate. Garnish with the remaining peanuts and serve immediately.

¼ yellow onion, sliced paper-thin and rinsed (about ¼ cup)

2 or 3 Thai bird chilies, cut into thin rings (optional)

1 tablespoon fish sauce

3 tablespoons fresh lime juice

½ teaspoon salt

3 tablespoons sugar

3 tablespoons water

¼ head green cabbage

½ carrot, peeled

½ cucumber (preferably hothouse), halved crosswise

4 ounces cooked shrimp

4 ounces cooked pork (butt or shoulder) or chicken, cut into thin bite-sized strips

1 cup loosely packed *rau ram* leaves (Vietnamese coriander, page 45)

5 sprigs cilantro, chopped

3 tablespoons Fried Shallots (optional, page 33)

3 tablespoons chopped Roasted Peanuts (page 35)

GREEN MANGO SALAD WITH GRILLED BEEF

 goi xoai voi bo

SERVES 6

2 tablespoons minced lemongrass

½ tablespoon finely chopped
  shallot

2 teaspoons fish sauce

1 teaspoon soy sauce

1 teaspoon sugar

½ pound New York steak or
  another tender beef,
  sliced against the grain into
  ¼-inch-thick strips

1 green mango (about 1 pound),
  peeled and cut into thin
  1 by 3-inch rectangular pieces

⅓ cup Chili-Lime Dipping Sauce
  (page 30)

1 tablespoon chopped cilantro

¼ cup Asian basil leaves,
  cut into thirds

2 tablespoons Fried Shallots
  (page 33)

2 tablespoons whole Roasted
  Peanuts (page 35)

One of the most memorable dishes I had in Saigon in recent years is this tangy green mango salad. The crunchy ribbons of sour mango juxtapose nicely against the smoky grilled beef. Green mangoes are a special type grown to be eaten when they're green and tart. If you can't find them at Asian markets, substitute Granny Smith apples.

1. Combine the lemongrass, shallot, fish sauce, soy sauce and sugar in a bowl and stir well. Add the beef and marinate for 20 minutes.
2. Grill the beef over a barbecue grill or pan-sear in an oiled skillet over high heat until just done, about 1 to 2 minutes.
3. In a serving bowl combine the mango with the chili-lime sauce and toss gently. Add the beef, cilantro, basil, shallots and peanuts. Toss gently and serve.

Green mangoes.

BEEF WRAPPED IN PEPPER LEAVES

bo nuong la lot

SERVES 4

La lot (pepper leaf) is used extensively in Vietnam, as an aromatic leaf in stir-fries and soups and as a wrapper. A member of the wild betel family, it has shiny, dark green heart-shaped leaves. In the United States, these leaves have been showing up more frequently at Asian markets. If you can't find them, substitute red perilla or *shiso* or grape leaves.

This dish is part of *bo bay mon* (Beef in Seven Ways), a popular special meal, featuring multiple beef courses. To enjoy this dish, serve it as an appetizer or as a topping for Rice Noodles with Fresh Herbs (page 119).

These rolls are typically grilled over hot coals. However, I prefer to cook them in a pan because the *la lot* leaves available in the United States are too mature and burn more easily when cooked on a grill.

1. Heat 2 tablespoons of the oil in a pan over moderate heat. Add the garlic and onion and stir until softened, about 2 minutes. Transfer to a bowl. Add the lemongrass, peanuts, turmeric, sugar, fish sauce, salt and ground beef. Mix with a fork until well blended and sticky, about 2 to 3 minutes. Set aside for 30 minutes.

2. To make the rolls, place 1 heaping tablespoon of the meat mixture in the center of a pepper leaf. Using your fingers, shape the meat into a cylinder about 2 inches long and ¾ inch wide. Wrap the leaf around the meat but leave the sides open. (If necessary, use 2 leaves.) When done, place the roll seam side down. Make the remaining rolls in the same way.

3. Thread 5 rolls onto each bamboo skewer, positioning the

4 tablespoons vegetable oil

1½ teaspoons minced garlic

½ yellow onion, chopped (about ⅔ cup)

2 tablespoons finely chopped lemongrass

3 tablespoons chopped Roasted Peanuts (page 35)

1 teaspoon ground turmeric

2 teaspoons sugar

2 teaspoons fish sauce

¼ teaspoon salt

½ pound coarsely ground beef

30 large *la lot* (pepper leaves, page 44) or red perilla or grape leaves

4 (6- or 8-inch) bamboo skewers

Table Salad (page 80), for serving

Vietnamese Dipping Sauce (page 23), for serving

rolls so they touch one another at the seams. Set aside until ready to cook.

4. Heat the remaining 2 tablespoons oil in a large nonstick frying pan over low heat. (Make sure the pan is large enough to accommodate the skewers. If not, shorten the skewers.) Add the beef rolls and cook until the meat is done, about 5 to 7 minutes total. Do not overcrowd the pan. Reduce the heat as necessary to keep the leaves from charring.

5. Transfer the skewers to a platter. Remove the skewers and serve the rolls with Table Salad and Vietnamese Dipping Sauce.

VIETNAMESE SPRING ROLLS

 cha gio

MAKES 30 ROLLS

FILLING

2 eggs

2 tablespoons fish sauce

½ tablespoon minced garlic

¼ teaspoon sea salt

2 teaspoons plus 3 tablespoons sugar

½ teaspoon ground black pepper

2 ounces bean threads (cellophane noodles), soaked in hot water for 30 minutes, drained and cut into 2-inch pieces

5 or 6 dried wood-ear mushrooms, soaked in hot water for 30 minutes, drained, chewy stems trimmed and finely chopped (about ¼ cup)

Called *nem ran* in Hanoi and *cha gio* in Saigon, these crispy rolls are most memorable when served the traditional way—wrapped in lettuce leaves with fresh herbs and then dipped in a sauce and eaten out of hand. They can be enjoyed as an appetizer, or as a meal when served as a topping on Rice Noodles with Fresh Herbs (page 119).

Cha gio is best when it's made with pork and crab and wrapped in thin rice paper, which is now becoming easier to find in the markets with all the new products coming from Vietnam. (Previously, many of the imported rice papers were too thick and often cooked up too chewy.) If you can't find the thin rice sheets, try the frozen wheat-flour spring roll wrappers (page 229). (Use an egg wash to seal the edges of the rolls.) They aren't as flavorful but are easy to use and cook up quite nicely.

These rolls can be made in advance and cooked halfway. Just before serving, finish them in a preheated 325-degree oven for about 15 minutes.

1. Make the filling: Beat the eggs, fish sauce, garlic, salt, 2 teaspoons sugar and black pepper together in a large bowl. Add the bean threads, mushrooms, onion, taro root, scallions, crabmeat and pork. Using a fork, gently mix until the ingredients are well blended.

2. Fill a large bowl with the warm water. Add the remaining 3 tablespoons sugar to the water and stir to dissolve. (This helps the rice paper turn golden when fried.) Dip the rice paper into the water and turn to moisten the sheet completely. Lay the rice sheet on a damp kitchen cloth. Wet another rice paper sheet and place it side by side. (This allows you to work with one sheet while the second sets.) Place 1 heaping tablespoon of the filling on the bottom third of the sheet. Using your fingers, gently shape into a small cylinder. Lift the bottom edge over the filling, then fold in both sides. Roll into a small cylinder, about ⅔ inch wide and 2 inches long. Place seam side down. (If you're using the wheat-flour spring roll wrapper, brush a little egg wash on the edges to seal.) Do not stack the rolls. Continue to make the rolls with the remaining filling and paper in this way. If a wrapper has a tear, reinforce it by patching it with a small piece of dampened rice paper.

3. Pour about 1½ inches of vegetable oil into to a large skillet and heat to about 350 degrees. Test the temperature by carefully placing a spring roll in it. If the oil foams but not too vigorously upon contact, it is hot enough. Add the rolls without crowding, and fry until evenly golden, about 5 to 6 minutes. (Cook in batches, if necessary.) Remove and drain on paper towels. Serve the spring rolls immediately with the dipping sauce and table salad.

⅔ cup minced yellow onion, squeezed gently to remove excess liquid

1 taro root, peeled and finely grated (about 1 cup) or 1 cup grated carrots

3 scallions, cut into thin rings

⅓ pound cooked crabmeat, picked clean, or coarsely chopped raw shrimp

⅔ pound ground pork

2 quarts warm water

30 (6- or 8-inch) dried rice paper rounds, plus extras

Vegetable oil for frying

Vietnamese Dipping Sauce (page 23), for serving

Table Salad (page 80), for serving

Rice papers are sun-dried on bamboo mats.

VIETNAMESE SANDWICH

 banh mi thit

SERVES 4

2 tablespoons vegetable oil

1 tablespoon chopped garlic

1½ teaspoons five-spice powder

½ teaspoon ground dried chili
or to taste

1 tablespoon soy sauce

2 teaspoons sugar

⅓ pound ground pork

4 (6-inch) baguette pieces

⅓ pound cooked pork butt or
shoulder, thinly sliced

¼ pound *cha lua* (Vietnamese
sausage) or headcheese or
ham, thinly sliced

⅓ cup Marinated Daikon and
Carrots (page 38)

⅓ hothouse cucumber, seeded,
cut into ¼-inch strips

8 sprigs cilantro

1 serrano or jalapeño chili,
thinly sliced on the diagonal

Salt and pepper

There must be thousands of sandwich stands all over Vietnam, but the sandwiches that always stand out in my mind are the *banh mi* at the market in Hoi An. The vendor starts by first heating a small baguette on the charcoal brazier hidden underneath his wooden cart. Then he adds a delicious sauce made from ground pork followed by thinly sliced pork and *cha lua*, a dense pork sausage sold at Vietnamese markets. To finish, he garnishes the filling with fresh herbs and marinated vegetables. One bite into his sandwich and I'm in heaven.

This recipe is based on that delicious sandwich. Try to find a very airy baguette and do serve it with the marinated vegetables. Without them, this sandwich wouldn't be Vietnamese.

1. Heat the oil in a medium skillet over moderate heat. Add the garlic, five-spice powder, dried chili, soy sauce, and sugar and stir until fragrant, about 10 seconds. Add the ground pork and stir a few times. Reduce the heat and cook until the meat is done, about 3 to 4 minutes. Remove from the heat and set aside.

3. Reheat the baguette in a 300-degree oven so that the outside is warm and crusty, about 5 minutes. Cut each baguette in half lengthwise without separating. Spread 2 to 3 tablespoons of the ground pork mixture (including pan juices) on the bread. Add one-fourth of the pork slices and one-fourth of the pork sausage, making sure the meat is evenly spread on the bread. Garnish the sandwich with marinated vegetables, cucumber, cilantro and chili along with some salt and pepper.

RICE PAPER–WRAPPED SALAD ROLLS

goi cuon

SERVES 6 TO 8 AS AN APPETIZER

To me, this is one of Vietnam's greatest culinary treasures. Made with poached shrimp, pork and fresh mint, *goi cuon* are wrapped in rice paper and dipped in a sauce. Similar to a salad that has been rolled up, these are usually eaten as a snack, although they also make a lovely lunch.

The key is to roll these tightly and that requires practice. You can substitute chicken or beef, or tofu and mushrooms for the filling. Grilled fish, such as salmon, also works well. Traditionally *goi cuon* are served whole, but I like cutting them into smaller pieces because they're easier to serve and share. Notice I called for untrimmed pork because the dish benefits from a little fat. In Vietnam, these rolls are traditionally served with a heavier bean sauce, but you can also serve them with the lighter Vietnamese Bean Dipping Sauce (page 28), which I prefer.

⅓ pound pork shoulder, untrimmed, cut into two pieces

12 medium raw shrimp, unpeeled

4 ounces *bun* (rice vermicelli or rice sticks), boiled for 5 minutes, rinsed and drained (page 112)

1 cup bean sprouts

½ cup mint leaves

1 small head red-leaf lettuce, leaves separated and washed

8 (12-inch) dried rice papers, round, plus extras

½ cup Vietnamese Bean Dipping Sauce (page 28), for serving

1. Cook the pork in boiling salted water until it's done but still firm enough for slicing, about 30 minutes.

2. While the pork is cooking, bring another small pot of water to a boil. Add the shrimp and cook until they turn pink, about 3 minutes. Rinse under running water and set aside to drain. When cool enough to handle, peel, devein and cut in half lengthwise. Refresh in cold water and set aside.

3. Remove the pork from the heat and drain. When it's cool enough to handle, slice into thin slices, about 1 by 2½ inches. Place on a small plate and set aside.

4. Set up a salad roll "station." Line a cutting board with a damp kitchen towel. Fill a large bowl with hot water and place it nearby. (Keep some boiling water handy to add to the bowl.) Arrange the ingredients in the order they will be used: the shrimp, pork, rice vermicelli, bean sprouts, mint and lettuce.

5. Working with 2 rice paper rounds at a time, dip one, edge first, into the hot water and turn it to wet completely, about 10 seconds. Lay the round down on the towel. Repeat with the second rice paper and place it alongside the first. This allows you to work with one while the second is being set.

6. Line the bottom third of the rice paper round with 3 shrimp halves, cut side up, and top with 2 slices of pork. Add 1 tablespoon rice vermicelli, 1 tablespoon bean sprouts, and 4 to 5 mint leaves. (Arrange the ingredients so the rolls will end up being about 5 inches long and 1 inch wide.) Halve a lettuce leaf lengthwise along the center rib. Roll up in one piece and place on the filling. (Trim if it's too long.) While pressing down on the ingredients, lift the bottom edge over the filling, then fold in the two sides. Roll into a cylinder about 1½ inches wide and 4–5 inches long. If the paper feels thick, stop three-quarters of the way and trim the end piece. (Too much rice paper can make the rolls chewy.) Repeat with the remaining rice papers and filling.

7. To serve, cut the rolls into 2 or 4 pieces and place them upright on a plate. Serve with the sauce on the side.

Rice Paper

In Vietnam, *banh trang* (rice paper) is still made by hand, one sheet at a time. In the village of Trang Bang, about fifty miles north of Saigon, there are several dozen families that specialize in this ancient art. Using the same recipes that have been handed down from one generation to another, they work tirelessly, usually in a small corner of the house near a window. The equipment is very basic—a big pot of simmering water sitting on top of a rice husk–burning stove.

To make *banh trang,* the rice paper–maker (usually the mother or eldest daughter) ladles a thin layer of rice flour batter on a cloth tightly stretched over the pot. The rice batter is allowed to steam for about 20 seconds after which it's transferred to a bamboo mat to be sun dried. It is during this process that rice papers take on their beautiful pattern from the weave of the mats. Once fully dried, the rice papers pop loose, creating a succession of faint cracks. The women then trim the sheets into perfect rounds by hand. Finally, they're loaded on a bicycle and taken to the village distribution house. In addition to plain rice papers, *banh trang* are available in different flavors such as coconut, ginger and pandanus. Some varieties are made with *bot nep* (glutinous rice flour) and once toasted, they puff up and have a great chewy texture.

Making rice paper by hand.

MUSTARD LEAF–WRAPPED SALAD ROLLS

 cuon diep

12 medium cooked shrimp,
    peeled and deveined

2 tablespoons vegetable oil

1 teaspoon minced garlic

½ teaspoons ground chili paste
    (page 225)

3 tablespoons peanut butter

¼ cup hoisin sauce (page 226)

2 tablespoons fermented whole
    soybeans (optional, page 225)

2 tablespoons rice vinegar

3 tablespoons water

12 Chinese mustard leaves

1½ cups cooked *bun*
    (rice vermicelli, page 112)

1 cup bean sprouts

24 Asian basil leaves

5 ounces cooked pork butt, cut
    into 1½ x 1 x ⅛-inch slices

12 scallions plus extras, blanched
    in hot water for 5 seconds,
    drained

GARNISHES

2 Thai bird chilies or
    ½ serrano chili,
    finely chopped (optional)

2 tablespoons ground Roasted
    Peanuts (page 36)

This beautiful dish epitomizes the elegance and meticulousness of Vietnamese royal cuisine. Similar to other delicacies of Hue (the former imperial capital city), these rolls are filled with shrimp and pork, then wrapped with tender Chinese mustard leaves. These greens add a delicious spicy undertone to the dish, but if you can't find them, substitute romaine lettuce leaves. If you are lucky enough to find *gai choy,* the narrow-stemmed variety of mustard leaf, use it.

1. For the sauce, mince 6 of the shrimp. Heat the oil in a small pot over moderate heat. Add garlic and minced shrimp and stir until fragrant, about 20 seconds. Add the chili paste, peanut butter, hoisin sauce, fermented soybeans, rice vinegar and water. Stir to blend in the ingredients, then reduce the heat. Simmer until the sauce is slightly thickened, about 4 to 5 minutes. (Add more water if necessary.) Set aside until ready to serve.

2. To make the rolls, cut the remaining shrimp in half lengthwise. Place a mustard leaf on a cutting board, with the bottom stem pointing at you and the smooth side facing down. Place 1 tablespoon rice vermicelli on the leaf, followed by 4 or 5 bean sprouts, 2 basil leaves, 1 pork slice and 1 shrimp half. Roll the leaves into a small cylinder, about ⅔ inch wide. Run the scallion around the roll twice, then tie into a knot. Repeat until all the rolls are made.

3. Trim the ends so the rolls are all the same length. Garnish the dipping sauce with chilies and peanuts, then serve on the side with the rolls. *Cuon diep* can be made in advance and refrigerated until ready to serve.

HANOI SHRIMP CAKES

banh tom

In Hanoi, a popular weekend outing is to head out to West Lake and eat *banh tom* (shrimp cakes) at one of the many outdoor cafés along the water. There must be at least a dozen restaurants featuring the same *banh tom*—all in full view of the sunset and the ancient pagoda towers nearby.

This dish is usually made with small unpeeled shrimp that cook up very crisp and moist. To eat, you wrap the shrimp cakes with the herbs and lettuce, then dip in a sauce. Because it's hard to find such small shrimp, I've substituted medium shrimp. For a more elegant twist, serve these cakes on a small bed of baby greens and herbs. It makes a beautiful and delicious appetizer.

½ cup all-purpose flour

⅓ cup rice flour

½ teaspoon baking powder

2 teaspoons sugar

½ teaspoon salt

½ teaspoon freshly ground
   black pepper

2 scallions, cut into thin rings

1 cup water

⅔ pound sweet potatoes,
   peeled, cut into thin
   matchstick strips

½ pound shrimp, peeled,
   deveined and cut into
   ½-inch pieces

Vegetable oil for frying

Table Salad (page 80), for serving

Vietnamese Dipping Sauce
   (page 23), for serving

1. In a bowl, combine the flour, rice flour, baking powder, sugar, salt, pepper, scallions and water. Set aside for 10 minutes. Fold in the sweet potatoes and shrimp. Do not overmix.

2. Heat 1 inch of oil in a medium skillet until it reaches about 330 degrees on a deep-fat thermometer. Place 2 heaping tablespoons shrimp batter in the middle of a flat metal spatula. Pat the batter down slightly to form a loose, irregular cake about ¼ inch thick.

3. Gently push the cake into the hot oil. Fry the cake, turning it over once, until evenly brown and cooked, about 2 to 3 minutes. Drain on paper towels. Repeat with the remaining batter, cooking only 3 or 4 cakes at a time. Keep the cakes warm in a preheated low oven until ready to serve.

4. To eat, place a piece of the shrimp cake and some herbs on a lettuce leaf from the Table Salad. Fold into a packet, dip into the sauce and eat.

chapter four

Mrs. Red's Rice Cakes

Rice Noodles, Cakes and Rolls

Steamed Rice Cakes with Shrimp

Rice Rolls with Shrimp and Wood-Ear Mushrooms

Rice Rolls—The Traditional Steamed Method

Fresh Rice Noodles

Scallion Noodles

Wok-Seared Noodles with Chicken and Mushrooms

Sizzling Saigon Crepes

Rice Noodles with Fresh Herbs

Lemongrass Beef on Cool Noodles

Hanoi Rice Noodles with Grilled Pork

Rice Noodle Stir-Fry with Pork

Noodle Pillows with Chicken and Shrimp

Grilled Shrimp on Sugarcane

Bean Thread Noodles with Crab

Hanoi Grilled Fish with Rice Noodles and Fresh Herbs

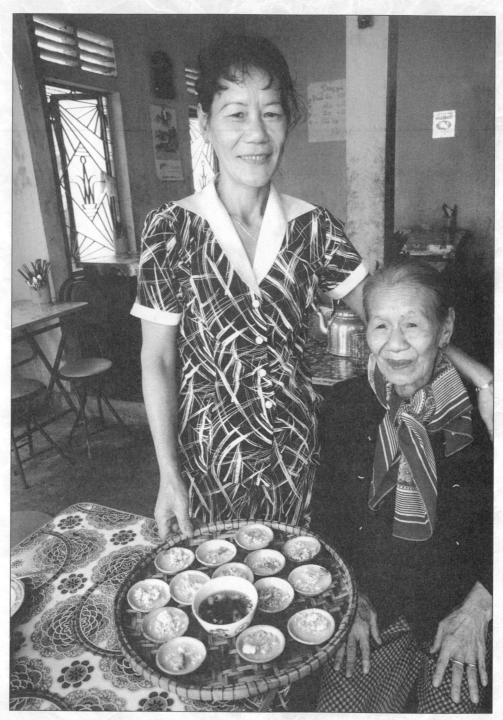

Ba Do and her daughter have been making banh beo *for more than fifty years.*

I t's hard to be in Hue without coming here to Quan Ba Do (Mrs. Red's Restaurant), probably the country's most famous place for *banh beo,* a local specialty of steamed rice cakes served with shredded shrimp.

"Come on in!" shouts Nguyen Thi Mai, as some friends and I climb out of our vehicle. Ba Mai, or Mrs. Mai as she's called, eagerly points us to a table up front, the red shawl on her head slipping as she excitedly pulls out the chairs. Around here, she's considered a master of *banh beo,* a dish that she learned from her mother, who first sold them at the market more than fifty years ago. (The restaurant was named after her mother, who was always seen wearing a red shawl.)

Several years ago, Ba Mai and her sister decided to open a restaurant at home so they could work together under one roof and still be able to care for their eighty-year-old mother. Every day, while the children frolic on the nearby divan, the women toil in the kitchen, preparing endless batches of *banh beo.*

Knowing that we're hungry, Ba Mai fires up the stove and starts to load the steamer with tiny ramekins. She vigorously stirs the rice flour batter—one moment moving left, another moving right—the sloshing sounds thumping and echoing from the huge vat. "You have to constantly stir because the rice flour loves to settle at the bottom," she explains while ladling a tiny amount into the dishes.

Ba Mai says a good *banh beo* should fit perfectly in the mouth, not be so thick and intrusive that it throws off the balance of the toppings. That's why she only puts two

Rice and rice flour noodles form the heart of Vietnamese cuisine.

tablespoons batter in each dish. "You have to start with good *bot gao* [rice flour] and you have to have an excellent sauce," she says.

The whole process begins early each morning when she hauls two large pails of rice to a nearby mill. The rice, which was soaked overnight to soften and slightly ferment, is then ground into a smooth paste. Once mixed with water, it can be made into *banh beo,* or any of the many noodle products eaten throughout the country. In fact, most Vietnamese rice noodles are prepared this way.

I can see why Ba Mai is so proud of her *banh beo.* When they emerge from the steamer, they look translucent, silkier and shinier than those that I make at my restaurant. The intense heat around the rim of the dish has made the edges puff up, creating a little crater in the center for the delicious sauce to collect.

Watching her makes me think of how my own mother used to make these rice cakes. In the southern part of Vietnam, cooks often use coconut milk to enrich the batter. Sometimes, when my mother didn't have enough round dishes, she would use porcelain spoons, creating cakes that looked like fat ears.

In our home, my mother unmolded the cakes before serving them. But in keeping with Hue traditions, Ba Mai serves them right in the ramekins, with the shredded shrimp and pork cracklings on top. To eat, I drizzle some *nuoc cham,* then loosen the cake with a long-handled spoon. The *banh beo* practically melts in my mouth and the shrimp, probably still jumping this morning, have a sweet, almost buttery flavor.

By now a few kids are swarming around us, totally in awe of our presence. "Don't you have this food over there in the U.S.?" asks one little girl while trying to peek through the lens of my camera.

"Yes, we do, but it's not quite the same," I reply. How could it be the same, I'm wondering, if you take this *banh beo* dish outside of this home? As I'm pondering the idea, I can see Ba Mai loading more dishes into the steamer rack. She's mumbling something about lunch for her mother upstairs. Her sister, while holding a baby in one arm, adds more firewood to the stove.

STEAMED RICE CAKES WITH SHRIMP

banh beo tom chay

SERVES 4 AS A MAIN DISH (ABOUT 48 LITTLE CAKES)

Based on a recipe from Mrs. Red's Restaurant, these delicious little rice cakes can be made in advance and reheated. You can serve them as an appetizer, or as a main course. You will need a large two-tier steamer, either aluminum or bamboo, and at least one dozen shallow dishes about 3 to 4 inches in diameter. Cook the first dozen cakes, remove them, then reuse the dishes for the next batch. Or, if you have a lot of dishes, serve the cakes right in the molds, as it's done in Hue.

1. Make the batter: Whisk the rice flour, water and salt in a bowl and set aside for at least 30 minutes.
2. Make the topping: Place the shrimp in a food processor and pulse until finely shredded. Alternatively, pound the shrimp with a mortar and pestle.
3. Heat the oil in a small nonstick pan over moderate heat.

BATTER

2 cups rice flour

2¾ cups water

½ teaspoon salt

TOPPING

4 ounces cooked shrimp,
    peeled and deveined

1 tablespoon vegetable oil

1 shallot, finely minced

½ teaspoon fish sauce

½ teaspoon sugar

Pinch salt

⅓ cup Scallion Oil
    (page 33)

GARNISH

1¼ cups Light Vietnamese
    Dipping Sauce (page 26)

Making banh beo, *steamed rice cakes with shrimp.*

Finished steamed rice cakes with shrimp topping.

Add the shallot and stir until fragrant, about 1 minute. Reduce the heat, add the shredded shrimp and stir until the mixture is dry and fragrant, 5 to 6 minutes. Add the fish sauce, sugar and salt. Stir for another minute. Transfer to a bowl and set aside until ready to use.

4. Fill the steamer pan halfway with water and bring to a boil. Arrange as many ramekins as will fit on the two steamer racks. Stir the rice batter well, then ladle 1½ to 2 tablespoons batter into each dish. Carefully place the racks on the pan. Cover and steam until the rice cakes are white and shiny, about 4 to 5 minutes. Remove and set aside to cool.

5. To unmold the cakes, dip the tip of a small knife in water and run it along the edge of each dish. Transfer the cakes to a plate. Arrange in a circular pattern, with one slightly touching the next. Rinse and wipe the dishes clean and continue to make rice cakes until the batter is finished.

6. To serve, sprinkle each cake with ½ teaspoon Scallion Oil and ½ teaspoon shredded shrimp. Invite guests to drizzle the dipping sauce on each cake before eating.

RICE ROLLS WITH SHRIMP AND WOOD-EAR MUSHROOMS

banh cuon chao

SERVES 4 AS A MAIN DISH (28 ROLLS)

Next to *pho,* this is my all-time favorite dish. Made with thin, almost transparent rice sheets wrapped around pork or shrimp and mushrooms, these delicious rolls are eaten all over Vietnam. There are two basic versions—one is stuffed, as in this recipe, and the other is the plain, unstuffed rice sheet served with *cha lua* (pork sausage). I love both versions, but the former is more sumptuous.

The best way to prepare this dish is to recruit a helper: One person makes the rice sheet and the other stuffs it while it's still warm and easy to work with. Traditionally, the sheets are steamed in a special pot (see page 111), but in this simplified version, they're cooked in a nonstick pan. I recommend trying the pan version first, then moving on to the steamed method. Make sure the pan is just moderately hot and that the amount of batter is consistent with each sheet. *Banh cuon* can be made in advance, refrigerated, and reheated in a microwave oven.

The addition of the potato starch strengthens the batter and helps it cook better in a pan.

1. Make the batter: Combine the rice flour, potato starch, water, salt and 1 tablespoon oil in a bowl and whisk until smooth. (The batter will be thin and watery.) Strain to remove any lumps and let stand for 30 minutes.
2. Make the filling: Place the 1½ tablespoons oil in a skillet and heat over moderate heat. Add the shallots and stir for 10 seconds. Add the onion and mushrooms and cook until the onion bits are translucent and soft, 3 to 4 minutes. Add the shrimp, fish sauce, sugar and white pepper and stir

BATTER

1½ cups rice flour

½ cup potato starch

3¼ cups water

½ teaspoon salt

1 tablespoon vegetable oil
    plus extra for cooking and
    oiling sheet

FILLING

1½ tablespoons vegetable oil

3 tablespoons minced shallots

½ yellow onion, minced
    (about ½ cup)

3 tablespoons dried wood-ear
    mushrooms, soaked in warm
    water for 30 minutes, drained,
    chewy centers removed and
    finely chopped

½ pound minced raw shrimp
    or ground pork

½ tablespoon fish sauce

1 teaspoon sugar

¼ teaspoon white pepper

GARNISHES

3 cups bean sprouts, blanched
    in boiling water for
    10 seconds

⅓ cup green perilla (page 45) or red perilla (page 44), or mint leaves, cut in thirds

⅓ cup Asian basil leaves, cut in thirds

¼ cup Fried Shallots (page 33)

1¼ cups Light Vietnamese Dipping Sauce (page 26)

until the shrimp turns pink, 2 to 3 minutes. Transfer to a bowl and set aside.

3. Oil a cookie sheet and place it near the stove. Heat ½ teaspoon oil in an 8-inch nonstick pan over low heat. Use a paper towel or brush to distribute the oil evenly. Stir the batter thoroughly and ladle 2½ tablespoons into the pan. Quickly swirl the pan so the batter completely covers the surface. The batter should set immediately upon contact. If it sizzles and develops bubbles beyond the edges, reduce the heat slightly and start again. Cover and cook until the rice sheet pulls away from the pan, 30 to 40 seconds. Invert the pan over the oiled cookie sheet and tap lightly to loosen the rice sheet. Rice flour settles to the bottom readily so it's important to stir the batter vigorously before making each rice sheet. Also allow the pan to reheat for at least 1 minute between making a new rice sheet. Repeat until you have used up the batter. Do not stack the sheets. (After you get the hang of it, you may want to use two pans to expedite the process.) Let the rice sheets cool for 30 seconds, then proceed to stuff them.

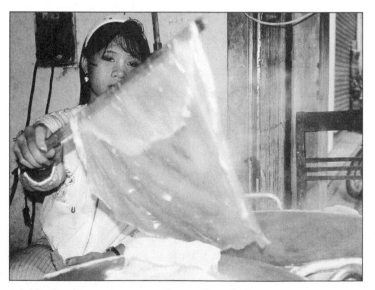

Making banh cuon, *or steamed rice rolls with shrimp.*

4. To make the rolls, make a 1-inch fold from the bottom of the rice sheet and neatly place 1½ teaspoons filling on top. Fold the sides over and roll into a cylinder about 2½ inches long and ⅔ inch wide. *Banh cuon* can be made in advance up to this point and stored in the refrigerator for 2 days.

5. To serve, divide the rice rolls among 4 plates. (You can reheat them in a microwave at this point until just warm, not hot.) Top each plate with one-quarter of the bean sprouts and herbs, then garnish with Fried Shallots. Invite guests to drizzle several tablespoons of sauce on top before eating.

RICE ROLLS—THE TRADITIONAL STEAMED METHOD

banh cuon hap

SERVES 4 AS A MAIN DISH (ABOUT 28 ROLLS)

This version is based on an ancient recipe that calls for ladling a thin rice batter on a piece of cloth stretched tightly over a *banh cuon* pot. Prior to owning this special pot, which is essentially a tall pot with a hoop and a pointed lid, I devised my own pot, which works quite well. (See How to Make a Rice Roll Pot on page 111.)

Steamed rice rolls are much more moist and silky than those made in a pan. This recipe may appear daunting but once you're set up, it's really quite simple—and the results are absolutely delicious. As with the previous recipe, find a helper to stuff the rice rolls.

1. Make the batter: Combine the rice flour, water, 2 teaspoons oil and salt in a bowl and whisk until smooth. (The batter will be thin and watery.) Strain to remove any lumps and let stand for at least 30 minutes.

2. Make the filling: Heat the 2 tablespoons oil in a skillet over moderate heat. Add the shallots and stir for 20 seconds.

BATTER

2 cups rice flour

2½ cups water

2 teaspoons vegetable oil

½ teaspoon salt

FILLING

2 teaspoons vegetable oil, plus
  extra for oiling cookie sheet

3 tablespoons minced shallots

½ yellow onion, minced

3 tablespoons dried wood-ear
  mushrooms, soaked in warm
  water for 30 minutes, drained,
  chewy centers removed and
  finely chopped

½ pound minced shrimp
  or pork

½ tablespoon fish sauce

1 teaspoon sugar

¼ teaspoon white pepper

GARNISHES

3 cups bean sprouts, blanched in
boiling water for 10 seconds

⅓ cup coarsely chopped mint
leaves

⅓ cup coarsely chopped Asian
basil leaves

¼ cup Fried Shallots (page 33)

1¼ cups Light Vietnamese
Dipping Sauce (page 26)

Add the onion and mushrooms and stir until the onion is soft, 3 to 4 minutes. Add the shrimp, fish sauce, sugar and pepper and cook until the shrimp turn pink, 2 to 3 minutes. Transfer to a bowl and set aside.

3. Bring the homemade rice roll pot (make sure it's been filled halfway with water) to a boil. (If you're using the traditional *banh cuon* pot, prepare the pot and the hoop attachment in a similar fashion.) Oil the cookie sheet and place it near the stove along with the filling.

4. Stir the batter well before making each rice sheet. Using a shallow ladle, spoon 2 tablespoons batter onto the center of the cloth. Using the bottom of the ladle, spread the batter to make a 6-inch-wide round sheet. (Work quickly and try not to put pressure on the cloth.) Cover and steam until the sheet is translucent, about 40 seconds. Uncover. (Be very careful removing the lid as the steam is very hot.) Hold a thin spatula at a 45-degree angle and push gently against the side of the rice sheet. When about ½ inch has gathered on the spatula, lift the sheet off in a steady motion and transfer to the oiled cookie sheet. (Do not stack the sheets.) Gently scrape the cloth clean and repeat. After cooking several rice sheets, tighten the cloth by pulling on the sides. Refill the pot with hot water as necessary by pouring it through one of the slits in the cloth.

5. Let the rice sheet cool for 30 seconds. To stuff the rice rolls, make a 1-inch fold from the bottom edge of the rice sheet. Neatly place 1½ teaspoons filling on top of this double layer. Fold the sides over and roll into a cylinder about 2½ inches long and ⅔ inch wide. *Banh cuon* can be made in advance up to this point and stored in the refrigerator for 2 days. Before serving, reheat in a microwave oven until just warm, not hot.

6. To serve, divide the rolls among 4 plates. Top each plate with one-quarter of the bean sprouts, mint and basil, and shallots. Invite guests to drizzle the sauce on top.

How to Make a Rice Roll Pot

Probably the most important thing about making a rice roll pot is to find a soup pot that is 10 to 11 inches wide with a dome-style lid. It should have a protruding rolled rim to help secure a string in place. You will also need 1 round piece of smooth cloth (cotton or cotton blend is fine) at least 4 inches wider than the pot; some heavyweight kitchen string; and a thin long metal spatula (about 12 inches or longer) or nonserrated carving or slicing knife. You will also need a shallow ladle for pouring the batter.

Fill the soup pot halfway with water. Then, with someone helping you, stretch the cloth across the top with drum-like tightness. Secure with 2 or 3 loops of string and tie into a knot. Pull the sides of the cloth again to stretch it as tight as possible. Using a very sharp paring knife or a razor blade, make three 1-inch-long slits crosswise in the cloth, about 1 inch from the edge. These incisions help distribute the steam for cooking the rice sheets and provide an opening for replenishing the water. Your rice roll pot is now ready for action.

Vietnamese Noodles

In Vietnamese cuisine, rice and noodles are the heart of every meal. For most families, dinner is built around rice, but at breakfast and lunch the preferred starch is often noodles. The following noodles are the ones most commonly used. With the exception of egg noodles and cellophane noodles, all are made with rice flour.

Choosing the right noodles to buy can be tricky. For example, *bun* and *banh pho* are distinctly different, yet both are sold in the West under the same "rice stick" label. When purchasing noodles, make sure you know the correct kind and size.

RICE VERMICELLI (ALSO KNOWN AS RICE STICKS) BUN

Bun is a popular type of noodle used extensively in Vietnamese cuisine. It resembles vermicelli and comes in two sizes—small or thin (similar to capellini), which is used in salads and room temperature dishes, and a fatter wider size (similar to spaghetti and larger), which is preferred in soups. *Bun* is used in dishes like Hanoi Rice Noodles with Grilled Pork (page 121) and in the filling for Rice Paper–Wrapped Salad Rolls (page 95). Dried *bun* is readily available, and now some Asian markets carry it fresh. There are many brands, but the most consistent one I've found is Bun Thap Chua from China. It has the right thickness and, similar to the fresh *bun* in Vietnam, takes on a "bouncy" feel when cooked.

To cook *bun*, boil until the noodles are white and softened but still resilient, about 4 to 5 minutes, drain, rinse immediately in cold water and drain completely before serving. (See Rice Noodles with Fresh Herbs, page 119.)

In Vietnam, there's another similar rice noodle called *banh hoi*. Available at some

Vietnamese markets in the United States, these fresh thin (almost hair-like) noodles are sold in small skeins. They're delicious when served with grilled pork.

RICE NOODLES (ALSO AS KNOWN AS RICE STICKS) BANH PHO

Banh pho is a flat rice noodle that resembles linguine. It's used in soups such as *pho* as well as in stir-fries. It's also the same noodle used in Thai cuisine to make *pad Thai*. Many Asian markets now stock both the dried and fresh varieties.

To prepare dried rice noodles for stir-fries, soak in cold water for 15 minutes. Then rinse and drain completely before adding to the pan. This technique helps remove the excess starch, thus preventing stir-fried noodles from getting gummy. If using fresh noodles, just add them directly to the pan. For instructions on how to prepare these noodles for soups such as *pho,* see page 53.

EGG NOODLES MI

Mi is made with wheat flour and eggs and is used in recipes of Chinese origin. Firmer and denser than rice noodles, it comes in various widths. *Mi* is easily available fresh. If using in soup, boil them about 1 to 2 minutes, depending on their size. If using the thicker chow mein–style noodles in stir-fries, cook about 2 to 3 minutes, then drain. Toss in a little oil to prevent sticking.

BEAN THREAD NOODLES OR CELLOPHANE NOODLES MEIN

Also known as glass noodles, cellophane noodles are made from mung bean starch. Available only in dried form and in various widths, these noodles are stiff and wiry and should be soaked in warm water for about 30 minutes before being used. Although they look fragile, *mien* are actually quite sturdy and can absorb a lot of water. They're used in many soups, salads and stir-fried dishes. Cellophane noodles will take anywhere from 1 to 5 minutes to cook, depending on their size. For a superb example of how to use them, see Cilantro Shrimp in Claypot, page 173.

FRESH RICE NOODLES

 banh pho tuoi

MAKES ABOUT 2 POUNDS

3 cups rice flour

3½ cups water

1 tablespoon vegetable oil
plus extra for stacking and
oiling cookie sheet

½ teaspoon salt

Simple and fun to make, these noodles are great for stir-fry dishes such as Wok-Seared Noodles with Chicken and Mushrooms (page 115). They're much more delicate than dried noodles, so try to stir them gently and be careful not to overcook. These are best eaten right away. You will need the rice roll pot for this recipe (page 111).

1. Place the rice flour, water, 1 tablespoon oil and salt in a bowl and whisk well. Strain to remove any lumps. Let stand for 30 minutes.

2. Prepare the rice roll pot as directed on page 111. Bring the water to a boil over moderate heat. Oil a cookie sheet.

3. Stir the batter well before making each rice sheet. Ladle about 3 tablespoons batter onto the cloth, spreading it so the rice sheet is about 6 inches wide. Cover and steam until the rice sheet becomes translucent and is done, about 1 minute. (Be very careful removing the lid as the steam is very hot.) Hold a thin spatula or knife at a 45-degree angle, then push gently against the side of the rice sheet. When about ½ inch has gathered on the spatula, lift the sheet off the cloth in a steady motion and transfer to the oiled cookie sheet. (You should be able to easily lift and peel the rice sheet. If not, the rice sheet needs to steam longer or the heat isn't high enough.) Brush each sheet with a little oil before stacking it. Scrape the cloth clean and repeat until the batter is finished. After several rice sheets, tighten the cloth by pulling on the sides. Refill the pot with hot water as necessary by pouring it through one of the slits in the cloth.

4. Cut the rice sheets into 1-inch or wider noodles. If not using right away, cover with plastic wrap.

SCALLION NOODLES

mi kho hanh

SERVES 4 AS A SIDE DISH

It seems like there's a version of this noodle dish everywhere in Asia. Originally from China, it calls for tossing fresh egg noodles with oil that's been infused with scallions. It can be served as a snack by itself or as a wonderful accompaniment to grilled meats such as Grilled Five-Spice Chicken or crab dishes such as Salt-and-Pepper Crab with Ginger (page 166).

1 bunch scallions

3 tablespoons vegetable oil

2 shallots, thinly sliced

2 tablespoons soy sauce or
    to taste

Pinch salt

1 pound fresh egg noodles,
    boiled 2 to 3 minutes, rinsed
    and drained

1. Remove the white part of the scallions and cut into thin rings. Cut the green part into 2-inch lengths and set aside.
2. Heat the oil in a large nonstick skillet over moderate heat. Add the shallots and the white and green parts of the scallions. Stir until fragrant, about 1 minute. Add the soy sauce, salt and noodles. Stir gently, being careful not to break the noodles. Turn several times so the noodles are coated evenly with the oil and are thoroughly heated. Transfer to a serving plate and serve immediately.

WOK-SEARED NOODLES WITH CHICKEN AND MUSHROOMS

pho ap chao

SERVES 4

The term *ap chao* means "pressed into the pan." Traditionally, that's how these noodles were made—seared until they became charred and stuck to the pan. This dish is probably a version of the Chinese *char kway tiow,* rice noodles stir-fried with soy sauce and spices, which is eaten all over Asia. In this recipe, the

⅓ pound boneless, skinless
    chicken, cut into bite-sized
    strips

1 teaspoon cornstarch

2 tablespoons water

3 tablespoons vegetable oil

1 tablespoon coarsely chopped
   Thai bird chilies, or to taste

1 tablespoon chopped garlic

1 cup Asian basil or sweet basil

10 dried black mushrooms,
   soaked in warm water for
   30 minutes, drained and
   halved if large

½ tablespoon fish sauce,
   or to taste

1 tablespoon oyster sauce

⅓ cup fresh Chicken Stock
   (page 39), store-bought low
   sodium chicken broth or
   water

⅔ pound dried ¼-inch-wide rice
   sticks (*banh pho*), cooked,
   drained and rinsed (page
   112), or 1 pound fresh rice
   noodles

1 tablespoon dark soy sauce
   (page 31) or regular soy sauce

⅓ pound Chinese mustard
   greens or bok choy, sliced on
   the diagonal into 2-inch
   pieces, blanched in boiling
   water for 1 minute and
   drained

½ cup Soy-Lime Dipping Sauce
   (page 29)

addition of fresh herbs and fish sauce gives it a Vietnamese touch.

1. Combine the chicken, cornstarch and water and toss to coat the meat evenly. Set aside to marinate for 10 minutes.

2. Heat 1 tablespoon oil in a large nonstick skillet over moderate heat. Add the chilies and garlic and stir until fragrant, about 10 seconds. Roughly tear half of the basil leaves and add to the pan. Stir in the mushrooms and chicken and cook until the meat turns white, about 2 minutes. Add the fish sauce, oyster sauce and chicken stock. Cook for another minute, transfer to a bowl and keep warm.

3. Wipe the pan clean and heat the remaining 2 tablespoons oil over moderate heat. Add the noodles and soy sauce. Cook until the noodles are brown and heated through, 3 to 4 minutes. (If using fresh noodles, don't stir too much.) Add the Chinese mustard greens, the remaining ½ cup basil and the cooked chicken (along with its juices) and stir gently so all the ingredients heat through. Transfer to a platter and serve immediately with the dipping sauce.

SIZZLING SAIGON CREPES

banh xeo

MAKES 4 LARGE CREPES

In Saigon, there's a small restaurant in the Dinh Cong Trang area that specializes in this dish. Upon arrival at this jam-packed outdoor eatery, guests are greeted by the smells and sounds of *banh xeo* sizzling on a bank of charcoal braziers. To eat, diners tear off a piece of the crepe, then wrap it with lettuce and herbs and dip it in a sauce. For a more authentic flavor, substitute mustard greens for the lettuce in the accompanying Table Salad. Traditionally, this dish is made with pork and shrimp, but other fillings would work nicely, including chicken, tofu and vegetables, or other seafood.

In the summer, instead of a barbecue, set up an outdoor stove, assemble the necessary ingredients and let your guests take turns cooking the crepes. It's a lot of fun and a good way to eat since you can enjoy the crepes just as they come out of the pan. You will need a 12-inch nonstick skillet for this recipe. If you need to use a smaller one, decrease the portion of batter accordingly.

1. Make the batter: Place the rice flour, coconut milk, water, turmeric, sugar, salt, curry powder and scallions in a bowl and stir well to blend. Set aside.
2. Make the filling: Heat 1 tablespoon of the oil in a large nonstick skillet over high heat. Add one-quarter each of the onion, the pork and the shrimp and stir until fragrant, about 15 seconds. Whisk the batter well, and ladle about ⅔ cup into the pan. Swirl so the batter completely covers the surface. Neatly pile about 1 cup bean sprouts and ½ cup mushrooms on one side of the crepe, closer to the center than to the edge. Reduce the heat slightly, cover the pan and cook until the edges pull away from the sides of the

BATTER

2 cups rice flour

½ cup unsweetened coconut milk

2⅓ cups water

1½ teaspoons ground turmeric

1 teaspoon sugar

½ teaspoon salt

½ teaspoon curry powder, preferably Vietnamese Golden Bells brand

3 scallions, cut into thin rings

FILLING

4 tablespoons vegetable oil

¼ yellow onion, thinly sliced (½ cup)

4 ounces pork shoulder or chicken breast, thinly sliced

12 medium raw shrimp, peeled and deveined

4 cups bean sprouts

2 cups sliced white mushrooms, lightly sautéed, drained

ACCOMPANIMENTS

1 cup Vietnamese Dipping Sauce (page 23)

Table Salad (page 80)

A street food vendor sells banh xeo, *or sizzling Saigon crepes.*

pan, about 5 minutes. Reduce the heat to low. Uncover and cook until the crepe is crisp and the chicken and shrimp are done, another 2 to 3 minutes. Slip a spatula under the crepe to check on the bottom of the crepe. If it's not brown, cook another minute or two.

3. Lift the side of the crepe without the bean sprouts and mushrooms and fold it over the covered side of the crepe. Using a spatula, gently slide the crepe onto a large plate. Wipe the pan clean and make the remaining crepes in the same way. Be sure to oil the pan before beginning the next crepe.

4. To serve, place the crepes, Vietnamese Dipping Sauce and Table Salad on the table. To eat, tear a piece of the *banh xeo* and wrap with lettuce or mustard leaves and herbs. Roll into a packet, then dip into the sauce and eat.

NOTE: In Hue, this dish is called *banh khoai* (happy pancakes). The crepes are smaller, about 6 inches in diameter, and are served with a heavier sauce of fermented soybeans. If you want to try this version, use a small pan and reduce the amount of ingredients accordingly. When the crepe is half-done, drizzle beaten egg around the edges and serve open face or folded, with the same accompaniments.

RICE NOODLES WITH FRESH HERBS

bun voi rau thom

MAKES 4 MAIN-COURSE SERVINGS WITH TOPPINGS

If there's one dish that exemplifies just how flavors and textures are contrasted in Vietnamese cuisine, it would have to be *bun*. Made with small rice vermicelli layered on a bed of shredded fresh herbs and greens, it can be served with a variety of meat or seafood toppings. In Vietnam, *bun* is usually a meal in itself but it certainly can be served in smaller, appetizer-sized portions.

To create a complete *bun* meal, make this recipe and serve it with a topping (see the following two recipes.) Make sure that the noodles are completely dry before assembling the bowls. Otherwise, the noodles will not adequately soak up the sauce.

2⁄3 pound small dried rice
    vermicelli (*bun*)
2 cups shredded red- or
    green-leaf lettuce
1½ cups bean sprouts
1⁄3 cucumber, seeded and
    cut into matchsticks
1⁄3 cup green or red perilla leaves,
    fish mint (pages 45, 44 and
    42) or mint leaves,
    cut into thirds
1⁄3 cup Asian basil leaves,
    cut into thirds

1. Bring a large pot of water to a rolling boil. Add the rice vermicelli and stir gently to loosen them. Cook until the noodles are white and soft but still slightly resilient, about 4 minutes. Drain and rinse under cold running water. Gently fluff the noodles and set them aside for at least 30 minutes. The noodles should be dry and sticky before serving.
2. Gently toss together the lettuce, bean sprouts, cucumbers, perilla and basil leaves. Divide the salad mixture among 4 bowls. Top each with one-quarter of the rice noodles. The bowls are now ready for the topping.

NOTE: Ideally, *bun* should not be refrigerated because the noodles become dry and stiff. However, if you need to, store the noodles and greens separately. Just before serving, reheat the noodles (preferably in a microwave oven) just until slightly warm. This will help them become soft and a little sticky again.

LEMONGRASS BEEF ON COOL NOODLES

 bun bo xao

SERVES 4

Rice Noodles with Fresh Herbs
(page 119), ready for serving
in noodle bowls

TOPPING

⅔ pound beef sirloin or another
tender cut, thinly sliced into
bite-sized strips

2 tablespoons minced lemongrass

2 tablespoons oyster sauce

1 tablespoon fish sauce

3 tablespoons vegetable oil

2 cloves garlic, minced

¼ red onion, thinly sliced
lengthwise

GARNISHES

2 tablespoons Scallion Oil
(page 32)

4 tablespoons chopped Roasted
Peanuts (page 35)

1½ recipes Vietnamese
Dipping Sauce
(page 23)

The last time I was in Saigon, I went back to the lively Cho Vuon Chuoi market near our house. I was so excited to find the same stall that my mother used to take me to for noodles. The lady who once fed me had retired and her daughter had taken over. After squeezing myself onto a low community bench in front of the hot charcoal stove, I found myself indulging in a delectable bowl of noodles with beef that had just come off a sizzling pan. These days, this dish remains a favorite, both for lunch and for a light dinner. For a delicious variation, try it with shrimp or pork.

1. Combine the beef, lemongrass, oyster sauce and fish sauce in a bowl and let the meat marinate for 20 minutes.
2. Heat the oil in a large skillet over high heat. Add the garlic and stir until fragrant, about 20 seconds. Add the red onion and stir for 1 minute, then add the meat. Stir and cook until the meat is cooked and the onion is soft, 3 to 4 minutes.
3. To serve, divide the beef topping among the 4 prepared noodle bowls. Garnish each bowl with ½ tablespoon Scallion Oil, 1 tablespoon peanuts and about ¼ cup dipping sauce. Toss several times before eating.

HANOI RICE NOODLES WITH GRILLED PORK

bun cha Hanoi

SERVES 4

In Hanoi, if you arrive at Bun Cha Hang Manh a little after the noon hour, chances are you'll have a tough time finding a seat. That's because this restaurant is known to have the best *bun cha* (noodles with grilled pork) in the city. Nguyen Doan Cam Van, a well-regarded television cooking teacher in Vietnam and advocate of northern regional cooking, says locals are quite particular about how *bun cha* should be eaten. Some soak the grilled pork slices and pork patties in the dipping sauce before adding them to their noodles. Others prefer to experience each ingredient with clarity and distinction, dipping and eating each item one by one.

1. Combine the scallions, shallot, fish sauce, Caramel Sauce, salt and pepper in a bowl and stir to blend. Divide the marinade equally between 2 bowls. Add the oil and sliced pork to one bowl and toss to evenly coat the meat. Let marinate for 20 minutes. In the second bowl, add the

2 scallions, sliced into thin rings

1 shallot, minced

1 tablespoon fish sauce

1½ teaspoons Caramel Sauce (page 35) or 1 teaspoon brown sugar

¼ teaspoon salt

½ teaspoon freshly ground black pepper

1 tablespoon vegetable oil

½ pound pork shoulder, sliced thin across the grain

½ pound ground pork

¼ cup chopped yellow onions

ACCOMPANIMENTS

⅔ pound small, dried *bun* (rice vermicelli), cooked until soft but still firm, 4 to 5 minutes, rinsed and drained (page 112)

Table Salad (page 80)

2 recipes Vietnamese Dipping Sauce (page 23)

ground pork and onions and mix well. Shape the ground pork into patties about 2 inches wide and ½ inch thick. Set aside until ready to cook.

2. Set the dining table with a platter of noodles and the Table Salad. Divide the dipping sauce among 4 small bowls. Provide each guest with a bowl of sauce and another bowl.

3. Preheat a grill or broiler to high heat. Grill the pork slices and pork patties until the meat is done and the edges are nicely charred on both sides. (You can also cook the pork in a skillet.) Transfer to a serving plate.

4. To eat, place a few slices of pork and pork patties in the bowls of dipping sauce and let them marinate for a few minutes. Invite guests to serve themselves by placing the noodles, herbs and lettuce and meat in their bowls and drizzling some sauce on top.

RICE NOODLE STIR-FRY WITH PORK

 pho xao

SERVES 4

½ tablespoon cornstarch

2 tablespoons water

½ pound pork shoulder, or beef flank, excess fat trimmed, cut into ⅛-inch-thick slices

3 tablespoons vegetable oil

1 pound fresh rice noodle sheets, cut into 1-inch-wide strips, or ⅔ pound dried *banh pho* (rice sticks, page 113), preferably ¼ inch or wider, cooked 3 to 4 minutes, rinsed and drained

2 tablespoons sweet soy sauce (page 30)

This dish is especially wonderful if you can make the fresh rice sheets on page 114 or purchase the similar *chow fun* noodle sheets at Asian markets. For stir-fries like this one, I like to cut the noodle sheets into 1-inch-wide ribbons. If you can't find these fresh noodles, use dried rice sticks or even fresh egg noodles.

1. Combine the cornstarch and water in a small bowl and mix well. Add the pork and toss to coat the meat evenly. Set aside until ready to use.

2. Heat 1½ tablespoons of the oil in a large nonstick skillet over moderate heat. Add the noodles, stirring slightly to loosen them. Drizzle the sweet soy sauce over the noodles, turning them 2 or 3 times to help absorb the sauce. Stir

gently until they're hot and the edges are slightly brown, about 2 to 3 minutes. (If using dried noodles, cook a little longer. If the pan is a little dry, sprinkle in 2 to 3 tablespoons water.) Transfer the noodles to a platter and keep warm.

3. Wipe the pan clean. Heat the remaining 1½ tablespoons oil in the pan over moderate heat. Add the onion wedges, soybeans and garlic and stir until fragrant, about 20 seconds. Add the pork and cook for 2 minutes. Add the oyster sauce, sugar, fish sauce, soy sauce and stock and stir for 30 seconds. Add the Chinese broccoli. Cover and cook until the ingredients are thoroughly hot, 2 to 3 minutes. Add the reserved noodles to the pan and stir until thoroughly hot, about 2 minutes. Transfer to a platter, then garnish with the cilantro sprigs and serve immediately with the dipping sauce on the side.

¼ yellow onion, cut into wedges

1½ tablespoons fermented whole soybeans (page 225)

2 teaspoons minced garlic

2 tablespoons oyster sauce

1 teaspoon sugar

1 teaspoon fish sauce

1 teaspoon soy sauce

⅓ cup fresh Chicken Stock (page 39) or store-bought low-sodium chicken broth

⅔ pound Chinese broccoli or regular broccoli, bottom stems discarded, cut on the diagonal into 2-inch pieces and blanched in boiling water for 20 seconds

5 sprigs cilantro, cut into 2-inch lengths

½ cup Soy-Lime Dipping Sauce (page 29)

NOODLE PILLOWS WITH CHICKEN AND SHRIMP

mi xao don

SERVES 4

In Vietnam, street vendors cook these noodles in a wok with a lot of oil, which creates a very crisp and airy pillow. This version is much lighter, but just as delicious. For best flavor, use the fresh egg noodles sold in Asian markets or in the produce sections of some supermarkets. The dried egg noodles will also work.

½ tablespoon cornstarch

2 tablespoons water

¼ pound skinless, boneless chicken breast, cut into thin bite-sized strips

4 tablespoons vegetable oil

1 pound fresh egg noodles,
cooked, or ½ pound dried
egg noodles, boiled for
3 to 4 minutes, depending
on the thickness, drained

2 teaspoons minced ginger

1 teaspoon minced garlic

1 to 2 teaspoons fermented black
beans (page 225), rinsed

½ teaspoon dried chili flakes

12 dried black mushrooms,
soaked in warm water for
30 minutes, drained,
stemmed and halved

¼ pound raw shrimp, peeled
and deveined

2 tablespoons oyster sauce

1 tablespoon soy sauce

1 small carrot, peeled, cut on the
diagonal into thin slices and
blanched in boiling water for
about 30 seconds

¼ yellow onion, thinly sliced
lengthwise

⅓ pound baby bok choy, cut on
the diagonal into ½-inch
pieces and blanched in hot
water for 10 seconds

⅓ cup fresh Chicken Stock
(page 39) or store-bought
low-sodium chicken broth

2 tablespoons rice wine or
dry sherry

5 sprigs cilantro, cut into
2-inch lengths

1. Combine the cornstarch and water in a bowl and stir well. Add the chicken and toss to coat the meat evenly.

2. Heat 2 tablespoons of the oil in a large nonstick skillet over moderate heat. Divide the noodles into 4 equal piles and transfer to the pan. Press gently on the noodles to create a flat round pillow. Cook until the noodles are golden and crisp around the edges, 3 to 4 minutes on each side. Add more oil if necessary. Drain on paper towels and keep warm.

3. Heat the remaining 2 tablespoons oil in a wok or large skillet. Add the ginger, garlic, black beans and chili flakes and stir until fragrant, about 10 seconds. Add the chicken and black mushrooms and cook 2 minutes. Add the shrimp, oyster sauce and soy sauce and stir a few times. Add the carrot, onion, bok choy and chicken stock. Cook until the sauce is slightly thickened and the vegetables are thoroughly hot, another 2 minutes. Splash the pan with rice wine and remove it from the heat.

4. To serve, place one noodle pillow on each of 4 plates and top with the chicken and shrimp stir-fry. Garnish with the cilantro and serve.

GRILLED SHRIMP ON SUGARCANE

chao tom

MAKES 24 PIECES OR 4 MAIN-DISH SERVINGS

This fabulous dish is both delicious and beautiful. Eaten throughout Vietnam, it's made with shrimp mousse wrapped around sugarcane, which is then grilled. This recipe calls for pork fat, which tenderizes and enriches the paste. Traditional cooks like my mom insist that once the pork fat is poached, it should cool down completely before being folded into the paste. That way, speckles of the translucent fat will still show through the cooked paste. (The best fat to use is fresh bacon, not the white chewy stuff from pork butt or pork shoulder.)

To properly enjoy this dish, tear off a piece of the shrimp paste, then wrap it in lettuce with some herbs before dipping in a sauce. And when the shrimp paste is all eaten, chew on the sugarcane and enjoy its sweet, smoky juice. You can use either canned sugarcane or fresh cane, which is more fragrant but a bit harder to find and handle. The canned sugarcane is packed in water and holds up well on the grill.

You will need a steamer for this recipe. *Chao tom* makes a lovely appetizer, but the Vietnamese typically serve it as the main dish, with a big table salad and plenty of rice vermicelli on the side.

1. If using pork fat, bring a small saucepan of water to a boil. Add the pork fat and cook just until the edges turn translucent, 2 to 3 minutes. Remove the pan from the heat and drain the pork on paper towels. Coarsely chop the fat and set aside. If using egg white, start with step 2.
2. Heat the oil in a small saucepan over moderate heat. Add the onion and shallots and sauté until slightly wilted, about 1 minute. Transfer the onion mixture (not the juice) to a bowl and add the fish sauce, salt, sugar, garlic, white

1 (2-ounce) piece pork fat,
  or 1 egg white
2 teaspoons vegetable oil
¼ cup chopped yellow onion,
  drained of excess water
3 shallots, minced
1 tablespoon fish sauce
¼ teaspoon sea salt
1 tablespoon sugar
1 teaspoon minced garlic
½ teaspoon ground white
  pepper
2 tablespoons cornstarch
½ teaspoon baking powder
1 pound raw medium shrimp,
  peeled, deveined and patted
  extremely dry
2 scallions, chopped
1 (20-ounce) can 4-inch-long
  sugarcane, drained

ACCOMPANIMENTS
½ pound small dried *bun*
  (rice vermicelli), cooked
  (page 112)
Table Salad (page 80)
Vietnamese Bean Dipping Sauce
  (page 28) or Vietnamese
  Dipping Sauce (page 23)

pepper, cornstarch, baking powder and pork fat. Add the shrimp and toss well.

3. Transfer the shrimp mixture to a food processor and process until almost smooth but still lumpy. Transfer the paste to a bowl, scraping the work bowl clean. Stir in the scallions. (If the paste is not cold, refrigerate at this point to stiffen it.)

4. Quarter the sugarcane pieces lengthwise, or halve them if they're small. Wet your hands with cold water. Place 2 tablespoons of the shrimp paste in the middle of your palm. Place a piece of the sugarcane on top and mold the paste around it. (The paste should be about ¼ inch thick and about 2½ inches long.) Gently press the paste against the stick so that the edges are sealed. Set the shrimp stick aside on an oiled plate. Repeat with the remaining sugarcane and paste.

5. Oil a steamer basket and place the sugarcane sticks in a single layer. (If necessary, steam in several batches.) Steam until the shrimp paste turns pink, 2 to 3 minutes. You can make this dish in advance up to this point. To finish, grill or broil the shrimp sticks until the paste is hot inside and slightly charred around the edges. Serve immediately with Table Salad, rice vermicelli and dipping sauce.

BEAN THREAD NOODLES WITH CRAB

 mien xao cua

SERVES 4

3 tablespoons vegetable oil

3 shallots, thinly sliced

2 cloves garlic, minced

⅓ pound cooked crabmeat
    or ⅔ pound raw shrimp,
    peeled and deveined

2 tablespoons oyster sauce

Mien xao cua is a very special dish, especially if you can see how it's prepared at one of the seafood restaurants on Dinh Tien Hoang Street in Saigon. The kitchens are located in front and diners can watch the cooks turn and toss the transparent noodles while adding big handfuls of fresh, chunky crabmeat. After watching the cooks, it's impossible not to order at least one plate!

If you can't get crabmeat, use shrimp. It won't be as decadent, but will be delicious just the same. Bean threads vary and some can absorb more liquid than others. If they seem dry in the pan, add more stock.

1. In a large nonstick skillet, heat 1 tablespoon of the vegetable oil over moderate heat. Add half the shallots and garlic and stir until fragrant, about 20 seconds. Add the crabmeat and cook for 2 minutes. Transfer to a plate and keep warm.

2. Heat the remaining 2 tablespoons oil in another skillet over moderate heat. Stir in the remaining shallots and garlic. When fragrant, add the oyster sauce, soy sauce, bean threads, mushrooms and chicken stock. Stir a few times, then reduce the heat. Cover and cook until the noodles are soft and have absorbed almost all of the sauce, 5 to 7 minutes.

3. Add the carrot strips and crabmeat. Cook until the carrots are just hot, about 2 minutes. (If the pan is dry, sprinkle with 2 or 3 tablespoons Chicken Stock.) Stir in the scallions and toss gently several times. Transfer to a serving plate and garnish with the cilantro and black pepper.

1 tablespoon soy sauce

4 ounces dried bean threads (cellophane noodles, page 113), soaked in warm water for 30 minutes, drained and cut into 12-inch pieces

¼ cup dried wood-ear mushrooms, soaked in warm water for 30 minutes, chewy centers removed and cut in half or thirds

1½ cups fresh Chicken Stock (page 39), store-bought low-sodium chicken broth or water

1 carrot, peeled, cut into matchstick strips (about 2 cups), blanched for 30 seconds and drained

3 scallions, cut into 2-inch lengths

6 sprigs cilantro, cut into 1-inch lengths

Freshly ground black pepper

HANOI GRILLED FISH WITH RICE NOODLES AND FRESH HERBS

cha ca Hanoi

SERVES 4

Every time I enter Cha Ca La Vong, a tiny landmark restaurant in Hanoi, I know I'm in for a special treat. Owned by the same family for several generations, it serves only one dish—*cha ca,* which comes to the table on a small charcoal brazier. To enjoy the dish, one adds the just-cooked fish and wilted

MARINADE

1 (1½-inch) piece galangal or 1 teaspoon galangal powder

2 tablespoons plain yogurt

2 teaspoons ground turmeric

2 teaspoons sugar

2 teaspoons rice vinegar

1 teaspoon shrimp sauce
(page 229)

½ teaspoon salt

1½ pounds catfish fillets, cut
into 3-inch chunks

⅔ pound small dried *bun*
(rice vermicelli), boiled for
4 to 5 minutes, rinsed and
drained (page 112)

½ head red-leaf lettuce, torn into
bite-sized pieces

2 bunches Asian basil or mint
leaves (about 3 cups),
preferably tender leaves only

4 scallions, cut into 2-inch
lengths

2 bunches fresh baby dill, bottom
tough stems removed and cut
into 1-inch lengths
(about 2½ cups)

½ cup whole Roasted Peanuts
(page 36)

½ cup Vietnamese Dipping
Sauce (page 23)

2 tablespoons vegetable oil and
extra oil for grilling

dill to the rice noodles and herbs and eats it with *mam tom* (a pungent sauce made from shrimp sauce and pineapple) or Vietnamese dipping sauce, which I much prefer.

Chef and owner Ngo Thi Tinh, who claims it was her grandmother who first popularized this dish, marinates *ca lang,* a local fish from the Red River in *me,* a souring agent made from fermented rice. In this adaptation, I call for catfish and yogurt instead.

1. Make the marinade: Peel the galangal and cut into thin slices. Pound in a mortar until mushy. Using your fingers, squeeze the pulverized galangal to extract as much juice as you can from the pulp. You should have about 1 table-spoon. (You can also use a Japanese ginger grater.)

2. In a large bowl, combine the galangal juice, yogurt, turmeric, sugar, rice vinegar, shrimp sauce and salt. Add the catfish and toss to evenly coat the fish. Set aside to mar-inate for 30 minutes.

3. Before cooking the fish, set the dining table with a plate of rice vermicelli and a platter of lettuce and Asian basil. Combine the scallions and dill and put on a plate. Put the

Cha ca as served in Hanoi.

peanuts and dipping sauce in separate bowls. Provide each guest with a small bowl and chopsticks.

4. Start a charcoal fire or preheat a gas grill to high. Grill the catfish pieces just until halfway done, about 2 minutes on each side. (The fish will finish cooking at the table.) Transfer the fish to a plate and keep warm.

5. To serve, place a portable gas or electric stove in the middle of the dining table. Heat the oil in a small skillet over moderate heat. Add some catfish pieces, but do not crowd the pan, and a generous amount (a cupful) of dill and scallions. Using chopsticks or a long-handled spoon, stir gently until the fish is hot and the dill and scallions wilted. Invite the guests to assemble their own condiments by placing some noodles, lettuce and herbs in their bowls. Top with the catfish, herbs, peanuts and sauce. When the catfish has all been eaten, cook another batch.

NOTE: If you don't have a tabletop stove, finish the dish in the kitchen. Heat the oil in a skillet until hot. Add the fish pieces and dill and scallions and stir until the fish pieces are cooked through, 2 to 3 minutes. Do not crowd the pan; cook in batches if necessary. Transfer to a platter and serve immediately.

chapter five

Inviting the Ancestors for Tet

Rice Dishes with Poultry and Meat

Poached Whole Chicken with Ginger-Lime Dipping Sauce

Perfect Steamed Rice

Vietnamese Fried Rice

Chicken Curry with Sweet Potatoes

Lemongrass Roasted Chicken

Ginger Chicken

Stir-Fried Chicken with Lemongrass and Chilies

Grandmother's Chicken with Wild Mushrooms

Grilled Five-Spice Chicken

Braised Duck with Pineapple

Broken Rice with Shredded Garlic Pork

Aunt Tam's Pork in Claypot

Vietnamese Rice Cakes in Banana Leaves

Shaking Beef

Beef Stew with Star Anise and Basil

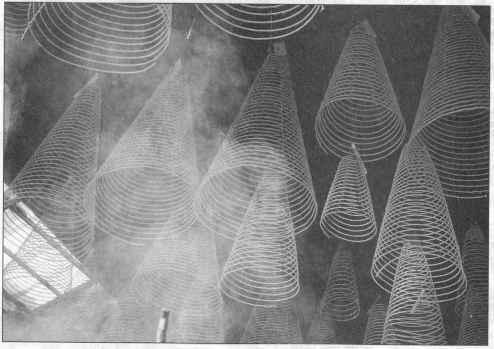

A round Tet (Vietnamese New Year), a whole chicken is a prized food. Symbolizing abundance and prosperity, it sits prominently on the ancestor worship altar, along with the flowers, candles and incense sticks. Since Tet combines the spirit of Thanksgiving, Christmas, New Year's and everyone's birthday (a person is considered one year older on this day) all in one, our family goes to great lengths to welcome our ancestors into our home.

Raised in a traditional Vietnamese home, I was taught that our ancestors are as important as, if not more important than, living members of the family. Because their presence and blessings are considered critical to our well-being, we involve them in our everyday life, remembering them through daily offerings of food and prayers, and inviting them to join us for important holidays.

We were taught that by connecting with them, our purpose in life would become clearer. We were told that every deed and action affects the whole family—including those who have passed on. A good deed makes them happy and proud and therefore eager to watch over us. On the other hand, a misdeed is considered an act of dishonor, a serious offense to the family lineage. Growing up with such taboos and belief systems, I never once dared jeopardize that tradition or embarrass the family in any way.

So, on the first day of Tet, we prepare a sumptuous meal to *ruoc ong ba* (welcome back the ancestors). Besides whole chicken, we cook dozens of other enticing dishes such as Caramelized Garlic Shrimp (page 174) and a traditional pork stew with hard-boiled eggs called *thit kho dua*. For dessert, we serve *che khoai mon* (sticky rice pudding with taro root, page 215) and fresh fruits like watermelon and tangerines. A small portion of each dish is then placed as an offering on the altar.

When we light the incense and say our prayers, the spirits are invoked and the ancestors begin their journey back to Earth. In our prayers, we thank them for watching over us and giving us good luck and health. It is only after these prayers that we can begin to eat.

Then, on the third day of Tet, when the ancestors get ready to depart, we prepare another extravagant send-off meal, this time with different dishes and wine. Towards the end of the ritual, we all go outside and gather around our parents and watch as they dutifully burn beautifully decorated paper tunics and clothes and even symbolic paper money—items which our ancestors will need in Heaven. And once our ancestors are gone, we go back to our own lives but with the lingering thoughts of Tet and a strong reminder that we must, as always, live up to their expectations.

One of the things you'll notice as you cook from this chapter is that, with the exception of steamed dishes and Chinese-style stir-fries, a typical, traditional Vietnamese meat recipe will call for few, if any, vegetables. Vietnamese cooks believe that in order to heighten the flavor of a particular meat or seafood, it should be cooked by itself, with a few spices and aromatics. The addition of vegetables would only dilute the flavor. So, from a Vietnamese perspective, a meat dish should taste like a meat dish and a vegetable dish should be served separately. Meat is generally expensive, so it's usually generously salted so it can be stretched and eaten with a lot of rice (which is unsalted) and other foods. Since rice is at the heart of these meals I've included a foolproof recipe for steamed rice. When serving steamed rice as part of a meal, allow 1 to 2 cups person.

POACHED WHOLE CHICKEN WITH GINGER-LIME DIPPING SAUCE

ga luoc nuoc mam gung

SERVES 6

This recipe uses an old Chinese technique of submerging a whole chicken in boiling water, turning off the heat, and letting it steep. The technique produces a moist and succulent bird, ready to be served or used in any recipe calling for cooked chicken. Many Chinese chefs cook the chicken so the meat is white but the bones are still red. I like chicken well done, so I've increased the cooking time.

When boiling or poaching foods, Vietnamese cooks typically do not use salt because the dish is often served with a dipping sauce and the last-minute balancing of flavors is done at the table. To serve, cut the chicken through the bones into large chunks and arrange them on a plate. To eat, remove the skin and dip the meat in a sauce. The Chinese vendors in Saigon like to serve this with Sweet Soy Sauce with Chilies and Ginger, but I also love it with Ginger-Lime Sauce. Steamed or fried rice and a vegetable dish are the traditional accompaniments.

1 fresh whole chicken
(about 2½ pounds),
preferably free range,
trimmed of excess fat

5 sprigs cilantro

2 recipes Sweet Soy Sauce with
Chilies and Ginger (page 30)

1 recipe Ginger-Lime Sauce
(page 27)

1. Place 5 quarts water in a large soup pot and bring to a rolling boil. Add the chicken and bring to a boil again. Boil for 10 minutes, then turn off the heat. Cover the pot and let the chicken steep, undisturbed, until cooked through, about 1 hour.
2. Remove the chicken and transfer to a deep dish. Loosely wrap a piece of plastic wrap around it to prevent the skin from drying out. When cool enough to handle, use a cleaver or heavy knife to cut the chicken into the desired-sized pieces. Arrange on a plate and garnish with the cilantro. Serve with the dipping sauce of choice on the side.

PERFECT STEAMED RICE

 com

SERVES 4 TO 6

2 cups jasmine rice

3 cups water

It's ironic that many times, the most important food at the table—the rice—gets the least amount of attention. To ensure that this critical part of the meal is as good as the rest of the dishes, start with quality rice and make sure it's properly cooked each time. I prefer jasmine rice from Thailand and Vietnam but, even then, each batch differs in quality: Some are fragrant, some are too mushy, and some are dry and bland. In an effort to avoid bad rice, I buy from the busy Asian markets with high turnover and stick to the brands that I'm familiar with, like Phoenix and Three Ladies.

Good rice is fresh-cooked rice. Period. You can start with the best batch of grains, but if it's been cooked even half an hour in advance, its taste and texture will be less than optimal. Try to time the cooking of the rice so that it's done just minutes before you eat.

The easiest way to make great rice is to boil it in an automatic insulated rice cooker. (Even though cooked rice is often referred to as steamed, it is actually boiled.) With an automatic cooker, the heat is more evenly distributed, and the insert creates more steam, thus resulting in better rice. Besides, if the most important part of the meal can be taken care of by this machine, why not use it and save your energy for other dishes?

Whether you are using an automatic rice cooker or the traditional stovetop method, I strongly suggest rinsing your rice before cooking, as the Vietnamese cooks do. Rinsing removes the excess starch that tends to mask the delicate flavor of rice. Once the rice is rinsed, measure out the water. The amount needed can vary because each batch of rice has a different moisture level. If it's from a new crop, the rice will be high in moisture and will need less water. Jasmine rice often falls in this category. But as a general guideline, use 1 part rice to 1½ parts water. Properly cooked rice is soft and fluffy with the grains still maintaining their shape.

1. If using a rice cooker, place the rice in the insert and rinse with cold water until the water runs clear. Tilt the insert to drain the rice, using your hand to keep the rice from spilling. Drain completely. Add the water and cook the rice. Serve the rice minutes after the timer goes off.

   To cook in a regular pot, place the rice in the pot and wash with several changes of cold water. Drain the rice, then add the water. Bring the pot to a boil and let it continue to boil for about 2 to 3 minutes. Stir gently once, then cover the pot. Reduce the heat to very low and simmer, covered, until all the water is absorbed and the rice is done, about 20 minutes. Turn off the heat and let it sit for 5 minutes before serving.

VIETNAMESE FRIED RICE

com chien

SERVES 4 TO 6

Unlike the more traditional recipes for fried rice that call for ham or Chinese sausage, this family favorite has a bit of a Western influence: It's stir-fried in butter, with a little ketchup. This makes a great accompaniment to barbecued meats such as Grilled Five-Spice Chicken (page 147) and Lemongrass Roasted Chicken (page 142). It also makes a wonderful lunch dish when embellished with cooked meat and vegetables (or even eggs) and served with Soy-Lime Dipping Sauce (page 29).

3 tablespoons butter

1 teaspoon chopped garlic

3 tablespoons chopped yellow onion

2 tablespoons ketchup

½ tablespoon fish sauce

Salt to taste

1 teaspoon sugar

4 cups cold cooked rice,
    preferably long grain
    (page 228)
2 scallions, cut into thin rings
5 sprigs cilantro, cut into
    2-inch lengths

1. Heat the butter in a wok or nonstick skillet over moderate heat. Add the garlic and onion and stir until fragrant, about 20 seconds. Add the ketchup, fish sauce, salt, and sugar and simmer until the sauce is slightly reduced, 2 to 3 minutes. Add the rice and stir-fry until it is hot, 4 to 5 minutes. Add the scallions and stir another 2 minutes. (Sprinkle on some water if the pan is dry.) Transfer to a serving dish, garnish with the cilantro and serve immediately.

CHICKEN CURRY WITH SWEET POTATOES

 ca ri ga

SERVES 4

3 tablespoons curry powder,
    preferably Three Golden
    Bells brand
½ teaspoon salt, or to taste
2 pounds skinless chicken thighs
2 tablespoons vegetable oil
1 tablespoon chopped shallot
2 teaspoons minced garlic
2 teaspoons ground chili paste
    (page 225) or dried chili
    flakes, or to taste
3 tablespoons fish sauce
1 tablespoon sugar
2 lemongrass stalks, cut into
    3-inch pieces and bruised
    with the flat side of a knife
1 (1-inch) piece ginger, peeled,
    cut into 3 slices and bruised
    with the flat side of a knife

True to the Vietnamese style of curry-making, this recipe is milder and lighter than Indian or Thai curries. You can make this with chicken stock, but the coconut milk adds body and enhances the overall flavor. Depending on my mood and the time of year, I sometimes serve this with a warmed baguette (a French influence) instead of steamed rice. Other times, I just make the curry with more broth and serve it with rice noodles. Like other curries, it's delicious the next day.

1. Combine 2 tablespoons of the curry powder and the salt in a bowl. Add the chicken and turn to coat the meat evenly. Set aside for 30 minutes.
2. Heat the oil in a medium pot over moderate heat. Add the shallot, garlic, chili paste and the remaining 1 tablespoon curry powder, and stir until fragrant, about 10 seconds. Add the chicken and cook until the edges of the pieces are golden, 3 to 4 minutes. Add the fish sauce, sugar, lemongrass, ginger and chicken stock. Bring to a boil, then re-

duce the heat. Add the carrots and cook for 10 minutes. Add the coconut milk, onion and sweet potato and cook until the vegetables are tender, about 15 minutes. Transfer to a serving bowl, garnish with Asian basil, cilantro and scallions, and serve.

1½ cups fresh Chicken Stock (page 39) or store-bought low-sodium chicken broth
3 carrots, peeled, cut on the diagonal into ⅔-inch pieces
1½ cups unsweetened coconut milk or cow's milk
1 yellow onion, cut into thin wedges
1 medium sweet potato (about 1 pound), peeled and cut into 1-inch cubes

GARNISHES
½ cup Asian basil leaves, cut in half
8 sprigs cilantro, cut into 2 inch pieces
2 scallions, chopped

Making Fresh Coconut Milk

My grandmother, who owns a coconut plantation in the Mekong Delta, grows two main varieties of coconuts. One is harvested for the sweet juice, used as a beverage and cooking liquid, and the other is used to make *nuoc cot dua*, or coconut milk.

To make coconut milk the traditional way, Co Muoi (Tenth Aunt), who now does all the cooking for my grandmother, relies upon a special tool. Using a round serrated blade, she scrapes the inside of the coconut flesh, turning the fruit as she goes. To extract the milk, she steeps the grated coconut in hot water, then squeezes it over a bamboo basket. The first pressing yields a rich creamy liquid commonly used in desserts. The second and third pressings, made by adding additional boiling water, are used to make curry sauce, soups and lighter desserts.

If you want to make fresh coconut milk, you can use the same basic technique. To crack open a coconut, hold it with a towel over the sink and use the back of a cleaver to whack crosswise along the middle. It usually takes several whacks (depending on its thickness) before the nut cracks. Using the tip of the cleaver, pry it open just enough to drain the juice. Drink the juice or use as a cooking liquid.

Bake the cracked coconut in a

A market vendor uses a dao bao *to slice fresh coconut.*

preheated 325-degree oven for about 30 minutes. Remove and let cool. Once cool, wrap a towel around it and lay it on a hard surface. Using a hammer or mallet, give it a few whacks to break it into several pieces. Remove the flesh with a screwdriver, then use a vegetable peeler to peel the outside brown skin.

Chop the coconut into coarse pieces, then add to a food processor. Grind as fine as you can, gradually adding 1 cup hot water. (You may have to do this in batches.) Transfer to a bowl and add 1 cup boiling water. When the coconut mixture is cool enough to handle, use your hands to massage and squeeze the pulverized coconut for about 5 minutes. Place a fine-mesh strainer over a bowl and pour the coconut mixture through. Again using your hands, squeeze the solids over the strainer, extracting as much liquid as possible. The creamy coconut milk is now ready for use. To make a less creamy version, add 2 more cups boiling water to the solids and repeat the process. Fresh coconut milk is highly perishable and should be used within 2 days.

These directions may sound daunting but it's really hard to beat fresh coconut milk. It's worth doing at least once so you can taste the difference between fresh coconut milk and the canned products. The good news about canned coconut milk is that the number of brands available these days is increasing. Many are quite good and consistent, like Mae Ploy and Chao Koh, both from Thailand.

LEMONGRASS ROASTED CHICKEN

ga nuong xa

SERVES 4 TO 6

4 tablespoons minced lemongrass

2 tablespoons minced shallot

2 tablespoons minced garlic

2 tablespoons soy sauce

2 tablespoons sugar

2 tablespoons fish sauce

1 tablespoon dried chili flakes,
   or to taste

1 teaspoon kosher salt,
   or to taste

1 whole chicken (about
   3 pounds), preferably
   free range, rinsed and
   patted dry

2 tablespoons minced cilantro

3 tablespoons vegetable oil

½ cup Soy-Lime Dipping Sauce
   (page 29)

In Vietnam, most homes don't have an oven, so chicken is usually cut into chunks for easy grilling or stovetop cooking. However, for this dish, I prefer using a whole chicken. Just imagine pulling out of the oven a freshly roasted chicken, its golden skin covered with a last-minute basting of aromatic lemongrass and cilantro. For a satisfying meal, serve this with steamed or fried rice (pages 136 and 137) and a salad such as Cabbage Salad with Shrimp and Pork (page 89).

1. Remove 2 tablespoons of the lemongrass and set aside in a small bowl. Combine the remaining lemongrass, shallot, garlic, soy sauce, sugar, fish sauce, chili flakes and salt in a large bowl. Add the chicken and turn to coat, tucking some marinade underneath the skin. Pour any excess marinade into the bird cavity. Cover the chicken with plastic wrap, then marinate in the refrigerator for at least 4 hours, preferably overnight. Bring the chicken to room temperature before baking.

2. Preheat the oven to 350 degrees. Put the chicken, breast side down, on a rack in a roasting pan. Bake for 40 minutes. Turn the bird over and roast until the chicken is cooked and nicely browned, about 20 to 30 minutes more. About 10 minutes before the chicken is done, combine the remaining 2 tablespoons lemongrass with the cilantro and oil. Brush the mixture on the bird, then continue to roast until it is done and the juices run clear. Let the chicken rest 10 minutes before carving. Serve with Soy-Lime Dipping Sauce and fried or steamed rice. (The pan juices are delicious on the rice.)

GINGER CHICKEN

ga kho gung

SERVES 4

Kho (braised) dishes are an important part of Vietnamese cuisine, particularly in the south. They're usually prepared in a claypot, with pork, chicken or seafood, without any vegetables. For working families in the villages, a *kho* dish is ideal because if generously salted, it can be stretched to feed lots of people. This simple recipe will surprise you with its robust flavors.

For this recipe, it's best to use a 1-quart Asian claypot (page 144), but you can also prepare this in a regular covered pot or casserole. Serve with a vegetable dish and steamed rice.

1. Peel the ginger and cut on the diagonal into ⅛-inch-thick slices. Take a few slices and finely chop enough to measure 1 tablespoon. Combine the minced ginger and the chicken in a bowl. Set aside to marinate for 30 minutes.
2. Heat the oil in a large skillet over moderate heat. Add the garlic, onion and chilies and stir until fragrant, about 10 seconds. Add the chicken, ginger slices, fish sauce, sugar and salt and stir for 2 to 3 minutes. Transfer to a preheated claypot, if using, at this point.
3. Add the chicken stock and Caramel Sauce and reduce the heat to a simmer. Cover and cook until the chicken is done halfway, about 5 minutes. Uncover and continue cooking until the sauce is thickened, another 5 minutes. Stir in the scallions. Remove the pot from the heat. Garnish with the cilantro and serve.

1 (2-inch) piece ginger
⅔ pound boneless, skinless chicken thighs or breast, cut into bite-sized strips
2 tablespoons vegetable oil
2 teaspoons minced garlic
¼ yellow onion, thinly sliced lengthwise
1 teaspoon chopped fresh red chilies or dried chili flakes
1½ tablespoons fish sauce
2 teaspoons sugar
¼ teaspoon salt
½ cup fresh Chicken Stock (page 39) or store-bought low-sodium chicken broth
½ tablespoon Caramel Sauce (page 34) or 1 tablespoon light brown sugar
2 scallions, cut into 2-inch lengths
6 sprigs cilantro, cut into 1-inch pieces

Cooking with Claypots

Made of sand and clay, the claypot is an ancient Chinese creation used throughout Asia. It imparts a deep, smoky flavor to foods and is especially good for slow braising recipes, such as stews and casserole-type dishes. The pot comes in two styles: one with a single thick handle, the other with two smaller handles. Some pots have a protective wire brace, a clever feature since they do sometimes crack. Both styles have an unglazed off-white exterior, while the lid and the interior are glazed dark brown.

Claypots are available in many different sizes, but I recommend getting the 1- and 3-quart sizes since most recipes call for one or the other. The smaller size is suitable for dishes with only a few ingredients like Aunt Tam's Pork in Claypot (page 150), while the larger one is better for rice dishes that need more steam, such as Vegetarian Claypot Rice with Ginger (page 195). When cooking, you can set the claypot right on the gas stove, then bring up the heat gradually. If you have an electric range, use a heat diffuser to be on the safe side. To prevent sudden cracks, avoid setting a cold pot on a very hot stove and always cook on moderate, not high, heat. Also, refrain from washing a hot claypot in cold water.

Claypots don't need to be seasoned in any special way, although I've found that boiling water in a new pot helps remove the smell of the clay. Over time, if you use claypots often, they will blacken and start to have a few unharmful cracks. It's all part of the beauty of claypot cooking.

STIR-FRIED CHICKEN WITH LEMONGRASS AND CHILIES

ga xao xa ot

SERVES 4

I was raised on this dish, eating it almost twice a week. I never grew tired of it, especially the gooey sauce. The secret is lots of onions, lemongrass and chilies: Not only do the onions impart a savory sweetness, but they help bring out the flavors of the spices and herbs. You can also make this dish with pork, seafood or eel, which is quite popular in Vietnam. Make sure the lemongrass is very fresh.

1. Combine the cornstarch, water and chicken in a bowl. Toss to coat the meat evenly. Set aside to marinate for 15 minutes.
2. Heat 1½ tablespoons of the oil in a skillet over high heat. Add the chicken and stir until the edges turn white, about 3 minutes. Transfer to a plate and keep warm.
3. Wipe the pan clean. Add the remaining 1½ tablespoons oil and heat over moderate heat. Add the garlic, chilies and half of the lemongrass and stir until fragrant, about 10 seconds. Add the onion and chicken stock and cook until the onion is soft, about 10 minutes.
3. Stir in the chicken, remaining lemongrass, fish sauce, sugar and Caramel Sauce and cook until the chicken is cooked through, about 3 to 4 minutes. Transfer to a plate, garnish with the cilantro and serve immediately.

2 teaspoons cornstarch

1 tablespoon water

⅔ pound boneless, skinless chicken thighs or chicken breast, cut into thin bite-sized strips

3 tablespoons vegetable oil

2 cloves garlic, chopped

2 teaspoons chopped fresh chilies or dried chili flakes

2 lemongrass stalks, bottom white part only, finely chopped (about ¼ cup)

1 yellow onion, thinly sliced lengthwise (about 1 cup)

½ cup fresh Chicken Stock (page 39) or store-bought low-sodium chicken broth

1 tablespoon fish sauce

1 teaspoon sugar

2 teaspoons Caramel Sauce (page 34) or 1 teaspoon light brown sugar

5 sprigs cilantro, cut into 2-inch lengths

GRANDMOTHER'S CHICKEN WITH WILD MUSHROOMS

 ga xao nam

SERVES 4

2 tablespoons soy sauce

2 teaspoons fish sauce

2 teaspoons sugar

2 teaspoons cornstarch

½ pound boneless skinless
chicken breasts and/or thighs,
cut into thin bite-sized strips

3 tablespoons vegetable oil

2 shallots, sliced

8 dried black mushrooms,
soaked in warm water for
30 minutes, drained,
stemmed and halved

1 cup white or brown mushrooms, clean and halved

1 cup oyster mushrooms,
cleaned and cut into
bite-sized pieces

½ teaspoon salt

2 teaspoons chopped garlic

½ cup fresh Chicken Stock
(page 39) or store-bought
low-sodium chicken broth

5 sprigs cilantro, cut into
2-inch lengths

At my grandmother's house, many of the best meals are those made with *nam moi*, a type of wild mushroom that grows profusely on her coconut plantation during the rainy season. Resembling a small but leggy straw mushroom, it has a distinct, earthy flavor. Since it's not available in the U.S., I've substituted other delicious mushrooms. This dish is typically made with young coconut juice (not milk) as a cooking liquid but since it's difficult to find, I've substituted chicken stock.

1. Place the soy sauce, fish sauce, sugar and cornstarch in a bowl and stir well. Add the chicken and toss to coat the meat evenly.

2. Heat 1½ tablespoons of the oil in a large skillet over moderate heat. Add the shallots and stir until fragrant, about 20 seconds. Add the black mushrooms, white mushrooms, oyster mushrooms and salt. Cook until the mushrooms are soft, 3 to 4 minutes. (Add 2 to 3 tablespoons water if the pan gets too dry.) Transfer the mushrooms and their juices to a bowl and keep warm.

3. Wipe the pan clean. Add the remaining 1½ tablespoons oil over moderate heat. Add the garlic and the chicken and stir-fry until the meat turns white, about 2 to 3 minutes. Add the chicken stock and mushrooms and cook until all the ingredients are cooked, about 3 minutes. Transfer to a serving plate, garnish with the cilantro and serve.

GRILLED FIVE-SPICE CHICKEN

ga ngu vi huong

SERVES 4

The best five-spice chicken I have had in Vietnam was made by a street food vendor in the port town of Hoi An in the central region. The vendor used a spice mix of freshly toasted star anise and turmeric. When she grilled the chicken, the whole neighborhood was perfumed with the most enticing fragrance. This is my version of that dish. It's great with Vietnamese Fried Rice (page 137) and Cucumber Salad (page 81).

1. Cut the chicken into 6 pieces and make 1 or 2 slashes in each piece for faster cooking. Trim and discard any excess fat. Pat the chicken dry.
2. In a bowl, combine the oil, soy sauce, ginger, garlic, sugar, turmeric, five-spice powder and salt. Stir well to blend. Add the chicken pieces and turn several times to coat them evenly. Marinate in the refrigerator for at least 4 hours.
3. Start a charcoal grill or preheat a gas grill to moderate heat. (You can also use a broiler.) Thirty minutes before cooking, add the freshly toasted star anise powder to the marinated chicken, turning so the meat is coated evenly.
4. Place the chicken, skin side up, on the grill. Cook 10 minutes, then turn over and grill until the chicken is cooked and the juices run clear, another 10 minutes, depending on the thickness. While grilling, move the chicken pieces around so that they cook evenly. Transfer the chicken to a serving platter and serve with the dipping sauce.

1 whole chicken (about 2½ pounds), preferably free range, rinsed

3 tablespoons vegetable oil

2 tablespoons soy sauce

3 tablespoons minced ginger

2 tablespoons minced garlic

2 tablespoons sugar

2 teaspoons ground turmeric

1 teaspoon Chinese five-spice powder (page 226)

½ tablespoon sea salt

4 whole star anise, lightly toasted in a dry pan for 3 minutes, pounded or ground into a fine powder

½ cup Soy-Lime Dipping Sauce (page 29)

BRAISED DUCK WITH PINEAPPLE

 vit nau thom

SERVES 6

3 shallots, minced

3 cloves garlic, minced

1 tablespoon fish sauce

2 tablespoons soy sauce

1 teaspoon sea salt, or to taste

½ teaspoon freshly ground
   black pepper

1 whole duck, excess fat
   trimmed, cut into 8 pieces

1 ripe pineapple

2 tablespoons vegetable oil

1 yellow onion, cut into
   thin wedges

2 carrots, peeled and cut on the
   diagonal into ⅔-inch slices

2 tablespoons dark rum

5 sprigs cilantro

At my grandmother's house, this dish often appears during *do ong noi* (paternal grandfather's death anniversary). My aunts think it's an adaptation of duck *à l'orange,* one of many dishes left behind from the French colonial days. Since oranges, except for the green-skinned variety, are not grown in Vietnam, pineapples are used.

1. Combine the shallots, garlic, fish sauce, soy sauce, salt and pepper in a large bowl. Add the duck and turn to coat the meat evenly. Cover and marinate for at least 4 hours but preferably overnight.

2. Peel the pineapple and cut in half lengthwise. Save one half for another use. Cut the remaining half in two and remove the core. Cut crosswise into ¼-inch-thick slices. Set aside half of the pineapple slices. Finely chopped the other half. Using your hands, squeeze the finely chopped pineapple over a strainer into a bowl, extracting as much juice as possible. Reserve the juice.

3. Heat 1 tablespoon of the vegetable oil in a skillet over high heat. Add the reserved pineapple slices and sear until the edges are slightly browned, 2 to 3 minutes on each side. Remove from the heat and drain on paper towels.

4. Wipe the pan clean. Heat the remaining 1 tablespoon oil in the pan over moderate heat. Add the duck, skin side down (do not crowd the pan) and cook until slightly browned, about 3 to 4 minutes. If necessary, cook in batches.

5. Transfer the duck and any marinating liquids to a pot and add the reserved pineapple juice. Add enough water to cover the duck. Bring the liquid to a boil, then reduce the

heat. Simmer for 20 minutes. While the duck cooks, skim the surface of any foam or fat.

6. Add the onion, carrots and dark rum. Continue cooking until the duck and carrots are tender, about 15 minutes. Stir in the reserved pineapple slices and cook until thoroughly hot, 2 to 3 minutes. Transfer the mixture to a serving dish, garnish with the cilantro and serve with steamed rice.

BROKEN RICE WITH SHREDDED GARLIC PORK

com tam bi

SERVES 2

The pork is very tasty in Vietnam, especially when it's made as it is in this dish, which is served at market kitchens and street cafés all over the country. It calls for broken rice—the grains that break when the rice is milled. It's often served with a combination of pork toppings, from the basic *bi,* or shredded pork, to grilled pork chops, pork sausage and pork meatloaf. In this version, the pork skin, which is cooked and available frozen at Asian markets, adds texture. However, the dish is also delicious without it. What makes this particularly enticing is the wonderful oil, dipping sauce and salad accompaniments. If you don't have broken rice, use regular rice. The texture is different but the flavors are just as delicious. Toasted rice powder is available at Asian markets.

1. Rinse the broken rice. Place in a pot with 2 cups water. Bring to a boil, stir a few times, then reduce the heat to the lowest possible temperature. Cover and cook for 20 minutes. (If you use regular rice, use 2¼ cups water and cook in a similar fashion.)

2. Heat the oil in a skillet over moderately low heat. Add the pork pieces. Cover and cook until the edges are golden,

2 cups broken rice or regular long-grain rice

3 tablespoons vegetable oil

⅔ pound pork shoulder, excess fat trimmed, cut into two 1-inch-thick pieces

10 whole cloves garlic, peeled

1 cup loosely packed shredded cooked and frozen pork skin, rinsed in hot water and very well drained

1 tablespoon sugar

½ teaspoon sea salt

1½ tablespoons toasted rice powder (page 231)

GARNISHES

½ cup Scallion Oil (page 32)

½ cup Chili-Lime Dipping Sauce (page 30)

Cucumber Salad (page 81)

about 5 minutes. Turn the meat and add the garlic. Cook until the pork is just done, another 5 to 7 minutes. When the garlic starts to brown, remove and drain on paper towels. Remove the meat and drain on paper towels.

3. Cut the shredded pork skin into 2-inch lengths and set aside.

4. When the pork is cool enough to handle, cut into thin narrow strips about the length and width of a short matchstick. Place the shredded pork in a bowl. Finely chop the garlic and add it to the bowl. Add the pork skin, sugar, salt and roasted rice powder and stir to combine.

5. To serve, place the hot broken rice in the center of a plate. Top with the shredded pork and Scallion Oil (scallions and a little oil). Drizzle with the dipping sauce and serve with the Cucumber Salad on the side.

AUNT TAM'S PORK IN CLAYPOT

 thit kho tieu

SERVES 4

2 tablespoons fish sauce

1½ teaspoons Caramel Sauce
    (page 34)

1 tablespoon sugar

½ pound boneless pork shoulder
    or butt, sliced into thin
    bite-sized strips

3 tablespoons water

1 teaspoon freshly ground
    black pepper

4 sprigs cilantro, cut into
    1-inch pieces

If there's such a thing as Vietnamese comfort food, this would be it. Every cook has his or her own recipe for this delicious pork, but Aunt Tam's is my favorite. Cooked in a rustic claypot or sandpot, the meat is simmered with fish sauce and caramel sauce, which adds a distinctive sweetness and smokiness to the dish. Then a generous amount of black pepper is added at the end. For a thoroughly authentic menu, cook this in a claypot and serve it with Sweet-and-Sour Shrimp Soup with Fresh Herbs (page 71) and a vegetable dish.

1. Combine the fish sauce, Caramel Sauce and sugar in a bowl and stir well to blend. Add the pork and marinate for 30 minutes.
2. Place the pork and any of the marinating juices in a 1-quart claypot. Bring to a boil, then reduce the heat to a simmer. Add the water and cook, uncovered, until the sauce is slightly thick, about 7 to 10 minutes. Stir in the black pepper. Remove the pot from the heat. Garnish with the cilantro and serve right in the claypot.

VIETNAMESE RICE CAKES IN BANANA LEAVES
banh chung

MAKES 1 CAKE OR 4 SERVINGS

Almost synonymous to Tet, the lunar new year, *banh chung* is a highly regarded food in Vietnam. It's said to have originated centuries ago when King Hung Vuong VI challenged his many sons that whoever came up with the best recipe for Tet would inherit his throne.

The eldest one, eager to impress his father, traveled far and wide to procure the most exotic recipes. But the youngest son, the shy and quiet one, stayed closed to home and cooked a dish based on a dream. A genie had told him to take sticky rice (which symbolized the earth), wrap it around a ball of mung bean paste (which represented the sun), then boil it for one day and one night. Upon tasting the dish and hearing the story, the king was so impressed he proclaimed his youngest son the heir to his throne and ordered the recipe to be shared with all commoners.

Since that day, *banh chung* has enjoyed a central place in Vietnamese culture—at the family table and on the ancestor worship altar. Since it's considered taboo to work or cook during the first three days of Tet, these cakes are usually made

1¾ cups sticky (glutinous) rice, preferably long-grain

1 drop of green food coloring (optional)

¼ cup dried split mung beans

¼ teaspoon salt

2 tablespoon chopped shallots

1½ tablespoons fish sauce

1 teaspoon ground black pepper

5 ounces pork shoulder or butt, cut into ¼-inch-thick chunks

1½ tablespoons vegetable oil

2 (14" x 16") sheets plastic wrap plus extra

1 (14"x 16") sheet aluminum foil

2 (14" x 14") pieces banana leaf

before the festivities begin. Serve this dish at room temperature with a side of salt and pepper or reheat slightly in the microwave and serve as part of a meal.

1. Place the sticky rice in a large bowl and cover with 3 inches of water. Stir in the food coloring, if using, and let the rice soak overnight. (Once soaked, the rice will double to about 4 cups.) In a separate bowl, soak the mung beans for at least 4 hours. Drain both just before using and set aside in separate bowls. Add the salt to the rice and stir to blend.

2. Combine the shallots, fish sauce, black pepper and pork pieces and let marinate for 30 minutes.

3. Heat the oil in a frying pan over moderate heat. Add the pork pieces and all the marinade and stir just until the meat is brown around the edges, about 3 to 4 minutes. Remove the pan from the heat and set aside.

4. Using a steamer basket, steam the mung beans until they're soft, about 10 minutes. Remove from the heat and set aside.

5. To make the packet, neatly lay down the wrappers in this order: 1 sheet of plastic wrap (leave the other for use later), the aluminum foil, 2 sheets of banana leaves (one perpendicular to the other). Place 1 cup of rice in the center of the banana leaf, spreading it to cover a 5-inch square. Place half of the mung beans on top, then add the pork pieces. Cover with the remaining mung beans and place 1 cup rice on top. Bring the narrow sides of the wrappers together. Fold the gathered edges over twice, then flatten against the packet. (You now have two open ends.) Fold one end over and hold the packet upright. Add half of the remaining rice, tapping it and pushing it down so that the packet will be an even square. Fold the end over and repeat on the other side.

6. Place the packet with the folded sides down in the center of the remaining plastic sheet. Wrap tightly so that water will not seep into the packet during cooking.

Banh chung *can be made as square or cylinder-shaped cakes.*

7. Tightly tie the packet with two parallel strings in both directions (as in a tic-tac-toe pattern).
8. Fill a large stockpot with water. Add the packet and bring to a boil. Reduce the heat to a simmer. Place a colander or something heavy on top of the packet to keep it submerged in the water. Cook uncovered until done, about 6 hours, adding more water as necessary. Remove from the heat and set aside to cool for 1 hour.
9. To serve, cut the packet (without unwrapping) into ½ inch slices. Remove the wrapping and arrange the slices on a serving plate. Serve warm or at room temperature. If wrapped in plastic and refrigerated, the cake will keep for 1 week.

SHAKING BEEF

 bo luc lac

SERVES 4

1½ tablespoons fresh lime juice

1 tablespoon fish sauce

1 tablespoon sugar

2 Thai bird chilies or
  ½ serrano chili, chopped

1 tablespoon oyster sauce

2 teaspoons soy sauce

⅔ pound beef sirloin or flank
  steak, cut into ½-inch cubes

2 to 3 tablespoons vegetable oil

2 cloves garlic, sliced

¼ ripe pineapple (about ½ cup),
  cut into bite-sized slices
  about ¼ inch thick
  (optional)

½ cup Asian basil leaves,
  cut in half

¼ red onion, thinly sliced
  lengthwise

3 cups watercress, washed,
  picked over and torn into
  bite-sized sprigs

1 ripe tomato, cut into
  thin wedges

For most families in Vietnam, the dish that comes closest to a steak is *bo luc lac,* which is made by shaking the beef in a pan over high heat. Inspired by the French, who introduced and popularized beef, it can be served either as a snack or as part of a meal. I remember my sister Denise and I often ate this at a French country club where we used to go swimming after school. The salad, which was served with warm baguette, was always the highlight of our outing. We'd eat everything on the plate, finishing by taking bread and soaking up every single drop of the dressing.

To me, this dish makes an easy and delicious light supper in the summer. I like it with either bread or steamed rice.

1. Combine the lime juice, fish sauce, sugar and chilies in a large bowl. Set aside.

2. Place the oyster sauce, soy sauce and beef in a medium bowl and toss to coat the meat evenly.

3. Heat the oil in a large skillet over high heat. Add the garlic and stir until fragrant, about 5 seconds. Add the beef and quickly stir-fry it until just charred on the edges, about 2 to 3 minutes. Add to the bowl with the lime sauce.

4. Add the pineapple slices, if using, Asian basil and red onion to the beef mixture. Spread the watercress and tomatoes in an attractive manner on a serving platter. Arrange the beef mixture and all its juices on the watercress and serve immediately.

NOTE: Another way of presenting *bo luc lac* is to omit the lime dressing completely and serve the beef with a dipping salt mixture made with 1½ tablespoons sea salt, 1 teaspoon freshly ground black pepper, and 1 tablespoon fresh lime juice.

BEEF STEW WITH STAR ANISE AND BASIL

thit bo kho

SERVES 6

In Vietnam, there are people who would travel great distances each morning just to get a perfect bowl of *thit bo kho,* an aromatic beef stew simmered with chilies and lemongrass and made with annatto oil, which gives it a reddish-orange color. Although hearty, this dish gets its refreshing twist from the last-minute addition of fresh basil and onion. At breakfast, *thit bo kho* is served with a French baguette, but at other meals it's usually accompanied by noodles or steamed rice.

1. Heat the oil in small saucepan over low heat. Add the annatto seeds, stir a few times and remove immediately from

3 tablespoons vegetable oil
2 tablespoons annatto seeds (page 223)
2 tablespoons chopped shallots
½ tablespoon chopped garlic
1 pound beef chuck roast, cut into 1½-inch cubes
3 cups fresh water, Chicken Stock (page 39) or store-bought low-sodium chicken broth, boiling

2 lemongrass stalks, lightly crushed with the flat side of a knife and cut into 3-inch pieces

2 tablespoons fish sauce

1 tablespoon soy sauce

1 tablespoon sugar

3 whole star anise

1 tablespoon curry powder, preferably Vietnamese Three Golden Bells brand

2 teaspoons chopped fresh red chilies or dried chilies, or to taste

3 carrots, peeled and cut on the diagonal into ½-inch rounds (about 3 cups), blanched in boiling water for 3 minutes and drained

½ cup Asian basil leaves

¼ small yellow onion, sliced paper-thin

5 sprigs cilantro, cut into 2-inch lengths

the heat. (The seeds should foam upon contact but not burn.) Let stand for 10 minutes, then strain the oil and discard the seeds.

2. Heat half the annatto oil in a medium pan over moderate heat. Add half the shallots and half the garlic and stir until fragrant, about 10 seconds. Add the beef and stir until lightly seared, about 3 to 4 minutes. Add the boiling chicken stock, lemongrass, fish sauce, soy sauce and sugar and bring to a boil. Reduce the heat to a simmer. Cook until the beef is tender, about 40 minutes, skimming the top occasionally.

3. While the beef is cooking, lightly toast the star anise in a dry pan over low heat until fragrant, about 3 to 4 minutes. Transfer to a mortar and pound to a fine powder. (You can also use a spice mill.)

4. Heat the remaining annatto oil in a small saucepan over moderate heat. Add the remaining shallots and garlic, star anise powder, curry powder, and chilies and stir until fragrant, about 20 seconds. Set aside until ready to serve.

5. Fifteen minutes before the beef is done, add the carrots and cook until they are tender. Add the spice mixture and stir a few times. Stir in half the basil and transfer the stew to a serving bowl. Garnish with the remaining basil, yellow onion and cilantro and serve immediately.

chapter six

Drifting and Dreaming

Seafood Dishes

Seafood Stew with Lemongrass and Dill

Tamarind Crab

Salt-and-Pepper Crab with Ginger

Southern-Style Catfish in Claypot

Sea Bass with Lily Buds, Mushrooms and Cellophane Noodles

Fish with Fresh Tomato Sauce

Grilled Lemongrass Shrimp

Steamed Striped Bass with Soy Sauce, Ginger and Scallions

Cilantro Shrimp in Claypot

Caramelized Garlic Shrimp

Pan-Seared Sea Bass with Ginger-Lime Sauce

Chili Clams with Fermented Black Beans and Basil

Steamed Mussels with Lemongrass

The canvas topsail of our junkboat flaps gently in the wind and the bamboo rods clang against one another. Underneath the deck, the waves ripple and splash.

Never before have I been so enchanted by nature. We have been sailing since dawn, drifting and floating on the calm Ha Long Bay. Just an hour ago this magical body of water, located just off the coast of northern Vietnam, was blanketed with misty fog. Then, as the blurry red sun rose above the silvery surface of the water, the fog slowly disappeared.

As we drift along, hundreds if not thousands, of limestone formations fade in and out of view—some clear, some in graduating shades of blue. No wonder this bay is named the Descent of the Dragon, where, according to one tale I often heard when I was a child, Vietnamese civilization was said to have originated.

In the beginning of time, so goes the tale, one hundred eggs were born to a dragon and a fairy. Fifty children went with the fairy mother and settled in the mountains and valleys where they cultivated rice. The rest followed the dragon father and conquered the sea. Growing up with such a tale, it's no wonder we're in awe of this panorama, especially when told we are *con rong chau tien* (children of the dragon and fairy).

As I look closely, I realize the formations do indeed look like the animals and objects after which they've been named—Fighting Roosters, Turtle, Rice Ball and Elephant. I can see now why Ha Long Bay is considered to be the Eighth Wonder. The

Ha Long Bay with rock formations in the background.

mountains seem to jut right out of the sea and touch the sky. Grottoes are filled with amazing stalactites and stalagmites, creating stunning temples of nature.

We manage to reach one such temple by squeezing through a passage underneath a rock that leads to a lagoon. Once inside, I'm captivated by the still of the warm water, the continuous cliffs that surround it, and the silence that breaks only when birds move from one treetop to another. Suddenly a voice startles me.

"How about some delicious crabs?" shouts a woman from a small fishing vessel, her hands grabbing the edge of our boat. She must have choked off the motor before getting close. Many fishing families around Ha Long Bay spend their entire life at sea, making a living by selling their catch to tourists like us.

The woman's husband waves a huge crab at me. His two toddlers, bundled in warm clothes and faces darkened by the sun, stare at me intently.

"Please, help our family and buy this fresh fish and shrimp. We just caught them this morning," the woman pleads. The crew already brought plenty to cook a big lunch with, including mackerel, squid, and clams, but I can't resist her offer. With these shrimp, I can make a pot of exquisite Vietnamese seafood stew, flavored with beer, lemongrass and dill. "Okay," I answer, "we'll take them both."

I can hardly contain my excitement as I pay for my purchases. I know that cooking and savoring this fresh seafood in this most breathtaking setting will truly be an experience of a lifetime.

Looking down at the fishing vessel, I can see the family watching us in such a poignant way. The couple stand motionless, their eyes fixated on us, their kids wrapped around their legs. Never mind the blue skies, the limestone peaks, the temples of nature. The family seems infinitely more interested in us than in anything else around them.

Seafood plays a critical role in the Vietnamese diet, thanks to the more than 3,000-kilometer-long coastline, stretching from the Gulf of Tonkin to the Gulf of Thailand, and all the rivers and tributaries that flow throughout the countryside. At any number of bustling fish markets, one can find all kinds of fish and shellfish—from the ordinary tuna and mackerel to the more exotic species such as angelfish, razor clams, and seaworms.

The seafood market at Ha Long Bay.

While many types of seafood are prized, fish, eel, crab and shrimp are the most commonly prepared. Fish—both saltwater and freshwater—are usually served whole, fried or steamed, and accompanied by a dipping sauce. When they are cut into smaller pieces, the bones and skin are left on to preserve flavor and moisture. At the Vietnamese table, it's acceptable to chew on a piece of fish and remove a bone or two, leaving them on the table. Shellfish and shrimp are cooked with their shells on for the same reason. The Vietnamese believe simplicity is the best approach to freshly caught fish and shellfish, so most of the recipes in this chapter are very uncomplicated.

SEAFOOD STEW WITH LEMONGRASS AND DILL

 lau bien

SERVES 6

2 tablespoons vegetable oil

2 shallots, thinly sliced

2 cloves garlic, thinly sliced

½ teaspoon dried chili flakes, or to taste

2 tomatoes, preferably vine ripe, cut into large chunks (about 2 cups)

2 tablespoons fish sauce

1 lemongrass stalk, cut into 3-inch pieces and lightly bruised with the flat side of a knife

2 cups Chicken Stock (page 39)

½ cup water

½ cup light beer

4 Asian celery stalks or 2 regular celery stalks (leafy parts included), cut on the diagonal into ¼-inch-thick slices

1 bunch fresh dill, leaves only, cut into 1-inch pieces (about ⅔ cup)

¼ pound raw medium shrimp, peeled and deveined

⅓ pound skinless red snapper fillets, or any firm fish, cut into large chunks

½ pound black mussels, scrubbed clean and debearded, or Manila clams

When I first had this delicious dish in Ha Long Bay, I was a little shocked. It came in a pot set on a tabletop stove and it was filled with all kinds of seafood, including live shrimp. When the broth boiled, the shrimp started jumping. Our server said this was the only sure sign of freshness. Like the Chinese, the Vietnamese prize live fish and shellfish.

This version of *lau*, which is a fairly new creation based on the Chinese hotpot, has become quite popular in recent years. It's considered status food, namely because it contains seafood that is cooked with beer or alcohol. Try to get the freshest seafood you can and use very ripe tomatoes. You can serve this dish with rice or bread, which is great for soaking up the wonderful broth.

1. Heat the oil in a medium pot over high heat. Add the shallots and garlic and stir until fragrant, about 20 seconds. Add the dried chili flakes, half of the tomatoes, the fish sauce and lemongrass and stir until fragrant, about 2 minutes. Add the stock, water, beer, celery and half of the dill. Bring to a boil, then reduce the heat to low. Cover and simmer for 15 minutes.

2. Add the shrimp, red snapper, mussels and the remaining tomatoes and dill, and cook until the fish turns white and the mussels have opened, about 3 minutes. Transfer to a large preheated bowl and serve immediately.

Tamarind

Tamarind is used extensively in Vietnamese cuisine as a souring agent. It's sold in three basic forms— dried pulp (sometimes labeled "candy") packaged in an 8-ounce or 1-pound plastic-wrapped block; liquid concentrate; and fresh pods. The dried pulp is readily available at Asian markets and is quite convenient to use. To make tamarind juice, soften the pulp in warm water for about 30 minutes. Use 1 part tamarind to 3 parts water. If this is too sour, add more water. Put the mixture through a strainer, scraping the pulp to extract as much juice as you can. When buying this product, look for the "sweet" tamarind, which is not as sour as regular tamarind. That way, you can use a larger amount to get more tamarind flavor without making the dish too sour.

There's not much sense in using the liquid concentrate when the dried pulp is available. If you are able to find fresh ripe pods, handle them as you do the pulp: Scrape the flesh from the pods, soften it in hot water, then press through a sieve to extract the juice.

TAMARIND CRAB

 cua rang me

SERVES 4

3 tablespoons vegetable oil

2 shallots, minced

1 tablespoon chopped garlic

1 fresh Dungeness crab (about
2 pounds), cleaned, cut into
4 or 6 pieces and tomalley
reserved (see How to Clean
a Crab on page 165)

2 to 3 tablespoons tamarind
pulp, juiced (page 163)

1½ tablespoons fish sauce

1 tablespoon sugar

½ cup fresh Chicken Stock
(page 39), store-bought
low-sodium chicken broth
or water

2 scallions, cut into 2-inch
lengths

5 sprigs cilantro, cut into 2-inch
lengths

My aunt Co Tam serves me this dish every time I'm in Saigon. It's a little messy to eat because you have to pick up the crab with your fingers and suck on the gooey sauce before cracking the shells, but it's well worth the effort. In fact, this hands-on approach is the proper etiquette for crab-feasting. In Vietnam, this dish is made with the sweet and meaty mud crab, but because they are not available in the United States you can use Dungeness crab or blue crab instead.

1. Place the oil in a skillet large enough to hold all the crab pieces and heat over high heat until the oil is very hot. Add the shallots and garlic and stir until fragrant, about 10 seconds. Add the crab tomalley, reduce the heat slightly, and stir for 2 minutes. Add the crab, tamarind juice, fish sauce and sugar. Stir so that the crab is well coated with the sauce. Add the chicken stock and cover. Simmer until the meat of the crab turns white, about 10 minutes. (Add a little water if the pan gets too dry.) Stir in the scallions. Transfer to a serving plate and garnish with the cilantro.

How to Clean a Crab

If you're a crab lover like me, it's helpful to know how to select a good live crab and clean it. While cooked crabs also work in the recipes in this book, live ones are better because the meat is fresh, firm and sweet. In Vietnam, crabs are only sold live.

Nho and Suong Pham, the husband-and-wife team who have been supplying fresh seafood to our Lemon Grass Restaurant since day one, personally handpick every crab that we serve. They look for those with very firm legs, a sign that they're meaty and juicy. Holding a crab with tongs, they press against the upper part of a leg. If it's very hard and doesn't give, it's a good crab.

To kill a crab, bring a pot of water to a rolling boil. Drop the crab in and cook for 2 to 3 minutes. When it stops moving, remove it from the water. (If you want to parcook the crab, let it cook longer, about 10 minutes.) Set aside to cool.

To clean, turn the crab belly side up and remove and discard the "apron"—the V-shaped flap on the bottom. Holding the crab firmly, pull the top shell away from the body. Remove the soft, yellowish tomalley or liver located on the inside of the shell, behind the eyes. Called *gach*, it's a prized part of the crab that Vietnamese cooks use to enrich the flavor of a dish. Discard the sets of feathery gills in the body of the crab, then rinse with cool water. Snap off the legs and claws. Using a heavy knife, cut the body into 2 or 4 pieces, depending on the size. You can crack the claws and legs lightly, although I prefer to leave them uncracked because the meat remains more moist when cooked that way.

SALT-AND-PEPPER CRAB WITH GINGER

 cua rang muoi

SERVES 2 AS A MAIN DISH

2 tablespoons vegetable oil

2 cloves garlic, minced

1 shallot, minced

1 (1-inch) piece ginger, peeled
and cut into matchstick strips

1 live Dungeness crab (about
2½ pounds), parboiled for
10 minutes, cleaned and cut
into smaller segments,
tomalley reserved
(see How to Clean a Crab
on page 165)

2 teaspoons coarse sea salt

1 teaspoon sugar

½ teaspoon freshly ground
black pepper

1 teaspoon soy sauce

2 scallions, cut into 2-inch
lengths

5 sprigs cilantro, cut into
2-inch lengths

Often called salt-baked crab in restaurants, this dish of Chinese origin is traditionally made by first deep-frying the crab, then stir-frying it with garlic and ginger. In order to make it a bit lighter, I've eliminated the deep-frying step. Instead I simply parboil the crab, then add it to the stir-fry. For the best flavor, purchase crab—preferably live—at a reputable seafood market. When it comes to eating, don't be bashful. Use your hands, nibble on the garlic and ginger, and retrieve every morsel of meat from the crab that you possibly can. I can eat this at least once a week come crab season. Try serving this with a side of Scallion Noodles (page 115), or just steamed rice and Cucumber Salad (page 81).

1. Heat the oil in a large wok or skillet over moderate heat. Add the garlic, shallot and ginger and stir until fragrant, about 15 seconds. Add the reserved tomalley, stirring to break it up. Cook for 1 minute, sprinkling with 2 to 3 tablespoons of water if the pan is too dry.

2. Add the salt, sugar, pepper, soy sauce and crab, and stir so that the crab pieces are evenly coated with the seasonings. Add the scallions and cook until the crab is thoroughly hot, about 5 minutes. Transfer the crab and all the bits and pieces of the seasonings to a serving plate. Garnish with the cilantro and serve with lots of napkins.

SOUTHERN-STYLE CATFISH IN CLAYPOT

ca kho to

SERVES 4

To me, if there's one dish that best represents Vietnamese home cooking, it has to be this classic *ca kho to*. Made with catfish and fish sauce simmered in a claypot, it's a favorite at every family table. Originally a southern creation, it is now eaten throughout the country.

Every time our mother made this, my siblings and I would fight over the gooey, smoky sauce in the bottom of the claypot. Interestingly, many customers at our Lemon Grass Restaurant do the same thing. A claypot will enhance the flavor of this dish, but it's also delicious cooked in a regular pot. Serve it with steamed rice, a soup and a vegetable dish and you'll have yourself an authentic Vietnamese meal.

2 tablespoons sugar

1 tablespoon vegetable oil

1 clove garlic, minced

½ cup boiling water

3 tablespoons fish sauce

⅔ pound fresh catfish fillets, cut in halves or thirds

1 scallion, cut into 1-inch lengths

4 sprigs cilantro, cut into 1-inch lengths

½ teaspoon freshly ground black pepper

1. Place the sugar in a 1-quart claypot and add just enough water to barely wet it. Heat over moderate heat until the sugar starts to turn brown, about 3 to 5 minutes. Stir once, then add the oil and garlic. Stir for 1 minute, then add the boiling water, fish sauce and catfish pieces. Turn the pieces so that they're evenly coated with the sauce. Reduce the heat to a simmer. Cook, covered, until the catfish is firm and almost done, about 5 minutes. Uncover, and continue to simmer for another 2 to 3 minutes so that the sauce is slightly thickened.
2. Remove the claypot from the heat and garnish with the scallion, cilantro and black pepper. Serve immediately right in the claypot.

SEA BASS WITH LILY BUDS, MUSHROOMS AND CELLOPHANE NOODLES

 ca chung tuong

SERVES 4

35 dried lily buds (page 196), each tied into a knot

6 small dried black mushrooms

1 ounce dried wood-ear mushrooms, preferably the small black variety (optional)

1 ounce dried cellophane noodles (page 112)

2 tablespoons vegetable oil

1 shallot, sliced

1 clove garlic, minced

½ teaspoon dried chili flakes

½ teaspoon sugar

2 tablespoons soy sauce

⅔ cup fresh Chicken Stock (page 39) or store-bought low-sodium chicken broth

2 (6-ounce) skinless sea bass fillets

1 (2-inch) piece ginger, peeled and cut into slivers

1 scallion, cut into 2-inch slivers

5 sprigs cilantro, cut into 2-inch pieces

Freshly ground black pepper

This dish is as delicious as it sounds. The soy-infused broth, seasoned with ginger, brings out the delicate flavors of the fish. In Chinese cookery, dried ingredients are prized for certain flavors and textures, as well as for the medicinal qualities that fresh foods don't have. In this dish, the *kim cham* (lily buds) add delightful chewiness and are said to be a mild pain reliever. The traditional way of preparing this dish is in a steamer (page 172), but you can also cook it in a pan. Just prepare the aromatics and noodles, then add the fish toward the end so it doesn't overcook.

1. Soak the lily buds, black mushrooms, wood-ear mushrooms, if using, and noodles in hot water for 30 minutes. Drain and squeeze dry. Remove the tough knobs and stems from the mushrooms and slice into bite-sized pieces. Cut the noodles into 10-inch lengths. Set aside.

2. Heat the oil in a pan over moderate heat. Add the shallot, garlic and chili flakes and stir until fragrant, about 10 seconds. Add the sugar, soy sauce and black mushrooms. Stir a few times, then add the stock, wood-ear mushrooms and noodles. Quickly transfer the mixture to a deep casserole that will fit inside your steamer. Place the fish fillets on top, then sprinkle half of the ginger on the fish.

3. Place the casserole on a steamer rack. Fill a wok or steamer pan with 3 inches water. Cover and steam over high heat until the fish is just done, about 15 minutes. Remove from the heat and garnish with the remaining ginger, the scallion, cilantro and black pepper. Serve immediately.

FISH WITH FRESH TOMATO SAUCE

ca chien sot chua ngot

SERVES 4

Hot, crispy fish topped with fresh, tangy tomato sauce. In Hanoi, these simple ingredients come together in such a delightful manner. What makes this dish so special are the vine-ripe tomatoes and the freshly harvested young scallions from nearby villages. Prior to my trips, I had thought baby vegetables and greens were a uniquely Western phenomenon, but in Vietnam it's the only way many vegetables, especially the scallions and aromatic herbs, are sold.

Cu kieu (pickled scallion bulbs), a popular Vietnamese condiment, adds complexity to the sauce. It's available at Asian markets, but the dish will still be wonderful without it.

1. Heat 2 tablespoons vegetable oil in a small saucepan over moderate heat. Add the shallots, garlic and chili flakes and stir until fragrant, about 1 minute. Add the pickled scallions and juice, if using, fish sauce, sugar and two-thirds of the tomatoes. Reduce the heat and simmer for 3 to 4 minutes.
2. Combine the cornstarch and stock. While stirring, drizzle the cornstarch mixture into the sauce and cook until the sauce is thick enough to just coat the spoon. Remove the pan from the heat and set aside until ready to use.
3. Into a skillet large enough to hold the whole fish, pour ½ inch oil and heat it over moderate heat until it reaches about 350 degrees. Carefully add the fish and cook until the meat turns white, about 5 minutes on each side. (If using fillets, reduce the cooking time.) Remove and drain on paper towels. Transfer the fish to a serving plate.
4. Add the remaining chopped tomatoes to the sauce and re-heat. Spoon the sauce over the fish. Garnish with the scallion and cilantro and serve immediately.

Vegetable oil

2 shallots, minced

1 clove garlic, chopped

1 teaspoon dried chili flakes,
    or to taste

2 tablespoons pickled scallions
    with juice, sliced

1 tablespoon fish sauce

½ tablespoon sugar

2 ripe tomatoes, cut into
    ⅓-inch cubes

2 teaspoons cornstarch

⅓ cup Chicken Stock (page 39)
    or store-bought low-sodium
    chicken broth

1 whole red snapper or striped
    bass (about 2 pounds),
    cleaned, with or without head
    and tail, scored with 3 slashes
    on each side, or 1 pound
    sea bass fillets

1 scallion, cut into 1-inch pieces

5 sprigs cilantro, cut into
    2-inch pieces

GRILLED LEMONGRASS SHRIMP

 tom nuong xa

SERVES 4 AS AN APPETIZER

¼ cup minced lemongrass
   (page 43)

1 teaspoon minced garlic

1 teaspoon soy sauce

1 teaspoon fish sauce

½ teaspoon ground chili paste
   (page 225)

Pinch salt

1 teaspoon sugar

2 tablespoons vegetable oil

1 pound medium raw shrimp,
   peeled and deveined

4 (10-inch) bamboo skewers,
   soaked in hot water for
   30 minutes and drained

What can be more enticing than the aroma of sweet, plump shrimp with lemongrass on the grill? It's a fragrance I often encounter at the market stalls in Vietnam, and it's always hard to walk by without surrendering to a plateful. Fortunately, this delicious dish is easily prepared at home and gets rave reviews from everyone, including children. Just make sure that the shrimp is of high quality and the lemongrass is really fresh. Serve this as an appetizer or as a main dish with the shrimp as the topping for Rice Noodles with Fresh Herbs (page 119).

1. Combine the lemongrass, garlic, soy sauce, fish sauce, chili paste, salt, sugar, and oil in a bowl. Add the shrimp and marinate for 15 minutes. Thread the shrimp on the skewers and set them aside.

2. Start a charcoal grill or preheat a gas grill to moderate heat. Just before serving, grill the shrimp, turning the skewers, until just done, about 2 to 3 minutes total, depending on the size. If you don't have a grill, trim the skewers and cook in a pan with a little oil on the stovetop.

STEAMED STRIPED BASS WITH SOY SAUCE, GINGER AND SCALLIONS

ca hap gung

SERVES 6

Whenever I'm in the mood for this dish, I head out to an Asian market, pick out a live striped bass and have it killed and cleaned right on the spot. When a fish is that fresh, you want to serve it simply, as in this recipe. Any white-fleshed fish including red snapper, sea bass, cod or rockfish will work.

Look for the very young scallions and use young ginger, with the smooth pinkish skin. The best way to cook this dish is in a Chinese aluminum steamer (page 172). If you don't have one, improvise: Place a cake rack in a large pot (with water below the rack) and set your platter on top. Be sure the pot has a tight-fitting lid.

1. Rinse the fish. Rub it with the sea salt inside and out, rinse again and pat dry. If you like, or if your steamer is small, re-move the head and tail and use only the middle section of the fish. Place the fish in a heatproof dish and place on a steamer rack. Fill the steamer pan one third full with water and place the rack in the pan. Cover and steam on high heat until the fish flakes easily, about 12 to 15 minutes, depending on the thickness.

2. While the fish is steaming, prepare the sauce: Heat the oil in a pan over moderate heat. Add the shallot and stir until fragrant, about 10 seconds. Add the soy sauce, rice wine, chicken stock and half the ginger. Reduce the heat and simmer 2 minutes. Remove from the heat and set aside.

3. When the fish is done, turn off the heat and carefully remove the platter. Drain most of the liquid from the platter. Pour the sauce on top. Garnish with the remaining ginger, scallions, cilantro and chilies, if using, and serve immediately.

1 whole striped bass (about 2 pounds), cleaned and patted dry

2 tablespoons sea salt

2 tablespoons vegetable oil

1 shallot, thinly sliced

2 tablespoons thin soy sauce, or to taste

1 tablespoon rice wine or dry sherry

¼ cup fresh Chicken Stock (page 39) or water

1 (1½-inch) piece young ginger, peeled and cut into thin slivers

2 thin scallions, cut on the diagonal into very thin slivers

3 sprigs cilantro, cut into 2-inch lengths

½ teaspoon chopped red chili, or to taste (optional)

Chinese Steamers

The steamer is one of the best tools created for the Asian kitchen. It's ideal for steaming all different kinds of foods—fish, crab, vegetables or rice. There are two main types of steamers to consider: the modern two-tier aluminum steamer set and the bamboo steamer that requires a wok or a large pan to hold the water. I prefer the aluminum one (although I own both). The aluminum version, which is quite inexpensive and very practical, comes with a water pan, two steamer racks and a big dome lid. The perforated racks have sturdy handles and can be used as colanders, and the water pan can double as a pot. It's especially good for steaming whole fish or chicken, as well as for making desserts, such as sticky rice. It's important to purchase one that is big enough to hold a whole fish, 16 inches or larger.

The bamboo version is more traditional and attractive, but a large one can be difficult to find. The small sizes are most available and are more appropriate for steaming foods such as dumplings and other *dim sum* items.

A busy fish market in Ha Long Bay.

CILANTRO SHRIMP IN CLAYPOT

tom kho to

SERVES 4

Although this recipe is not Vietnamese, it's one of our family favorites. In the late sixties when our family lived in Thailand, our Thai nanny often spoiled us with this dish. It calls for simmering whole shrimp with a generous amount of cilantro, black peppercorns and ginger in a claypot. Just remembering the fragrance of this dish makes me hungry.

The shells add tremendous flavor and color, so before you're tempted to peel the shrimp, try them unpeeled first. At the Vietnamese table, it's perfectly acceptable to suck on the whole shrimp, peeling and discarding the shells as you go.

1. Place the peppercorns, garlic, ginger and half the cilantro in a mortar and pound into a coarse paste. (You can also grind the peppercorns in a spice mill, then chop the remaining ingredients by hand.)
2. Heat the oil in a 2-quart claypot over moderate heat. Add the herb paste and stir until fragrant, about 20 seconds. Add half the onion and all the shrimp and stir-fry until the shrimp just turn pink, about 2 minutes. Transfer to a plate and keep warm.
3. Return the claypot to the stove. Add 1 cup of the stock, the soy sauce, sugar, rice wine, fish sauce and sesame oil. Bring to a boil, then add the bean threads. Stir so the noodles are well coated with the sauce. Add the celery and remaining onion. Reduce the heat slightly and cook, uncovered, for 3 minutes. Stir in the cooked shrimp, scallions and the remaining ½ cup stock and simmer until thoroughly hot, another minute or so. (The claypot retains heat for a long time so it's best to undercook slightly.) Garnish with the remaining cilantro and serve immediately right in the claypot.

1 teaspoon black peppercorns, lightly toasted, or ½ teaspoon freshly ground black pepper

3 cloves garlic, chopped

2 teaspoons chopped ginger

4 tablespoons chopped cilantro

3 tablespoons vegetable oil

½ small yellow onion, cut into thin wedges

½ pound raw unpeeled shrimp, slit through the back and deveined

1½ cups fresh Chicken Stock (page 39) or store-bought low-sodium chicken broth

1½ tablespoons soy sauce

2 teaspoons sugar

1 tablespoon rice wine or dry sherry

2 teaspoons fish sauce, or to taste

2 teaspoons sesame oil

2 ounces bean thread noodles (page 113), soaked in hot water for 30 minutes, drained and cut into 12-inch lengths

2 celery stalks, leaves included, sliced on the diagonal into ¼-inch-thick pieces

3 scallions, cut into 1-inch pieces

CARAMELIZED GARLIC SHRIMP

 tom rim man

SERVES 4

⅔ pound raw medium shrimp,
    unpeeled

2 tablespoons vegetable oil

1½ tablespoons sugar

1 clove garlic, chopped

1 shallot, chopped

4 tablespoons water

1 tablespoon fish sauce

¼ teaspoon salt

5 sprigs cilantro, cut into
    2-inch lengths

While growing up in Vietnam, my aunts often made this dish using live freshwater shrimp caught from one of the tributaries on the Mekong River near my grandmother's house. They actually went shopping at the riverbanks, waiting as the fishermen came to shore with buckets of live shrimp. In this southern dish, the shrimp is first stir-fried in oil and sugar and then seasoned with garlic and fish sauce. What makes it is especially delectable is the intense caramelized flavor and the savoriness of the shell-on cooked shrimp. To enjoy this dish, just suck on the shells, peeling and eating as you go.

For a simple but satisfying country-style meal, serve this with steamed rice, a clear broth soup and a vegetable dish such as Chopstick Beans in Garlic (page 202).

1. Lay the shrimp on a cutting board. Holding the shrimp down securely, use a sharp paring knife and carefully make a shallow cut through the shell in the back. Remove the black vein (but not the shell), and rinse. Clean all the shrimp in this way. Pat the shrimp dry with paper towels.
2. Heat the oil in a skillet over moderate heat. Add the shrimp and sugar and stir for 1 minute. Add the garlic and shallot, stir 1 minute, and add the water, fish sauce and salt. Reduce the heat and cook until the shrimp are done and the pan is almost dry, about 1 minute or so. Transfer to a plate, garnish with the cilantro and serve immediately.

PAN-SEARED SEA BASS WITH GINGER-LIME SAUCE

ca chien nuoc mam gung

SERVES 4

Take one bite of this dish and you'll be amazed at how the ginger and fish sauce can enliven the flavor of fried fish. At the market food stalls that serve *com binh dan* (inexpensive home-style foods), this classic dish is prepared with just about any small whole fish, including yellow-fleshed catfish, perch, mackerel, and snapper.

What I love about this recipe is the cucumber garnish. It's a traditional Vietnamese touch, made by cutting the cucumber into long thin strands—about the thickness of angel hair pasta—and soaking them in the sauce. It's actually quite a clever concept because without the cucumber garnish, the sauce would just sit on the plate rather than on the fish.

½ hothouse cucumber, unpeeled
1 cup Ginger-Lime Dipping
    Sauce (page 27)
¼ cup vegetable oil
1 pound skinless sea bass fillets,
    cut into 2 or 3 pieces
6 small whole cloves garlic

1. Seed the cucumber and use a Japanese mandoline to cut it into long, thin strips about the thickness of angel hair pasta. Add the cucumber to the dipping sauce and set aside.

2. Heat the oil in a large nonstick skillet over moderate heat. Add the fillets and carefully sear them until golden and just done, 3 to 4 minutes on each side, depending on the thickness. Halfway into the cooking, add the whole garlic cloves and cook until soft. (If the fillets are thick, cover and cook a few minutes more.) Remove the fish and garlic and place on paper towels to drain.

3. Arrange the fillets on a serving dish. Scatter the garlic cloves on top. Remove the cucumbers strips from the sauce and place neatly on the fish. Pour half of the sauce on top and serve the remaining sauce on the side.

CHILI CLAMS WITH FERMENTED BLACK BEANS AND BASIL

 ngheu xao tau xi

SERVES 4

2 tablespoons vegetable oil

2 teaspoons chopped garlic

2 teaspoons minced ginger

1½ teaspoons fermented black
    beans, rinsed (see below)

6 Thai bird chilies or
    1 serrano chili, cut into
    slivers, or to taste

1 cup Asian basil leaves

1 tablespoon oyster sauce

2 pounds Manila clams,
    scrubbed

1 teaspoon cornstarch

¼ cup Chicken Stock (page 39)
    or water

The distinctive flavors of ginger and fermented black beans in this dish can be traced back to its Chinese roots. The addition of the Asian basil, however, gives it a refreshing Vietnamese touch. Be sure to soak and scrub the clams clean before using them. For variations, try mussels and shrimp. You can serve this as an appetizer or as part of a meal.

1. Heat the oil in a wok or large skillet over high heat. Add the garlic, ginger, black beans, chilies and half the Asian basil leaves. Stir until fragrant, about 10 seconds. Add the oyster sauce and clams and stir several times.

2. In a cup combine the cornstarch and stock, and stir into the pan. Cook until the clams are all opened, about 3 to 4 minutes total. Stir in the remaining basil. Transfer to a serving plate and serve immediately.

Fermented Black Beans

Called *tau xi,* this ancient Chinese seasoning is used to add pungent, savory flavor to food. Fermented black beans (also called salted black beans or preserved beans) are sold in 1-pound plastic bags, in round paper cartons or in earthenware jars. Rinse them briefly to remove any gritty substances but don't soak them because that will diminish their flavor. Asian markets carry a variety of brands but I find that the Yang Jiang Preserved Beans with Ginger (by Pearl River Bridge) are most aromatic and assertive in flavor.

    Fermented black beans will keep indefinitely if transferred to a clean, covered jar and stored in the refrigerator.

STEAMED MUSSELS WITH LEMONGRASS

so hap xa

In Vietnam, one of the most popular ways of preparing mussels, clams and snails is to steam them with lemongrass, or other aromatic leaves like ginger or guava, then serve them with a zesty and spicy dipping sauce. The traditional version calls for using a steamer with the herbs added to the liquid. This modified version is a little simpler and yields a more intense flavor because the lemongrass is actually cooked in the broth before the mussels are added.

1. Place the stock, salt, lemongrass and shallots in a medium pot and bring to a boil over moderate heat. Reduce the heat, cover and simmer for 10 minutes.
2. Add the chili and mussels. Cover and cook until the mussels open, about 2 minutes. Transfer to a preheated large bowl and serve steaming hot, with the dipping sauce on the side.

2 cups Chicken Stock (page 39) or water

¼ teaspoon sea salt

3 lemongrass stalks, cut into 2-inch pieces and lightly bruised with the flat side of a knife

2 shallots, sliced

1 red serrano chili or other fresh chili, seeded and cut into matchstick strips

2 pounds black mussels, scrubbed cleaned and debearded

½ cup Chili-Lime Dipping Sauce (page 30)

chapter seven

Return to the Grandmotherland

Vegetarian Favorites and Meatless Dishes

Salad Rolls with Jícama, Peanuts and Basil

Salad Rolls with Tofu and Mushrooms

Cucumber and Tofu Salad

Vegetarian Pho Noodle Soup

Vegetable Curry

Spicy Lemongrass Tofu

Rice Noodles with Stir-Fried Vegetables

Vegetarian Claypot Rice with Ginger

Black Mushrooms with Bean Threads in Claypot

Mustard Greens with Garlic

Water Spinach with Tofu

Twice-Cooked Eggplant with Garlic and Basil

Luffa Squash in Mushrooms

Chopstick Beans in Garlic

Taking my grandmother on her first wheelchair tour of her plantation.

Whenever I cook a vegetarian meal, I'm reminded of my grand-mother—who is 102 years old at this writing—and of that special reunion at her home in the Mekong Delta.

It was only my second trip back to Quoi Son, my ancestral village, since the war had ended in 1975. We had barely finished unloading a special gift from the van—a sparkling lightweight wheelchair that I had wanted to give my grandmother for years—when a crowd of relatives came running out. The well-wishers surrounded us, hugging us and hanging on to our clothes as we stumbled toward the house. I looked up and saw my grandmother standing in the doorway, calling and beckoning us to come inside. She waved, her face beaming and her eyes—though drowned in tears—still shining bright.

We embraced and chatted. Except for a cut on her forehead from a recent fall, she was in good health. Had the whole village not prayed by her bedside, she confided, she might not have pulled through. As we talked, the well-wishers quieted down. Their mouths dropped as they admired what must have been the first wheelchair to roll into the village. "Fancy!" "Must be expensive," said the onlookers as they touched and caressed the shiny chrome.

The commotion made my grandmother excited to try her new wheelchair. When her ninety-pound frame fell into the nylon seat, her eyes widened. She seemed a bit puzzled but quickly laughed, marveling at how comfortable it felt. I placed her

Grandmother's open-air kitchen in the Mekong Delta.

feet on the rest and started to push her toward the street. She giggled, but became nervous and fearful about falling into the potholes. "I'll be careful," I reassured her. I pushed her out to the front, then up and down the road where she's lived all her life. We rolled past the coconut plantations where she once worked, past the longan orchards that she helped plant, the ones that would later produce unusually big, juicy fruits.

She seemed overjoyed, her words barely understandable. Her bony arms flew, one moment pointing this way and another that. This village had been her home all these years, but only now was she able to see it again up close. The last time she had walked this land was more than two decades ago, before arthritis struck and left her practically immobile.

In the bright sunlight, my grandmother's face was pinkish-white. Her eyes squinted and her silvery hair glistened. Whenever the breeze blew her hair into her face, she seemed pleased as she pushed it behind her ears. She liked being out here. She loved the sun, the air, the feeling of movement. I tried to extend the moment, pushing the wheelchair slowly, step by step, basking in the happiness as it unfolded. I felt ecstatic, not only because I'd brought a meaningful gift but also because I was reunited with someone I've admired all my life.

When my grandfather died years ago at an early age, my grandmother was forced to raise seven kids by herself while running the family plantation. That twist of fate turned her into a vegetarian, in part because vegetarianism is a form of merit-making. In Asian culture, it's not uncommon for one to abstain from eating meat as a way to *duoc phuoc* (gain merit). In doing so, one's wishes would be granted. In my grandmother's case, she prayed for the well-being of her children, now made more challenging with the passing of her husband. To support all the kids, she had to work very hard. Even in her sixties she still went to the fields every day to harvest coconuts and other fruits. Despite her hard life and difficult circumstances, she remained compassionate, caring and generous.

Every time she visited our family in Saigon, she brought baskets of live chickens and ducks, fresh bamboo shoots, wild mushrooms and other vegetables from her garden. They were her gifts of love. Although she didn't eat meat, she spent endless hours in the kitchen, cooking up sumptuous meals. Then at night, she spoiled us even more, sharing fascinating and endearing stories about life on the coconut plantation.

She taught me that family is sacred, that food is love and love is food. Though I had a lot to say and thank her for, I felt awkward. I just kept my eyes on the wheelchair. My grandmother, too, didn't say much after that.

By the time I wheeled her back to the house, my aunts had finished cooking all my grandmother's favorites—salad rolls with *jícama* and peanuts and basil, spicy lemongrass tofu, and black mushrooms and bean threads in a claypot. While savoring the food, we chatted, joked and laughed with one another. But when my grandmother started to talk, the noise quickly subsided.

"That's a great wheelchair," she said, almost whispering, as she pointed to the prized gift parked beneath the side porch. "When I go, you all can take turns using it. It stays in the family." Since that reunion, I've been back to Quoi Son several times, but I still yearn to share many more meals with my grandmother. I want to go for that walk again, she in that wheelchair and me by her side, strolling up and down on her favorite road.

The Vietnamese have a high regard for vegetables, in large part because meat is too expensive to be consumed on a regular basis. But beyond that, we were raised with the notion that vegetables are just as important as meat proteins and starches. As kids we often heard our

Delta schoolgirls.

mother say, "*An rau cho mat va bo*" or "Eat vegetables so you will be strong." We learned to appreciate vegetables in every form imaginable—raw, cooked, pickled, salted and dried—and even as kids we were able to distinguish the different ways a vegetable could taste depending on how it was cut or prepared. For example, if the cucumbers were served with tender meat, they'd be cut thick for contrast. If they were used as a garnish with fried fish, they'd be cut into long thin strands so they could easily soak up the sauce and flavor the fish. In other words, we learned to treat and prepare vegetables with the same level of attention and care as one would treat meat.

This attitude also stems from the fact that many Vietnamese are Buddhists who practice vegetarianism on one level or another. At many temples and restaurants, cooks go to great lengths to make vegetarian meals look and taste as if they had meat. Tofu is pressed, molded and flavored to resemble a whole fish or pork chops. Spring rolls are stuffed with shredded coconut, taro root, and tofu instead of the usual crabmeat and pork. One time, just when I thought I was digging into catfish in a claypot, it turned out to be pressed tofu that had been simmered in soy sauce! With the shortage of animal protein and the pervasiveness of the Buddhist influence in the culture, it is not uncommon to find many Vietnamese dishes eaten in two ways—*man* (with meat) and *lat* (without meat). Indeed, almost every meat dish in this book can be made vegetarian.

This chapter includes many of my favorite meatless recipes. Some are hearty noodle soups and noodle main courses that can be served by themselves; others are smaller side dishes that are meant to accompany other foods. When making vegetable dishes, try the many varieties of vegetables that are becoming increasingly available at Asian markets, farmer's markets and even supermarkets around the country. For example, the recipes for luffa squash and long beans are delicious but they also can be made with just about any vegetables you like.

As you're cooking from the recipes, notice how the concepts of building flavors that I talked about in the first chapter—the layering techniques, the contrasting of textures and temperatures, and the use of dipping sauces and garnishes—still all apply to vegetable cooking. In fact, when you don't have that savory meat to work with, these techniques become even more important.

SALAD ROLLS WITH JÍCAMA, PEANUTS AND BASIL

bo bia chay

MAKES ABOUT 24 ROLLS

One of the biggest attractions in Saigon at night is the area around the main post office where the *bo bia* (salad roll) carts assemble. When the weather is warm, nothing is better than to sit on a low stool and watch the world go by while snacking on these delicious rolls. Unlike the more common *goi cuon,* which are stuffed with room-temperature shrimp and pork, these rolls are typically made to order, so that the filling is slightly warm.

The original recipe calls for Chinese sausage, which I've replaced here with tofu and eggs. If you want to make the dish vegan, omit the eggs. This is a great do-it-yourself finger food and is wonderful for outdoor events. Simply place the ingredients on a table and invite guests to make their own rolls. Note that this dish is not served with any sauce because the hoisin sauce is added to the rolls during assembly. Serve this as a snack or appetizer.

1. Heat 1 tablespoon of the oil in a large nonstick pan over moderate heat. In a bowl, combine the eggs and a pinch of salt and beat well. When the pan is hot, pour in half the beaten eggs and quickly swirl to cover the bottom of the pan. Cook until firm, about 1 minute. Flip the egg crepe and cook another minute. Transfer the crepe to a plate. Repeat with the remaining egg batter. When the crepes are cool enough to handle, cut into thin strips and set aside.

2. Heat the remaining 3 tablespoons oil in a large pan over high heat. Add the shallot and stir until fragrant, about 1 minute. Add the soy sauce, *jícama,* carrot, water and the remaining salt. Cook, uncovered, until the vegetables are

4 tablespoons vegetable oil

2 eggs

1 teaspoons sea salt

2 tablespoons chopped shallot

1 tablespoon soy sauce

1 *jícama,* peeled and cut into matchstick strips (about 2 cups)

1 carrot, peeled and cut into matchstick strips (about 1 cup)

½ cup water

¼ cup hoisin sauce

1 tablespoon ground chili paste (page 225), or to taste

1 head green-leaf lettuce, washed, drained and cut into 1-inch-by-3-inch pieces

1 (6-ounce) piece tofu, pan seared and cut into thin strips (page 188)

⅔ cup Asian basil leaves

⅓ cup chopped Roasted Peanuts (page 35)

24 (6- or 8-inch) dried rice paper rounds plus extras, page 97

soft, about 15 to 20 minutes. Transfer the vegetables to a dish.

3. Combine the hoisin sauce and chili paste in a small bowl and set aside. Set up a work station by placing the ingredients in the order in which they will be needed: rice papers, egg strips, lettuce, *jícama* mixture, tofu, hoisin mixture, basil, peanuts.

4. Fill a large bowl with hot water. Cover a cutting board with a damp towel and place it next to the bowl. Working with 2 rice paper rounds at a time, dip one, edge first, into the hot water and turn to wet it completely, about 10 seconds. Lay the round down on the towel. Repeat with the other round and place it next to the first. (This allows you to work with one while the second sets.)

5. Neatly place on the bottom third of the first round a few strips of egg crepe, 1 piece of lettuce, 2 tablespoons *jícama* mixture (no juice), 2 pieces of tofu, ½ teaspoon hoisin sauce mix, 2 or 3 basil leaves and a sprinkling of peanuts. Make sure the filling is neatly stacked. Fold the bottom edge over the filling, tuck in the sides and roll into a cylinder. A perfect *bo bia* is about 1 inch wide and 4 inches long. Repeat with the remaining ingredients. Serve the rolls whole or cut in half.

SALAD ROLLS WITH TOFU AND MUSHROOMS

 goi cuon chay

SERVES 6 TO 8 AS AN APPETIZER

2 tablespoons vegetable oil
2 shallots, sliced
¼ yellow onion, thinly sliced
    lengthwise

Goi cuon chay relies a great deal on how the mushrooms are prepared. To make this a standout dish, be sure the pan is extremely hot before adding the onions and mushrooms. If the soy sauce sizzles and caramelizes upon contact, you did it right.

You can prepare these rolls a couple of hours in advance and cover them with a damp towel or wrap them in plastic wrap until ready to serve. Do not refrigerate them, as the wrappers will get dry and hard.

1. Heat the oil in a pan over high heat. When the pan is very hot, add the shallots and onion and stir until fragrant, about 20 seconds. Add the mushrooms and stir vigorously. Create a well in the center of the mixture. Add the soy sauce and sugar, and stir until fragrant, about 30 seconds. Transfer to a bowl and set aside.

2. Set up a work station by placing all the ingredients in the order in which they will be needed: rice papers, lettuce, rice vermicelli, carrots, mushroom mixture, tofu, bean sprouts, and basil leaves.

3. Fill a large bowl with hot water. (Also keep some nearby to add to the bowl when the water cools.) Cover a cutting board with a damp towel.

3. Working with 2 rice paper rounds at a time, dip one, edge first, into the hot water and turn to wet it completely, about 10 seconds, taking care not to burn yourself. Lay the round down on the towel and pull to remove any wrinkles. Repeat with the other round and place it next to the first. (This allows you to work with one while the second round sets.)

4. Tear a lettuce leaf in half lengthwise and place it on the bottom third of the rice round. Place 2 tablespoons rice vermicelli, 4 carrot strips, 1 tablespoon mushroom mixture, 2 tofu strips, 2 tablespoons bean sprouts and 4 or 5 basil leaves on the lettuce. Make sure the ingredients are evenly spread out.

5. Fold the bottom edge over the filling, fold in the sides and roll into a tight cylinder. The rolls should be about 1 inch wide and 4 to 5 inches long. Repeat with the remaining rice paper and filling ingredients. To serve, cut the rolls into 2 or 4 equal pieces and place them cut side up on a plate. Serve with the dipping sauce of choice on the side. If you like, garnish with the basil or mint sprig tops.

6 dried Chinese black
   mushrooms, soaked in warm
   water for 30 minutes, drained
   and thinly sliced
1 tablespoon soy sauce,
   or to taste
1 teaspoon sugar
8 (12-inch) dried rice paper
   rounds plus some extra
1 small head red-leaf lettuce,
   leaves separated and washed
¼ pound *bun* (rice vermicelli)
   boiled 4 to 5 minutes, rinsed
   and drained (page 112)
1 carrot, peeled, cut into
   matchstick strips and
   blanched
4 ounces tofu, pan-seared
   (page 188) and cut into strips
   about ¼ inch thick
1 cup bean sprouts
1 cup Asian basil or mint leaves
   (tops reserved for garnish,
   optional)
1 cup Vietnamese Bean Dipping
   Sauce (page 28) or Soy-Lime
   Dipping Sauce (page 29)

Tofu

Since ancient times, tofu and other forms of soy foods have been regarded as essential foods. They provide not only the necessary amino acids, vitamins and minerals, but also other hormone-like chemicals that researchers now say can help combat cancer and illnesses related to high cholesterol and menopause.

Although tofu by itself is neutral tasting, it is highly versatile and easily adaptable to sautéing, stir-frying, steaming, simmering or grilling. It can also be puréed for use in sauces and dips. The most common form is fresh tofu that is sold packed in water. Pressed tofu, fermented tofu and tofu skins are other forms of this soy product.

In the United States, fresh tofu is available in three textures—soft, medium and firm. Soft tofu is used in soups and steamed dishes, while medium and firm tofu are best in stir-fries and braised dishes and for stuffing. A fourth but not as popular kind is silken tofu, which is served as a dessert, often with a light ginger-flavored syrup. Unless otherwise specified, use medium-texture tofu for the recipes in this book.

At Asian markets, you can often find deep-fried tofu, which is how a lot of tofu is typically sold and eaten. Many stir-fry and simmering recipes call for precooked tofu because it holds up better and adds flavor to the dish. One way to precook tofu at home is to pan-sear it, which I actually prefer because it's less oily. *To pan-sear tofu:* Cut the tofu slab into 2 or 3 manageable pieces and pat dry. Heat about 2 to 3 tablespoons vegetable oil in a nonstick pan over moderate heat. Add the tofu in one layer and cook, turning once, until golden, about 5 min-

Cutting fresh tofu, the main source of protein in a vegetarian diet.

utes. Drain on paper towels, then cut into the desired size and shape as directed in the recipe.

Another delicious product made from soybeans is *tau hu ky,* or dried bean curd (also called dried bean curd sticks). It's made by simmering soy milk until a very thin film forms on top. At one tofu factory in Vinh Long that I visited, the tofu maker used a long, thin bamboo stick to lift the skins to a clothesline. After several hours, the skins became dried and stiff, taking on the shape of a pair of tongs (hence the name "sticks").

Available at Asian markets in the dried food section, *tau hu ky* is cream colored, about 12 inches long and sold in plastic packages. To use, first soak them in warm water for about 30 minutes, depending on the brand and thickness, and then cut into smaller pieces and add to stews or soups. Like tofu, dried bean curd is delicate tasting but has a remarkable ability to soak up flavor and impart a unique savoriness to food. It's also available as sheets, which make wonderful wrappers and fillings for dishes such as vegetarian sausages.

CUCUMBER AND TOFU SALAD

goi chay

SERVES 4

This is the vegetarian version of a popular salad made with dried jellyfish. While it may sound unusual, it's really a very delicious salad, with the jellyfish adding a subtly flavored crunch. This recipe calls for *tau hu ky* (dried bean curd skin) and pan-seared tofu instead. Use small pickling cucumbers, as they're very crisp and take well to blanching.

1. Bring a pot of water to a rolling boil. Cut the carrot into bean sprout–sized strips. Cut the cucumbers into slightly

1 medium carrot, peeled

1 pound pickling cucumbers, unpeeled

4 tablespoons rice vinegar

3 tablespoons sugar

2 Thai bird chilies, cut into thin rings

½ teaspoon sea salt

2 tablespoons vegetable oil

¼ yellow onion, thinly sliced

2 pieces dried bean curd skin,
soaked in cold water for
15 minutes, drained and
cut into ½-inch pieces

2 teaspoons soy sauce

1 (6-ounce) piece tofu,
pan-seared (page 188)
and sliced

1 cup loosely packed Asian basil
leaves plus a few sprigs

3 tablespoons white sesame
seeds, lightly toasted

3 tablespoons whole Roasted
Peanuts (page 35)

2 tablespoons Fried Shallots
(page 33)

thicker strips. Place the vegetable strips in a sieve with a handle and lower them into the boiling water. Blanch for just 5 seconds, remove, rinse under cold water, and squeeze gently to remove the excess water.

2. Combine the vinegar, sugar, chilies and salt in a large bowl and mix well. Add the carrot and cucumber strips to the bowl and marinate for 10 minutes.

3. Heat the oil in a skillet over moderate heat. Add the onion and stir until fragrant, about 20 seconds. Add the dried bean curd skin and soy sauce and stir for 30 seconds. Remove from the heat and set aside to cool.

4. Add the bean curd skin, tofu, basil leaves, sesame seeds, peanuts and shallots to the bowl and toss well. Transfer to a serving dish and garnish with the basil sprigs.

VEGETARIAN PHO NOODLE SOUP

 pho chay

SERVES 4 AS A MAIN DISH

BROTH

3 celery stalks, cleaned and cut
into 4-inch pieces

4 carrots, peeled and cut in half

6 medium dried Chinese black
mushrooms, soaked in warm
water for 30 minutes and
drained

1 (2-inch) piece ginger, cut in
half lengthwise, lightly
bruised with the flat side of a
knife and charred (page 56)

When I first started writing about *pho,* I received a lot of mail and calls from readers asking about a vegetarian version. At first I was quite apprehensive, wondering how I could come up with such a recipe when the dish is so quintessentially beef oriented. But after much thought, I decided to use the approach that the nuns in Vietnam often resort to—when in doubt, use black mushrooms and tofu as meat substitutes. As with beef *pho,* the success of this soup depends on the garnishings: the paper-thin onions, the scallions, the cilantro, the Asian basil and the chilies.

1. Make the broth: Bring 4 quarts of water to a boil in a stockpot. Add the celery, carrots, mushrooms, and charred ginger and onions and simmer for 2 hours.

2. Thirty minutes before the broth is done, add the soy sauce and salt. Place the star anise and cloves in a spice bag and add to the broth. Simmer for 30 minutes, then remove and discard. (Simmering the spices any longer will make the broth too pungent.) Using a slotted spoon, remove the black mushrooms. Remove the chewy stems and slice the caps into strips.

3. To serve, place the cooked noodles in 4 preheated bowls. (If the noodles are not hot, reheat in a microwave or dip briefly in boiling water.) Divide the tofu and mushrooms evenly among the bowls. Pour a generous amount of hot broth over the noodles and garnish with scallions and cilantro. Invite guests to garnish their bowls with bean sprouts, basil, chilies and squeezes of lime before eating.

2 yellow onions, charred (page 55)

¼ cup light soy sauce (page 30)

½ tablespoon salt, or to taste

4 whole star anise, lightly toasted in a dry skillet

4 whole cloves, lightly toasted in a dry skillet

NOODLE ASSEMBLY

1 pound dried $1/16$-inch-wide rice sticks, cooked, drained and rinsed (page 113)

8 ounces tofu, pan-seared (page 188) and cut into ¼-inch-thick slices

3 scallions, cut into thin rings

½ bunch cilantro, chopped

1 pound bean sprouts

12 sprigs Asian basil

3 Thai bird chilies or 2 serrano chilies, cut into thin rings

6 lime wedges

SERVES 4

Some of the best vegetarian curries in Vietnam are those made at the temples. I think this has to do with two factors—the ingredients are often grown right on the temple grounds, and the nuns who prepare the curries are very serious cooks. Just imagine how a curry would taste if you could grate a freshly

VEGETABLE CURRY

ca ri chay

2 tablespoons vegetable oil

2 shallots, chopped

2 cloves garlic, chopped

2 to 3 tablespoons Vietnamese curry powder

2 teaspoons ground chili paste
or to taste (page 225)

2 tablespoons soy sauce

½ teaspoon sea salt

2 teaspoons sugar

2 cups unsweetened coconut
milk

½ teaspoon ground turmeric

1 cup water

2 pieces dried bean curd skin,
soaked in cold water for
30 minutes, drained and cut
into 1-inch pieces
(about 1 cup)

1 lemongrass stalk, cut into
3-inch lengths and lightly
bruised with the flat side of
a knife

1 (1-inch) piece ginger, peeled
and cut into 3 slices

1 carrot, peeled and cut into
½-inch rounds

½ yellow onion, cut into
wedges

1 sweet potato, cut into 1-inch
cubes (about 1½ cups)

½ head cauliflower, cut into
bite-sized florets

1 tomato, cut into thin wedges

5 sprigs cilantro, cut into
2-inch lengths

picked coconut to make coconut milk, grow your own sweet potatoes, and toast your own curry spices!

For this recipe, use the Vietnamese curry powder called Golden Bells, which is sold in plastic bags or small jars. It's milder (having less cumin and fewer fennel seeds) and won't overwhelm the lemongrass and ginger. The bean curd skin enhances the savoriness of the dish and is a real find for vegetarian cooks. For interesting variations, try different vegetable combinations here, such as yucca, taro, cauliflower, long beans and chayote.

1. Heat the oil in a large pot over moderate heat. Add the shallots, garlic and curry powder and stir until fragrant, about 20 seconds. Add the chili paste, soy sauce, salt, sugar, coconut milk, turmeric, water, bean curd skins, lemongrass and ginger. Let the mixture come to a boil, then reduce the heat to low. Add the carrot and onion, then cover and simmer for 5 minutes.

2. Add the sweet potato, cauliflower and tomato and cook until the vegetables are tender, another 15 minutes. Transfer to a serving bowl and garnish with the cilantro. Serve immediately with steamed rice.

SPICY LEMONGRASS TOFU

dau hu xa ot

SERVES 4

While traveling on a train one time to the coastal town of Nha Trang, I sat next to an elderly nun. Over the course of our bumpy eight-hour ride, she shared stories of life at the temple and the difficult years after the end of the war when the Communist government cracked down on religious factions. Toward the end of our chat, she pulled out a bag of food she'd prepared for the trip. It was tofu that had been cooked in chilies, lemongrass and *la lot,* an aromatic leaf also known as pepper leaf. When she gave me a taste, I knew immediately that I had to learn how to make it. This is my rendition of that fabulous dish. Make sure to pat the tofu dry before marinating it and use very fresh lemongrass. I always love serving this to friends who think tofu dishes are bland.

1. Combine the lemongrass, soy sauce, chilies, chili flakes, turmeric, sugar and salt in a bowl. Add the tofu cubes and turn to coat them evenly. Marinate for 30 minutes.
2. Heat half of the oil in a 12-inch nonstick skillet over moderately high heat. Add the onion, shallot and garlic and stir until fragrant, about 1 minute. Reduce the heat to low and cook until

2 lemongrass stalks, outer layers peeled, bottom white part thinly sliced and finely chopped (about ¼ cup)

1½ tablespoons soy sauce

2 teaspoons chopped Thai bird chilies or another fresh chili

½ teaspoon dried chili flakes

1 teaspoon ground turmeric

2 teaspoons sugar

½ teaspoon salt

12 ounces tofu, drained, patted dry and cut into ¾-inch cubes

4 tablespoons vegetable oil

½ yellow onion, cut into ⅛-inch slices

2 shallots, thinly sliced

1 teaspoon minced garlic

4 tablespoons chopped Roasted Peanuts (page 36)

10 *la lot,* or pepper leaves (page 44), shredded, or ⅔ cup loosely packed Asian basil leaves

the onions are soft, about 3 minutes. Transfer to a plate and keep warm.

3. Wipe the pan clean and heat the remaining oil over moderate heat. Add the tofu mixture and, using chopsticks or wooden spoons, turn so it cooks evenly, about 4 to 5 minutes. Add the onion mixture and cook, uncovered, for another 2 to 3 minutes. Add half the peanuts and all the pepper leaves.

4. Remove from the heat and transfer to a serving plate. Garnish with the remaining peanuts and serve immediately with steamed rice.

RICE NOODLES WITH STIR-FRIED VEGETABLES

 bun chay

SERVES 4 AS A MAIN DISH

1 recipe Rice Noodles with
   Fresh Herbs (page 119)
2 tablespoons vegetable oil
½ yellow onion, thinly sliced
   lengthwise
½ teaspoon minced garlic
8 dried Chinese black
   mushrooms, soaked in
   warm water for 30 minutes,
   drained, stemmed and sliced
2 tablespoons soy sauce
2 teaspoons sugar
3 tablespoons unsweetened
   coconut milk
1 small *jícama,* peeled and cut
   into matchstick strips
   (about 1½ cups)

It was our grandmother who first got our family interested in vegetarian food. Since she is a strict vegetarian, my mother would cook a special meal for her every time she came to stay with us in Saigon. After years of sharing many meals with her, my siblings and I grew fond of her vegetarian meals.

This popular dish is often served at my grandfather's death anniversaries and on other special occasions. *Bun chay* is great for entertaining because you can make the Rice Noodles with Fresh Herbs ahead of time, then stir-fry the topping just before serving.

1. Prepare the rice noodles according to the recipe on page 119. Divide them among 4 bowls for serving.

2. Heat the oil in a large pan over high heat. Add the onion and garlic and stir for 30 seconds. Add the mushrooms, soy sauce, sugar, coconut milk and *jícama.* Stir, then reduce

the heat slightly and cook until the *jicama* softens, 3 to 4 minutes. Add the tofu and carrot and cook until all the ingredients are hot, 2 to 3 minutes. Add a little water if the pan gets too dry.

3. Divide the vegetable topping among the 4 bowls of noodles. Garnish each with 2 tablespoons peanuts. Invite each guest to drizzle 3 to 4 tablespoons sauce over the noodles, and gently toss a few times before eating.

6 ounces tofu, pan-seared (page 188) and cut into ¼-inch strips

1 carrot, peeled, cut into matchstick strips (about 1½ cups), blanched for 1 minute and rinsed

½ cup chopped Roasted Peanuts (page 35)

1 cup Soy-Lime Dipping Sauce (page 29)

VEGETARIAN CLAYPOT RICE WITH GINGER

com tay cam chay

SERVES 4 WITH OTHER DISHES

In the cooler months, one of my favorite things to eat is *com tay cam chay*, which translates as "vegetarian handheld rice." It's sort of a Vietnamese rice pilaf, only cooked in a claypot. For this you can use any mushrooms available. To keep the rice moist, use fleshy vegetables like chayote or another squash. It's best to cook this in a large 3-quart claypot (the rice steams better in a larger pot), but if you don't have one, a regular pot will do. For a complete meal, serve with another vegetable side dish and a simple soup.

1. Place the rice in a medium skillet over low heat. Gently stir until it turns opaque, about 4 to 5 minutes. Set aside.
2. Heat the oil in a 3-quart claypot over moderate heat. Add the onion, ginger, five-spice powder, garlic and chili flakes and stir until fragrant, about 10 seconds. Add the soy sauce, salt, sugar, black mushrooms and bamboo shoots.

1¼ cups Thai jasmine or any long-grain rice, washed

3 tablespoons vegetable oil

½ small yellow onion, thinly sliced

2 tablespoons minced ginger

1½ teaspoons Chinese five-spice powder, lightly toasted in a dry pan

1 teaspoon minced garlic

½ teaspoon dried chili flakes, or to taste

2 tablespoons soy sauce

¼ teaspoon salt or to taste

2 teaspoons sugar

6 small dried Chinese black
mushrooms, soaked in hot
water for 30 minutes, drained,
stemmed and halved

½ cup canned bamboo shoot
slices, rinsed and drained

2 cups boiling water

1 chayote or 1 zucchini, cut into
¼-inch bite-sized slices,
blanched for 2 minutes
and drained

6 ounces tofu, pan-seared
(page 188) and cut into
⅔-inch cubes

6 sprigs cilantro, cut into
1-inch pieces

½ cup Soy-Lime Dipping Sauce
(page 29)

Add the boiling water and the rice and stir a few times. Let the mixture come back to a boil, then reduce the heat to a low simmer. Cover and cook until the rice is done, about 20 minutes.

3. Ten minutes before the rice is done, stir in the chayote and tofu and simmer until all the ingredients are cooked and thoroughly hot. Remove from the heat and garnish with the cilantro. Serve right from the claypot with the sauce on the side.

DRIED LILY BUDS

Known as *kim cham* in Vietnamese, the unopened buds of the lily are a favorite ingredient in vegetarian cooking and are prized for their earthy mushroom-like flavor. Considered both a food and an herb, *kim cham* are light yellow, 2 inches long and about ⅛ inch thick. They're used mainly in braised dishes and soups. Before using, Vietnamese cooks like to tie each bud into a knot in the center, then soak in water for about 30 minutes. This traditional technique keeps the lilies intact during cooking and makes them chewy.

BLACK MUSHROOMS WITH BEAN THREADS IN CLAYPOT

nam kho

If there's a noodle that loves sauce, it's bean threads, also called cellophane noodles. I suggest presoaking these dried, clear strands so they don't absorb all of the cooking liquid. For an interesting twist, add ginger and other vegetables like lotus root, bamboo shoots or long beans.

This dish is best when prepared in a 2-quart or larger clay pot but it's also delicious in a regular pot. For a complete meal, serve this dish with a salad or appetizer and a soup.

1. Heat the oil in a 2-quart claypot over moderate heat. Add the fermented soybeans and shallot and stir until fragrant, about 2 minutes. Add the onion, lily buds, black mushrooms, wood-ear mushrooms, chili flakes, soy sauce and sugar. Stir for 2 minutes. Add the bean threads, water, tofu and bamboo shoots. Stir gently, taking care not to break up the tofu or noodles. Reduce the heat to low, cover and cook until the vegetables are soft, about 15 minutes. Garnish with the cilantro and serve directly in the claypot.

3 tablespoons vegetable oil

2½ tablespoons fermented soybeans, page 225

1 shallot, minced

½ small yellow onion, cut into thin wedges

30 dried lily buds (page 196), each tied into a knot, soaked for 10 minutes, drained

4 dried black mushrooms, soaked in hot water for 30 minutes, stemmed and halved

3–4 wood-ear mushrooms, soaked in hot water for 30 minutes, chewy centers removed, cut into pieces

½ teaspoon dried chili flakes

2 teaspoons soy sauce, or to taste

2 teaspoons sugar

2 ounces bean threads, soaked in water for 30 minutes, drained and cut into 10-inch lengths

2½ cups water

6 ounces tofu, cut into 1-inch cubes

½ cup bamboo shoot strips, blanched in hot water, drained

2 tablespoons chopped cilantro

MUSTARD GREENS WITH GARLIC

 cai xao toi

SERVES 4 AS A SIDE DISH

⅔ pound Chinese mustard
    greens or another
    Asian green
2 tablespoons vegetable oil
5 cloves garlic, minced
2 tablespoons oyster sauce
    or mushroom sauce

Sometimes the best way to cook is the simplest way. In this recipe, you can use any Asian greens, such as Chinese mustard, Chinese broccoli, bok choy or water spinach. Serve this with roast chicken, steamed fish or claypot rice dishes.

1. Cut off the stems of the mustard greens and cut them on the diagonal into 1-inch-thick slices. Cut the leafy parts into 3-inch pieces.
2. Heat the oil in a large skillet or wok over high heat. Working quickly, add the garlic and stir until fragrant. Add the oyster sauce and mustard greens. Toss several times to coat the greens evenly in the sauce. Cook until the greens are done but still green and crunchy, 2 to 3 minutes. Remove from the heat and transfer to a serving plate.

WATER SPINACH WITH TOFU

rau muong xao

SERVES 4 AS A SIDE DISH

Rau muong, or water spinach (also known as morning glory or swamp cabbage), is a common vegetable in Vietnam. There it's harvested when the stems are still very young and tender and is stir-fried as in this recipe, or simply steamed and served with a dipping sauce. During my visits to Vietnam, I often ate this vegetable for days in a row because it was such a great side dish to every meal.

Another popular way of preparing water spinach is to make "curls" out of it. The hollow stems are split into long thin shreds. When soaked in cold water, they become crisp and crunchy and are used in salads or as garnishes for noodle soups. If you can't find water spinach, use regular spinach or substitute another leafy green. I think the flavor of this dish is even more intense when it's served cold.

1 pound water spinach

2 tablespoons vegetable oil

1 tablespoon chopped garlic

1 teaspoon chopped fresh
   Thai bird chilies (optional)

2 teaspoons fermented whole
   soybeans (page 225)
   or soy sauce

Salt to taste

6 ounces tofu, pan-seared
   (page 188) and cut into
   ½-inch cubes

1. Trim and discard the chewy parts of the water spinach stems, 1 to 3 inches from the bottom. Cut the stems and leaves into 3-inch pieces.
2. Heat the oil in a large skillet over high heat. Add the garlic, chilies, if using, and fermented soybeans and stir until very fragrant, about 30 seconds. Add the water spinach and salt and cook until tender, 2 to 3 minutes. If the pan gets too dry, add 2 to 4 tablespoons water. Add the tofu, toss and transfer to a serving dish.

TWICE-COOKED EGGPLANT WITH GARLIC AND BASIL

 ca tim xao rau que

SERVES 4 AS A SIDE DISH

Vegetable oil

⅔ pound Asian eggplant,
  preferably the small
  dark-purple variety,
  cut on the diagonal into
  ⅔-inch-thick slices

2 cloves garlic, chopped

1 shallot, thinly sliced

3 Thai bird chilies or
  1 serrano chili, chopped,
  or to taste

⅔ cup Asian basil leaves,
  roughly torn

6 ounces tofu, drained and cut
  into ⅔-inch cubes

1½ tablespoons mushroom
  sauce

1 tablespoon soy sauce

⅓ cup water

To me, there's something particularly enticing about the smokiness of eggplants cooked over a very hot fire. When I first had this dish in Hanoi, I was very impressed. Unlike many mushy eggplant dishes, this one stays firm and delicious, even after the eggplant has been stir-fried over high heat. I make this several ways, sometimes just with eggplant and at other times embellished with shrimp and pork. Either way, it is satisfying, especially if you are able to find sweet, firm eggplants.

1. Heat 2 tablespoons oil in a skillet over high heat and swirl to coat the entire surface. Add the eggplant slices in one layer (work in batches if necessary) and scar briefly on both sides, about 1 to 2 minutes total. Do not cook completely. Drain on paper towels and keep warm. Repeat with the remaining eggplant, adding more oil as necessary.

2. Heat 2 tablespoons oil in a pan over high heat. Add the garlic, shallot, chilies, one third of the basil, tofu, mushroom sauce and soy sauce and stir gently until fragrant, about 2 minutes. Add the water and continue to cook until the sauce is slightly reduced, another 3 to 4 minutes.

3. Add the eggplant slices and the remaining basil leaves and stir until the vegetables are thoroughly hot. Quickly transfer to a platter and serve immediately.

LUFFA SQUASH WITH MUSHROOMS

muop xao

SERVES 4 AS A SIDE DISH

Luffa squash (also known as silk squash or Chinese okra) is similar to zucchini but has a slightly sweeter, earthy flavor. It resembles a long cucumber covered with ridges from one end to another. Belonging to the same family as the vegetable used to make bath sponges, the edible luffa is harvested very young, long before those tough fibers develop.

In Vietnam, luffa squash, winter melon, fuzzy melon and kabocha squash are among the many vegetables used in stir-fries and soups. You can any one of them in this recipe.

1½ pounds luffa squash
2 tablespoons vegetable oil
1 shallot, sliced
2 cloves garlic, minced
1 cup white mushrooms, cleaned and halved or quartered
1 teaspoon soy sauce
1 tablespoon vegetarian mushroom oyster sauce
2 scallions, cut into thin rings
5 sprigs cilantro, cut into 2-inch lengths

1. Cut each luffa squash crosswise into 2 pieces for easier handling. Cut off the ridges and peel, taking care not to cut too deeply because most of the flavor is just under the skin. Cut on the diagonal into ¾-inch-thick pieces.

2. Heat the oil in a large skillet over high heat. Add the shallot and garlic and stir until fragrant, about 20 seconds. Add the mushrooms, soy sauce and mushroom sauce and stir for 30 seconds. Add the squash and reduce the heat slightly. Cover and cook until the squash is just softened, 3 to 4 minutes. Stir in the scallions and transfer to a serving dish. Garnish with the cilantro sprigs and serve.

CHOPSTICK BEANS IN GARLIC

 dau dua xao

SERVES 4 AS A SIDE DISH

2 tablespoons vegetable oil

1 clove garlic, chopped

1 egg, beaten

2 teaspoons fish sauce

1 teaspoon sugar

1 pound long beans, ends
trimmed, cut into 3- to 4-inch
pieces, blanched in boiling
water for 4 minutes, rinsed
in cold water and drained

¼ cup water

Pinch salt

5 sprigs cilantro, cut into
2-inch lengths

The Vietnamese call long beans *dau dua* (chopstick beans) for good reason. They're best when they're skinny (the width of a chopstick) and tender. In recent years I've seen other varieties in American markets, such as purple and black, but the green ones are still the best. Use long beans as you would regular green beans. They're great in curries and stir-fries, or blanched and added to salads.

The traditional recipe calls for eggs and fish sauce, but if you want to make it vegan omit them both and add 2 teaspoons soy sauce.

1. Heat the oil in a large pan over moderate heat. Add the garlic and stir until fragrant, about 20 seconds. Add the egg, fish sauce and sugar and stir a few times. Add the long beans, water and salt. Reduce the heat slightly, then cover and cook until done, about 4–5 minutes. Transfer to a serving plate, garnish with the cilantro and serve.

chapter eight

Sweet Things

Desserts and Sweet Drinks

Sweet Dumplings in Ginger Broth

Vietnamese Fried Bananas with Ice Cream

Sticky Rice with Mung Beans and Fresh Coconut

Iced Red Bean Pudding with Coconut Milk

Crème Caramel

Coconut Sticky Rice Pudding with Taro

Grandmother's Banana Stew with Tapioca Pearls

Fresh Coconut Ice Cream

Lychee Sorbet

Warm Soy Milk with Pandanus Leaf

Iced Pandanus Tea

Vietnamese Coffee

*C*hi Tu (Fourth Sister) is moving as fast as she can, filling up one bowl after another while her customers eagerly wait. It's hard to tell she's selling desserts because her stand looks no different from the savory food stalls here at the Ben Thanh Market in Saigon. There are no signs of cakes, candies or sweets, just big metal pots. Instead of holding soup or savory dishes, they're filled to the rim with warm *che* (sweet puddings). "*Ngon lam em*," she yells, telling me how delicious her pudding with fresh corn is. In fact, everything looks enticing—the young, green sticky rice pudding with taro root and coconut milk, the banana and tapioca stew and the mung bean pudding.

Chi Tu even has *che troi nuoc* (sweet dumplings in ginger broth), a dessert that my sister Denise and I used to love to eat as kids. Late at night, we would wait outside our front door for our favorite dessert vendor to come and serve us little bowls of this dessert. The dumplings were soft and warm and the mung bean filling inside was rich and creamy. Nothing could have prepared us better for a good night's sleep.

Like that vendor, Chi Tu serves most of her puddings at room temperature, although some can also be served hot or with ice. When served cold, they're mixed with coconut milk and ice and sometimes with tapioca strands. If you visit a *pho* shop, for example, you'll probably see diners finishing their noodle soups with tall glasses of red beans or white beans in sweetened coconut milk and crushed ice.

Besides puddings, the Vietnamese eat a lot of *banh* (cakes). Unlike the Western-style leavened breads and cakes, they're made with sticky rice or rice flour or tapioca starch and stuffed with ripe bananas, mung bean paste or shredded coconut, then steamed. Wrapped with banana or other leaves, they come in various sizes and shapes. Some are loaves, which can be sliced, and others are individual portion packages and triangles. Tea, the most common beverage, is often served with these *banh*.

Thanks to the French influence, our dessert repertoire also includes European-style cakes, pastries, breads and ice cream, although these items generally are served only on special occasions. Vietnamese coffee, another legacy from the French colonial days, is extremely popular and, because it's so rich and sweet, is certainly a dessert option.

Making Vietnamese coffee.

Despite the variety of desserts available, the Vietnamese do not, except for special occasions, eat sweets right after a meal. Instead, we prefer to snack on them throughout the day and late at night.

You can serve the recipes in this chapter either way. To finish a meal, fresh fruit (such as ripe mangoes) or ice cream or sorbet are always good choices. If you're looking for something more traditional, try a pudding like Grandmother's Banana Stew with Tapioca Pearls (page 217). You can serve a small bowl right after dinner, or do what the Vietnamese would do—serve it a little later, when you have more of an appetite and the energy to truly enjoy it.

SWEET DUMPLINGS IN GINGER BROTH

che troi nuoc

SERVES 6

At our home, my mother always prepared this dessert on Tet (Vietnamese New Year) and placed it on the ancestor worship altar as part of the celebration ritual. The dumplings are made with mung bean paste wrapped in sticky rice flour dough, then simmered in a ginger-infused broth. As a child, I especially loved the little "pearls" made from leftover dough.

This calls for both glutinous, or sticky, rice flour and regular rice flour, which are two distinctly different starches. Some northern cooks prefer to use only the sticky rice flour, although I think it makes the dumplings a bit too chewy. The mung beans called for here are the dried skinless, split variety.

1. Make the dumplings: Place the coconut milk, the ¼ cup water and the salt in a saucepan and bring to a boil. Add the mung beans and reduce the heat to low. While stirring occasionally, simmer until most of the liquid has evaporated and the mung beans are soft, almost 15 minutes. Remove from the heat. Whisk the beans until they're smooth. Set aside to cool.

2. Shape the mung bean paste into 12 little balls about ⅔ inch in diameter. Cover and refrigerate until ready to use. (The balls are easier to handle later, when they're cold.)

3. Place the glutinous rice flour and regular rice flour in a bowl. Stir in the 1 cup of hot water, a little at a time. Mix until the dough is well blended and sticky. Knead the dough for about 2 to 3 minutes. (The dough will be dense and stiff.) Place in a bowl, cover and let it rest while you prepare the broth.

4. Make the broth: Combine the sugar, ginger and the 2½

DUMPLINGS

½ cup unsweetened coconut milk, preferably Mae Ploy brand

¼ cup water

Pinch salt

⅓ cup dried split mung beans, soaked in warm water for 30 minutes and drained

1⅓ cups glutinous rice flour

1 cup rice flour

1 cup hot water

BROTH

8 ounces light brown sugar

1 (2-inch) piece ginger, peeled and bruised with the flat side of a knife

2½ cups hot water

3 tablespoons white sesame seeds, lightly toasted

cups hot water in a large saucepan. Bring to a boil, and reduce the heat to very low.

5. Roll the dough into a log about 2½ inches in diameter. Using a knife, cut it into ¼-inch-thick slices. Flatten each piece so it's thin and wide enough to wrap around one of the balls of the filling. Place a mung bean ball in the center and fold and seal the edges. With wet hands, roll the dumplings until they're smooth and round. Flatten the dumplings very slightly by pressing them between your palms. Make all the dumplings this way and set them aside until ready to cook. Roll leftover dough into pearl-sized balls.

6. Bring a pot of water to a boil and add the dumplings and pearls. Cook until they are translucent and rise to the surface, about 10 to 12 minutes. Raise the heat under the ginger broth to medium. Using a slotted spoon, transfer the cooked dumplings and pearls to the ginger broth. Simmer for 10 minutes. To serve, place 2 dumplings and some pearls in a small bowl and ladle some broth on top. Garnish with the toasted sesame seeds and serve warm.

VIETNAMESE FRIED BANANAS WITH ICE CREAM

 chuoi chien voi kem

SERVES 4

⅔ cup all-purpose flour, sifted

3 tablespoons potato starch
  or cornstarch

½ teaspoon baking powder

3 tablespoons sugar

⅔ cup water

Fried bananas are eaten all over Asia, either as a snack by themselves or a little more embellished as in this recipe. For variations, try using different types of bananas, such as the dwarf or saba variety that's becoming increasingly available at Asian markets. This recipe is best if made just minutes before serving.

1. Combine the all-purpose flour, potato starch, baking powder, sugar and water and stir well. Refrigerate for 30 minutes.
2. Peel the bananas and cut them in half lengthwise. Cut in half crosswise. Set aside until ready to use. If serving ice cream, have the chilled bowls ready.
3. Heat 2 inches of oil in a heavy skillet to about 375 degrees. Dredge the bananas in the flour mixture, then carefully slip them into the hot oil. Using chopsticks or tongs, turn the bananas once and fry until golden, 3 to 4 minutes total. (Do not crowd the pan.) Drain the bananas on paper towels.
4. To serve, place 3 banana pieces on each plate, sprinkle with confectioners' sugar, and serve with a small scoop of ice cream, if desired.

3 ripe-but-firm bananas
Vegetable oil for frying
3 tablespoons confectioners' sugar for garnish
1 pint coconut or vanilla ice cream (optional)

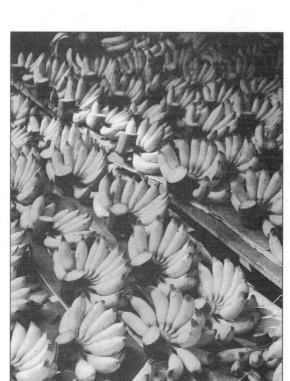

STICKY RICE WITH MUNG BEANS AND FRESH COCONUT

 xoi dau xanh dua

SERVES 4 TO 6

⅓ cup split and shelled mung
　beans, soaked for 2 hours
　and drained
2 fresh or frozen pandanus leaves,
　tied into a small bundle and
　lightly bruised with the flat
　side of a knife (page 213)
1 cup sticky rice or sweet
　(glutinous) rice, soaked
　overnight, drained
⅓ cup unsweetened coconut
　milk, preferably Mae Ploy
　brand
7 tablespoons sugar
2 tablespoons white sesame
　seeds, lightly toasted in a
　dry pan
¼ cup chopped Roasted Peanuts
　(page 35)
½ teaspoon salt
½ cup freshly grated coconut
　(page 140) or store-bought
　coconut flakes

My favorite sticky rice vendor in Saigon is indeed a true master chef. For the past thirty years, she has been coming to the same street corner to sell her fabulous *xoi* (sticky rice) to the many customers who stop by on their way to work each morning. Although a popular breakfast item, it's also eaten as a sweet during other times of the day. Traditionally *xoi* is served on a banana leaf with a variety of toppings, including this one with mung bean paste, shredded coconut and toasted sesame seeds.

For this recipe, you'll need a steamer and the long-grain sticky rice (sold as sweet or glutinous rice) from Thailand, not the short-grain variety that's more common in Japanese and Chinese recipes.

1. Place the mung beans and ½ cup water in a small saucepan over moderate heat. Bring to a boil. Reduce the heat and simmer until the beans are soft, about 20 minutes. Add a little more water if the pan gets dry. Using the back of a spoon, mash the beans until smooth and creamy. Set aside.
2. Fill the bottom of a steamer pan one-third full of water and bring to a boil. Add the pandanus leaves to the water. Line the steamer rack with a damp, double-layered piece of cheesecloth. Place the sticky rice on top, making sure to spread it out so that it cooks evenly. Cover and steam until the rice is cooked but still firm, about 20 minutes.
3. While the rice is steaming, combine the coconut milk and 4 tablespoons of the sugar in a small saucepan and heat just until the sugar is dissolved. Remove from heat and set aside.
4. Transfer the cooked sticky rice to a bowl. Add the coconut milk and stir gently with a fork or chopsticks.

5. Combine the sesame seeds, peanuts, salt and the remaining 3 tablespoons sugar in a small bowl. To serve, transfer about ½ cup sticky rice to each plate. Dab 1 tablespoon mung bean paste on top, then sprinkle with the shredded coconut and sesame seed mixture. Serve warm or at room temperature with the remaining sesame seed mixture on the side.

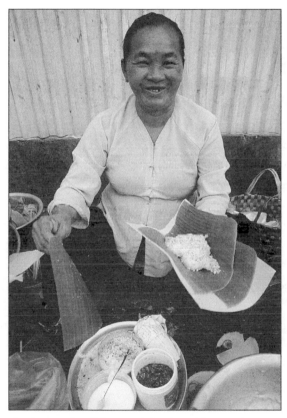

A street vendor dishes up sticky rice with mung bean paste and sesame seed topping.

ICED RED BEAN PUDDING WITH COCONUT MILK

 che dau do lanh

SERVES 6 TO 8

½ cup dried small red beans (adzuki), soaked overnight, drained and rinsed

¼ teaspoon baking soda (optional)

½ cup tapioca strands (page 231), soaked in cold water for 30 minutes and drained

1½ cups unsweetened coconut milk, preferably Mae Ploy brand

2 fresh or frozen pandanus leaves, folded into a short bundle and bruised with the flat side of a knife (facing page) or

½ teaspoon vanilla extract

¼ cup palm sugar or cane sugar

3 tablespoons granulated sugar

Pinch salt

3 cups shaved or crushed ice

My sister Denise and I used to run to our favorite dessert vendor after school and gulp down one of these before going home. Part drink, part dessert, this delightful pudding is particularly satisfying on long hot days and nights—whether in Vietnam or the United States. The soft red beans are bathed in a sweet coconut milk with chewy tapioca strands and shaved ice.

To enjoy this dessert, first stir the ingredients together, then use a long spoon to drink and eat. It can be made with different combinations such as mung beans, shredded seaweed, shredded agar-agar (a natural gelatin made from seaweed) and lotus seeds. If you prefer, you can also serve this hot. For a Vietnamese, a glass of *che dau do* after a bowl of *pho* constitutes a true happy meal.

1. Combine the beans and 4 cups water in a saucepan and bring to a boil. Reduce the heat to low and simmer until the beans are soft, about 1 hour. If they're not soft by then, speed them along by adding the baking soda. Set aside to cool, then refrigerate until cold.

2. While the beans are cooking, combine the tapioca strands and 2 cups water in a small pot. Cover and cook over moderate heat until the strands are soft, about 20 minutes. Drain.

3. Combine the tapioca strands, coconut milk, pandanus leaves, palm sugar, sugar and salt in a medium pot and bring to a boil. Stir to dissolve the sugar. Remove from the heat and set aside to cool. Chill.

4. To serve, place ¼ cup of the beans and some of the cooking liquid in a tall parfait glass. Top with ¼ cup of the coconut milk mixture and a heaping mound of shaved ice. Prepare the remaining glasses in the same way. Serve with long dessert spoons.

Pandanus Leaf

In Vietnam, the desserts are not only sweet but very aromatic, thanks to *la dua* (pandanus leaf), the vanilla of Asia. Also known as screw pine, it's used extensively to flavor puddings, cakes, sticky rice and sweet beverages. At the markets in Vietnam the vendor who sells coconuts also sells pandanus. The two ingredients are made for each other! The long, narrow green leaves, which resemble the leaves of a day lily, are tied together, then bruised with a knife before being added to the cooking liquids.

In the United States pandanus leaves are available frozen and, in some areas, fresh. If you're lucky enough to find them fresh, buy extra and freeze them for later use. Pandanus extract is a poor substitute, so it's best to use banana extract or vanilla extract if you can't find the real thing.

To make pandanus juice, pulverize the leaves (with a mortar and pestle or fruit blender), adding a little water to ease the job. Strain before using. One leaf will make about 1½ tablespoons juice.

CRÈME CARAMEL

1½ cups sugar

½ cup water

3 eggs

3 egg yolks

1½ cups milk

1½ cups half-and-half

¼ teaspoon salt

1 teaspoon vanilla extract

In Saigon, it's rather stylish to go to a French café and enjoy a strong cup of coffee and a *crème caramel,* or flan. The traditional method calls for steaming the custard in a Chinese steamer, but I prefer the flavor of baked custard. This recipe calls for six (6-ounce) ramekins but if you like, you can also make it in a bundt pan and bake it for about 1½ hours.

1. Preheat the oven to 325 degrees.
2. Combine 1 cup of the sugar and the water in a small saucepan and bring it to a boil. Reduce the heat slightly and let the mixture boil until it starts to bubble and turn brown but not black, about 10 to 12 minutes. Stir a few times so the edges don't become scorched. Remove from the heat and using a long-handled spoon, pour 2 to 3 tablespoons of the caramel into 6 ramekins. (Work fast before the caramel cools and sets.) Carefully tilt the ramekins so the bottoms are completely covered with caramel. Set aside.
3. In a bowl, whisk the eggs and egg yolks together until well blended. In a heavy-bottomed saucepan, heat the milk, half-and-half, remaining ½ cup sugar and salt over moderate heat. While stirring continuously, scald the milk until the sugar is dissolved. Remove from the heat and stir in the vanilla.
4. While whisking, gradually add all the hot milk to the eggs. Strain the custard into a bowl and divide it among the ramekins. Place the ramekins in a baking pan filled halfway with hot water. Bake until the tops of the custards are firm around the edges but slightly soft in the center, about 45 minutes. Remove the ramekins from the water bath and chill for at least 4 hours. To unmold the custard, run a knife along the edge of the ramekin and invert onto a dish.

COCONUT STICKY RICE PUDDING WITH TARO

che khoai mon

SERVES 6 TO 8

You can always tell where the dessert vendors sit at the market near my grandmother's house. It's where the schoolchildren congregate, peering excitedly at the big pots of *che*. This dish is typical of those served there. It calls for the sticky rice to be simmered with a root vegetable such as taro or yucca, with legumes such as black beans, red beans or black-eyed peas, or with fresh corn. Except for the corn, all legumes must be boiled before being added to the sticky rice. You can serve this dessert warm or at room temperature.

1. Place the water in a medium pot and bring to a boil. Add the glutinous rice and bring it to a second boil. Reduce the heat to low, then simmer until the rice is almost soft, about 10 minutes.

3½ cups water

⅓ cup glutinous rice (page 228), rinsed

½ pound taro (page 216), peeled, cut into ⅔-inch cubes and rinsed

⅓ cup sugar, or to taste

Pinch salt

1 (14-ounce) can unsweetened coconut milk, preferably Mae Ploy brand, not shaken

1 teaspoon cornstarch

1 tablespoon pandanus juice (page 213) or ½ teaspoon vanilla extract

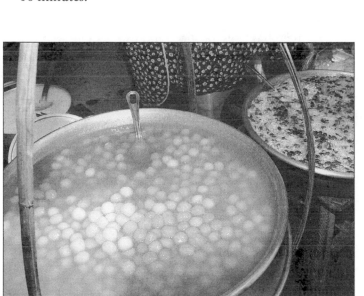

Sweet puddings made with sticky rice and root vegetables

Add the taro, sugar and salt. Cook until the taro is soft but not mushy, about 15 minutes.

2. Scoop off ½ cup of the thick cream from the surface of the coconut milk and place in a small saucepan. Stir in the cornstarch, then bring the sauce to a boil. Remove from the heat and set aside.

3. Add the remaining coconut milk and pandanus juice to the sticky rice and gently stir to blend. The pudding should be slightly thick, and the grains should be soft but still maintain their shape. Transfer the pudding to individual small bowls. Drizzle the coconut cream on top and serve.

Taro Root

Khoai mon, or taro, is used like a potato in Vietnam. It's mashed or shredded and added to soups and spring roll fillings, or sliced and used in simmering dishes. There are two varieties: one is a large brown-skinned tuber about 10 inches long and 5 inches wide, and the other is a shaggy egg-shaped root. The flesh ranges from light cream with flecks to pale lavender. Raw taro root is said to cause itchiness in some people, so you may want to use rubber gloves when handling it.

Taro is also delicious in soups, curries and desserts. It has a creamy texture and a delicate nutty flavor similar to young coconut. The Vietnamese also like to cook with the sponge-like stems of a different kind of taro, one that does not produce a tuber. Called *bac ha*, they add texture to soups and braised dishes.

GRANDMOTHER'S BANANA STEW WITH TAPIOCA PEARLS

chuoi chung

SERVES 6

One of my grandmother's favorites, this recipe has also become a big hit among friends to whom I've introduced it. In Vietnam, this dessert is made with the dwarf banana—a fat, stubby variety commonly used for puddings and cakes. It's starchier and won't collapse into mush when cooked. This modified recipe calls for regular bananas, which are sweeter and more fragrant, although very fragile. The tapioca pearls are available at Asian markets. They're slighter larger than the instant tapioca found at regular supermarkets. For an interesting variation, substitute the bananas with cooked chunks of kabocha squash (page 226).

3 cups water

⅓ cup tapioca pearls
   (¹/16 inch wide)

1 cup unsweetened coconut milk,
   preferably Mae Ploy brand

⅓ cup sugar, or to taste

Pinch salt

3 ripe but firm bananas

2 tablespoons chopped
   Roasted Peanuts (page 35)

1. Bring the water to a rolling boil in a medium saucepan over high heat. Add the tapioca pearls and stir to separate. Reduce the heat to low and simmer until the tapioca becomes translucent, about 20 minutes. Add the coconut milk, sugar and salt and stir well.

2. Five minutes before the end of the cooking time, peel the bananas and cut them in half lengthwise. Cut each piece again into 4 pieces. Add them to the pan and cook until just soft. At this point the tapioca pearls should be clear and cooked.

3. Remove from the heat and transfer to individual dessert bowls. Garnish with the peanuts and serve hot or at room temperature. (The pudding will thicken as it cools.)

FRESH COCONUT ICE CREAM

 kem dua

MAKES 1¼ QUARTS

2 cups unsweetened coconut
   milk

1 tablespoon tapioca starch
   or cornstarch

2 cups half-and-half

⅔ cup sugar

Pinch salt

1 cup freshly grated coconut
   (page 140) or ⅔ cup
   store-bought unsweetened
   coconut flakes, lightly
   toasted in a dry pan

4 tablespoons chopped Roasted
   Peanuts (page 35)

What can be better than finishing off a meal with fresh coconut ice cream? This recipe will be even more memorable if you go to the small trouble of finding a fresh coconut and grating the meat yourself. Fortunately, in recent years, fresh coconuts have become readily available at the supermarkets. When purchasing a coconut, pick out one that is heavy and with "eyes" that are fresh-looking and intact.

1. Combine the coconut milk, tapioca starch and half-and-half in a heavy medium saucepan. Heat over medium heat until the mixture starts to bubble around the edges and reaches 175 degrees. Stir in the sugar and salt. Remove from the heat. Strain through a fine-mesh sieve into a bowl and set aside to cool. Refrigerate overnight or for at least 4 hours.

2. Add the grated coconut to the coconut milk mixture, transfer to an ice-cream maker and freeze according to the manufacturer's instructions. Serve the ice cream in small bowls and garnish with a sprinkling of the peanuts.

LYCHEE SORBET

kem trai vai

MAKES I QUART

If there is one fruit that seems to survive canning, it is the lychee nut. Sweet, juicy and intensely aromatic, it is a beloved fruit in Asia and is enjoyed fresh, canned and dried. Here its fragrant flavors are well captured in the form of a sorbet. The flavor dissipates after a week so it's best to eat it soon after it's made.

5 (20-ounce) cans lychees
   in heavy syrup, drained,
   juice reserved
⅓ cup sugar
2 tablespoons fresh lemon juice

1. Measure ⅓ cup of the lychee syrup and set aside. Drain the lychees. (Save the extra syrup to flavor iced tea or to drink.)
2. Combine the ⅓ cup reserved syrup and sugar in a small saucepan and heat until the sugar dissolves. Remove from the heat and set aside until ready to use.
3. Place the lychees in a fruit blender and process as fine as possible. Add the syrup mixture and lemon juice and process for 1 minute. Strain the mixture through a fine-mesh sieve into a bowl. Using the back of a spoon, mash the fruit to extract as much juice as possible. Cover the lychee mixture and refrigerate for at least 4 hours. Transfer to an ice-cream maker and freeze according to the manufacturer's instructions.

WARM SOY MILK WITH PANDANUS LEAF

 sua dau nanh

MAKES 2 QUARTS

1 pound dried soybeans, soaked
    overnight and drained
2½ quarts water
2 pandanus leaves (page 213),
    folded and tied in a bundle
    and slightly bruised with
    the flat side of a knife, or
    1 teaspoon vanilla extract
3 tablespoons sugar, or to taste

I grew up on soy milk, but never thought of making it fresh until I started going back to Vietnam. There, fresh soy milk is sold at the markets and on street corners early in the morning and late at night. Sometimes I can walk into a market and just sniff my way to a soy milk vendor. I definitely have a nose for *sua dau nanh,* especially if it's been scented with pandanus leaf.

Since my trips to Vietnam, and after reading reports about the health benefits of soybeans, I have been making soy milk on a regular basis. It's a little time-consuming but well worth the effort. The difference between fresh soy milk and the shelf-stable commercial product is like the difference between canned orange juice and freshly squeezed. Although some Asian markets are now carry fresh soy milk, it, too, isn't the same as homemade. Often it's watered down and is too sweet for my taste.

To make this recipe, you can use a blender or food processor. But if you want fresh soy milk on a daily basis as I do, you might want to get a soy extracting machine like the Taiwanese-made "Pineapple," available at well-stocked Asian markets. It extracts and strains the milk, so all you have to do is boil it. To me, nothing is more soothing late at night than a bowl of warm soy milk.

1. Divide the soybeans into 4 batches. Place the first batch in the blender and add about 2 cups water. Process until the soybeans are broken down and the milk is thick and almost smooth, about 10 seconds. Transfer to a large bowl. Repeat with the remaining soybeans and water, taking care to not

overfill the blender. Transfer all the pulverized soybeans and any remaining water to the bowl.

2. Strain the soy milk mixture by pouring it through a fine-mesh sieve into a large pot. Using a spoon or spatula, scrape against the sieve to extract as much water as possible. Discard the solids. Repeat until the soy milk is all strained. Then rinse the sieve, line it with a piece of muslin and strain the soy milk again. Twist the ends of the muslin together and squeeze to extract the liquid. Discard any remaining solids.

3. Place the pot over moderate heat and bring to a slow boil. Add the pandanus leaves and sugar. Stir to prevent the bottom from burning. When the milk starts to bubble, reduce the heat to low and simmer for 10 minutes. Serve the soy milk hot or cold. If you need to store it in the refrigerator, make sure it's completely cool before chilling it. Fresh soy milk should be enjoyed within 2 days.

ICED PANDANUS TEA

nuoc la dua

MAKES ABOUT 10 SERVINGS

This is not a Vietnamese recipe, but it's a drink I grew up with during my childhood years in Thailand and it's too exceptional to be left out. You can serve this straight, as indicated here, or you can use it to flavor regular iced tea. If you're lucky enough to find fresh pandanus, float a few leaves in the pitcher or glass.

1 (4-ounce) packet frozen
   pandanus leaves, chopped
   into 1-inch lengths
10 cups water
½ cup sugar, or to taste
1 quart crushed ice

1. Place the chopped pandanus leaves and 1 cup of the water in a blender. Blend until the leaves are broken down, about 1 minute. (If necessary, add more water.) Transfer to a large bowl and add the remaining water. Strain the liquid through a sieve lined with a double layer of cheesecloth

into a pot. Add the sugar and bring the mixture to a boil. Remove from the heat and chill. To serve, fill a tall glass with ice and pour the pandanus tea over it.

VIETNAMESE COFFEE

 café sua da

SERVES 4

1 cup dark French roast coffee, medium grind
½ cup condensed milk
3 cups boiling water
4 cups ice

In Vietnam, stories abound about coffee roasters who add secret ingredients to their blend—salt, spice, roasted corn, butter and even fish sauce!

To make authentic Vietnamese coffee, use a very dark French roast and brew it in a special individual filter that sits on top of the cup. The slow-drip brewing process is what gives Vietnamese coffee its characteristic flavor. If you don't have a Vietnamese metal coffee filter, use a plastic drip filter, although the flavor—not to mention the ritual—isn't quite the same.

1. Divide the coffee grounds evenly among 4 individual filters. Place the inner screen on the coffee but do not pack it down. Place 2 heaping tablespoons condensed milk in each of the 4 coffee cups. Set the individual filters on top. Pour 2 to 3 tablespoons boiling water into each filter and let the grounds expand for 2 minutes.
2. Fill the filter with boiling water all the way to the rim once. The water should slowly drip through the filter, about 3 to 4 drops at a time. (If it drips much faster than that, the grounds are too large.) The brewing should take 4 to 5 minutes.
3. Fill 4 tall glasses with ice. Stir the coffee well so the condensed milk is dissolved and blended. Pour over the ice and serve with a tall spoon.

Glossary

This glossary highlights common ingredients used in Vietnamese cuisine. Many of the essential items are discussed in greater detail in the previous chapters and are noted here accordingly. Herbs, which the Vietnamese eat in huge quantities, almost as vegetables, are highlighted in a separate section on page 40 in the chapter on Essential Sauces, Condiments and Fragrant Herbs.

Annatto seeds *hot dieu*

In Vietnam, the rust-red seeds of the annatto tree are often used to color soups and stews. The seeds are fried in oil, then allowed to steep. Once the seeds are removed, the oil is used to make the aromatic base of braised or simmered dishes like *thit bo kho* (Beef Stew with Star Anise and Basil, page 155).

Bamboo shoots *mang*

The young shoots of the bamboo tree, they're usually harvested when they're about the size of a fist. The smaller they are, the more tender. (Bamboo shoots are often referred to as the winter or spring shoot, the former being more tender.) To prepare fresh bamboo shoots, cut and discard the tough, hairy outer layers. The inner core should be sliced and boiled for 15 minutes or longer. Canned bamboo shoots are widely available and are sold as whole shoots or tips, or as strips and slices. The latter works well for curries. For stir-fries, I like to buy the whole tips and cut them to the desired shape and thickness. Always blanch canned bamboo shoots to remove any tinny flavor they may have.

Banana blossom, banana flower *bap chuoi*

The deep purple flower of the banana tree is eaten as a vegetable throughout Asia. It's usually sliced thin and soaked in acidic water to prevent it from turning black. Banana blossom is served raw in salads, as in Banana Blossom Salad with Chicken (page 82), although in some recipes the tiny fruits are boiled beforehand.

Banana leaves *la chuoi*

The plastic wrap and aluminum foil of Asia, banana leaves are used to wrap both savory foods and desserts before steaming or grilling. In Thailand, they are used to make little molds, trays and bowls for desserts. In Vietnam, they're used to wrap sausages, sticky rice and desserts, even becoming plates from which to serve sticky rice. The broad center rib is removed and used as a spoon. You can find frozen banana leaves in 1-pound packages. To use, thaw and wipe clean. Do not wash under running water because the leaves tear easily. Remove the rib before wrapping food. For grilling or steaming foods, especially those that are saucy, it's best to use a double thickness.

Bean sauce *tuong*

Made from puréed fermented soybeans, this condiment seasons stir-fries and dipping sauces. In Vietnam, the traditional sauce for *goi cuon* (salad rolls) is made with this condiment blended with sticky rice, coconut milk, chilies and sugar. In the United States, however, hoisin (a mixture of soybeans, salt, sugar, five-spice powder and other spices and additives) has become the standard dipping sauce for salad rolls and for the meat toppings in *pho* (Vietnamese Rice Noodle Soup with Beef, page 47).

Bean threads/cellophane noodles *bun tau*

Also known as glass noodles, these thin, transparent and wiry noodles are made from mung bean starch. They become soft, plump and clear when cooked. They're used in soups, salads, stir-fries and fillings. They should be soaked in water for 30 minutes before using. (For more information, see page 112.)

Bitter melon *hu qua*

This bitter relative of the cucumber is an unusual-looking vegetable, with warty bumps and ridges running from one end to the other. Considered highly nutritious, it is thinly sliced and stir-fried, or stuffed and braised, or added to soups. The seeds and the whitish-to-pinkish skin that surrounds them should be removed as both are quite bitter.

Black mushroom *nam huong kho*

Also known as Chinese black mushrooms or dried shiitake mushrooms, these fungi are prized for their rich, meaty flavor and texture. Available in different grades and prices, the most flavorful are those with deep fissures on the caps. To use, soften in hot water for 30 minutes or longer. Remove and discard the rubbery stems. Black mushrooms can be added to soups, stews, stir-fries and fillings.

Chili paste, ground *tuong ot toi*

Made with coarsely ground (unseeded) red chilies, garlic, and vinegar, this versatile paste is a table condiment as well as a seasoning. The Vietnamese like to add a little dab of it to their *nuoc cham* dipping sauce. It is also an essential flavoring in Vietnamese stir-fries (along with oil and garlic).

Chili sauce, Sriracha sauce *tuong ot*

Similar in appearance to Tabasco, this bright-red fiery sauce is a smooth purée of seeded red chilies, vinegar, garlic and sugar. Packaged in glass or plastic squeeze bottles, it is a favorite condiment for Vietnamese *pho,* used as a dipping sauce for the meat toppings and to season the noodle broth itself. It's also popular as a dipping sauce for seafood and grilled meats.

Chili, Thai bird *ot hiem*

Although commonly referred to as Thai bird chilies, the Vietnamese also love this special variety of fresh chilies. Slender and tiny (about 1 inch long), they're extremely hot and flavorful. They're wonderful when smashed and added to dipping sauces and stir-fries. Thai bird chilies are available fresh, dried, and pickled and may be green or red.

Coconut milk *nuoc dua*

Unsweetened coconut milk is the cream and butter of Southeast Asian cooking. It is made by soaking grated mature coconut flesh with hot water and then squeezing the coconut to extract the liquid. (For information on how to prepare fresh coconut milk, see page 140.) *Nuoc dua* is an important ingredient in curries, soups and desserts. In the United States, the canned products are easily available although fresh coconuts are now also showing up at more supermarkets.

Fermented black beans *tau xi*

Fermented black beans are used in stir-fry dishes of Chinese origin. Also called preserved black beans, these dried loose beans are sold in plastic bags or in paper cartons. You can rinse them briefly to remove some of the salt, or use them as is.

Fermented soybeans *tuong hot*

Made from fermented whole soybeans (not to be confused with fermented *black* beans), this salty condiment is packed in small jars or long-neck bottles and is labeled as salted beans, bean sauce, or sweet bean sauce. All refer to the same product. It is an important seasoning ingredient in many Chinese-style dishes. The Vietnamese use this condiment to season steamed fish and to make dipping sauces such as Vietnamese Bean Dipping Sauce (page 28).

Fish sauce *nuoc mam*

The quintessential seasoning in Vietnamese cooking, fish sauce is used in practically every savory dish and dipping sauce. It is the clear, amber-colored liquid drained from fish fermented in brine. It is pungent but the odor quickly dissipates with cooking. In addition to providing flavor, fish sauce is rich in proteins and vitamins otherwise lacking in the Vietnamese diet. It will last indefinitely. (For more information, see page 24.)

Five-spice powder *ngu vi huong*

Five-spice powder is a traditional Chinese spice blend that can be made with more than five spices. This fragrant brown powder is principally made with star anise and cinnamon and several other ingredients such as Szechuan peppercorns, clove, and fennel. It's often used to season roasted and braised meats, especially chicken and duck.

Galangal *cu rieng*

This knobby rhizome is used in the same way as its cousin, the common ginger. Particularly important in Thai cuisine, it's often sliced and added to soups and used to make curry pastes. In Vietnamese cooking, it shows up only in some northern specialties such as *cha ca Hanoi* (Hanoi Grilled Fish with Rice Noodles and Fresh Herbs, page 127) and in dishes made with dog meat and other exotic meats.

Hoisin sauce *sot hoisin*

A versatile condiment made from soybean purée, sugar, five-spice powder and other spices, this brown sauce is used primarily in dipping sauces, marinades and stir-fries. You can make a particularly delicious dipping sauce by mixing hoisin sauce with onions, garlic, chilies, vinegar, and crushed peanuts. This product is sold in cans or small jars.

Jícama *cu san*

Jícama is used extensively in Vietnam in stir-fries, salads, fillings and soups. It resembles a large turnip and has a delicate taste with a pleasant crunchy texture similar to a water chestnut. Fresh *jícama* is heavy, full of liquid and free of blemishes. To use, peel and cut into the desired shape and size.

Kabocha squash *bi ro*

Also known as Japanese squash, this small (about 8 inches in diameter), squatty pumpkin-shaped vegetable has dark green skin with yellow spots and faint green lines. Its delicious and creamy flesh is used in a variety of recipes, including braised dishes, curries, soups and even desserts.

Lemongrass *xa*

A staple herb in Vietnamese cooking, this woody, fibrous stalk is finely chopped and used to make marinades or left in larger pieces to infuse soups and curries with its wonderful flavor. It imparts a delightful citrusy taste to grilled meats and stir-fries. (See page 43.)

Lily buds *kim cham*

Also known as "golden needles," lily buds are small, thin (imagine a dried bean sprout) and light golden in color. Available in 8-ounce packages, these dried delicacies should be pliable when you buy them, not dark brown and stiff. Soak the buds in warm water for about 30 minutes before using, then tie each into a knot to keep it from fraying while cooking. Lily buds have an interesting earthy flavor that blends perfectly with soy sauce, bamboo shoots and dried black mushrooms.

Long beans *dau dua*

Also known as yard-long beans or chopstick beans, these leggy beans (usually a foot or longer) are delicious in stir-fries, soups, curries and even salads. When buying this legume, look for young, thin pencil-like beans. There are several varieties: dark green, light green, and, in recent years, purple. To use, cut into 2- to 3-inch lengths.

Lotus stems *ngo sen*

In Vietnam, every part of the lotus is used or eaten, including the long stems that connect the main part of the plant to the flowers and leaves. Vietnamese cooks like to peel these stems and add them to soups and salads. In the United States lotus stems are available in jars in brine and are labeled "lotus rootlets." Lotus root can be substituted for lotus stems. (See page 88.)

Luffa squash *muop*

My favorite of the Asian squash family, this sweet, spongy, mild-tasting vegetable is used in stir-fries and soups. Similar to a long cucumber but covered with ridges and dark-green skin, luffa squash is generally harvested when it's about a foot long. To use, peel the skin, slice and cook as you would zucchini.

Mung beans *dau xanh*

The same beans used to grow bean sprouts, mung beans are prized in Vietnamese cooking. Sold husked or unhusked, they generally are soaked in warm water before cooking. Mung beans are used to enrich savory dishes such as Sizzling Saigon Crepes (page 117) and desserts such as puddings and iced drinks.

Pandanus leaf *la dua*

Also known as screw pine, this long, pleated, smooth pointed leaf is the vanilla of Southeast Asia. It appears in many desserts, from puddings and steamed cakes to iced drinks and soy milk. It is often folded and bruised, then steeped in coconut milk or syrup to extract its earthy vanilla aroma. Pandanus is available frozen and occasionally fresh. Substitute banana, jasmine or vanilla extract. (See page 213.)

Papaya, green *du du xanh*

When a recipe calls for this ingredient, it refers to the large green variety sold at Asian markets, not the unripe version of smaller papayas found in supermarkets. In Vietnam, green papaya is shredded and eaten raw in salads with lots of fresh herbs, such as *rau ram,* Vietnamese coriander.

Peanuts *dau phong*

Peanuts are used extensively in Vietnamese cooking, primarily as a garnish. Roasted and chopped, they are used to garnish *bun* and other Vietnamese rice noodle dishes, as well as salads and desserts. Boiled peanuts are also eaten as snacks.

Potato starch *bot khoai*

In Vietnam, potato starch is used as a binder in meatballs, pâtés and *goi lua,* the sausage wrapped in banana leaves that is used in Vietnamese sandwiches. In some instances potato starch is mixed with rice flour batter to make a firmer dough.

Preserved cabbage *cai man*

Preserved cabbage is a popular garnish for soups such as *hu tieu My Tho* and noodle dishes of Chinese origin. Often labeled as "Tianjin preserved vegetables," it is sold in squatty crocks or in plastic jars. Preserved cabbage is very salty, so use it sparingly.

Rice *gao thom*

The Vietnamese prefer the long-grain jasmine rice, which is eaten at almost every meal unless a noodle soup is served. Rice should be washed until the water runs clear. Although each batch is different, the standard ratio of 1 part rice to 1½ parts water should yield a good pot of rice. (See page 136 for how to cook perfect rice.)

Rice flour *bot gao*

Made from rice, this starch figures prominently in Vietnamese cooking. Most dumplings, cakes and noodles are made from rice flour. When purchasing this product, do not confuse it with glutinous rice flour (sweet rice flour), which is very different. For recipes in this book, use the Thai rice flour sold in 1-pound bags at Asian markets.

Rice noodles

Rice noodles are a staple food in Vietnamese cuisine. The most commonly used noodles are *banh pho* (rice sticks), *bun* (rice vermicelli) and *banh hoi* (tiny sheets of woven noodles). Rice noodles are more fragile than pasta and generally require less cooking time. (See page 112.)

Rice papers, dried *banh trang*

Another staple in the Vietnamese kitchen, these dried, transparent, rice-flour sheets are used to wrap *cha gio,* or spring rolls, and *goi cuon,* or salad rolls. They are available in several shapes (round, triangular and square) and sizes. Rice paper should be soaked in hot water until it softens and becomes pliable, about 10 seconds, before being used. (See page 97.)

Rock sugar/rock candy *duong phen*

Also known as lump sugar, rock sugar is a solidified mixture of refined and unrefined cane sugar and honey. The Vietnamese prefer this sugar in *pho* and in other savory dishes in which a touch of sweetness is desired. Rock sugar is also believed to keep meats firm and shiny.

Sesame seeds *hot me*

Hulled white sesame seeds are used extensively in Vietnamese sweets. They are often toasted and sprinkled on banana stews and puddings with coconut sauce. Mixed with roasted peanuts and salt, they are a common topping for steamed sticky rice.

Shrimp, dried *tom kho*

Dried shrimp are used much like dried fish, to flavor stocks, stews and stir-fries. They are available in different sizes, with the larger ones being more expensive. High-quality dried shrimp are pink and should yield slightly to the touch. Do not buy those that are rock hard. Pungent and salty, dried shrimp are used in small amounts. Vietnamese cooks like to add them to salad rolls or pound them into a paste for seasoning dumpling soups.

Shrimp paste, shrimp sauce *ruoc*

This pungent paste is made from fermented shrimp and salt. Sold in jars, tubs and dried cakes, shrimp paste keeps indefinitely, like fish sauce. In Thailand, a similar but firmer product (Kapi) is used in curry pastes and dipping sauces. The Vietnamese equivalent is wet and sold as shrimp sauce. It is also used to add savoriness to noodle broths and to make dipping sauces.

Spring roll wrappers *banh trang bot mi*

Made from wheat flour, these wrappers are often used for wrapping *cha gio.* Although not quite as tasty as rice paper, these wrappers are easier to use and cook up golden and crisp.

Available in 8-inch squares, they can be found in the frozen foods section of Asian markets. Before use, they're first thawed and separated into single sheets.

Squid, dried *muc kho*

In Asia, dried squid is appreciated both for its intensely fishy flavor and for its chewy texture. At the beaches in Vietnam, dried squid is roasted over hot coals, and then run though a hand-cranked press. The teeth of the press flatten the squid, tenderizing it at the same time. To eat, one tears off a piece and dips it into *tuong ot,* or Sriracha-style chili sauce. Besides eating it as a snack, dried squid can be reconstituted and used in stir-fry dishes and seafood soups. To flavor stocks for noodle soups, lightly toast the squid in a dry skillet and add to the pot. Sometimes labeled as dried cuttlefish, dried squid is packaged in plastic bags. Once opened, the bag should be sealed tightly so the strong odor doesn't overwhelm the pantry.

Star anise *hoi*

This beautiful eight-pointed spice pod lends a sweet licorice flavor to stews and soups, such as *pho.* It's best to add star anise towards the end of the cooking time as the wonderful aroma subsides with prolonged simmering.

Starfruit *khe*

Also called carambola, this star-shaped fruit is juicy and reminiscent of Asian pear with floral undertones. In Vietnam, ripe ones are eaten as snacks and the sour green fruits are sliced thin and used in table salads. Starfruit is a tasty accompaniment to grilled meats.

Straw mushrooms *nam rom*

Small and with oval caps, these mild-tasting, grayish-black mushrooms are preferred in Vietnamese cooking. Because they're harvested before the caps are open, the Vietnamese also call them *nam bup,* or bulb mushrooms. Outside of Asia, they are available canned.

Sugarcane *mia*

In Vietnam, sugarcane is often peeled and cut into 1-inch rounds, then skewered on a bundle of bamboo sticks. To enjoy, one pulls off a piece and chews it until all the juice is sucked out. The very fibrous and stringy meat is then discarded. Another way of using sugarcane is as a skewer onto which shrimp paste is molded and then grilled, as in Grilled Shrimp on Sugarcane (page 125). The sugarcane imparts a sweet, delicate flavor to the shrimp. Sugarcane may be pressed to make sugarcane juice or it may be refined into sugar. In this country, sugarcane is available canned and sometimes fresh. For skewers, the canned product works well.

Tamarind *me*

Tamarind is the sour-tasting pod of the tamarind tree. The pods are originally green but eventually turn dark brown. The pulp inside, which is similar to dried prunes in color and texture, is used to flavor soups and salads. In the West, tamarind pulp is packaged in compressed blocks. To use, soften the pulp in warm water for about 20 minutes, then push through a sieve. Occasionally you may be able to find fresh tamarind pods at Asian markets.

Tapioca *bot ban*

Made from the cassava root, tapioca is used as a thickener in desserts such as Grandmother's Banana Stew with Tapioca Pearls (page 217). In Asia, this product is usually referred to as tapioca pearls and generally comes in two sizes—small (about 1/16-inch pellets) or the larger pearl-like size. Tapioca strands or noodles must be soaked in water for 30 minutes before using, but the small pearls can be added directly to boiling water.

Tapioca starch *bot nang*

Made from the pulverized cassava root, this starch is used to make desserts and dumplings. When used in combination with other flours, it enhances the pliability and chewiness of the dough.

Taro *khoai mon*

Taro is used much like potato. It is a starchy root, with a creamy texture and a sweet, nutty flavor. The two common varieties are the large barrel-shaped tubers with cream-colored flesh and pink fibers, and the smaller egg-shaped tubers with purplish flesh. The larger variety is firmer; the smaller one is softer, creamier and more flavorful. In Vietnam and Thailand taro is used in soups and desserts. Some varieties will discolor after peeling so it's best to submerge the root in water if not used immediately.

Taro stems *bac ha*

In Vietnam, the stem of a variety of taro called *Colocasia gigantea* is used in soups. It looks identical to the stem of the regular taro—long, thick and sponge-like. Taro stems are often sold in long stalks, about 12 to 20 inches long. To use, peel the skin (as you would rhubarb) and cut on the diagonal into thin slices. It doesn't have any flavor, but is appreciated for its sponge-like sauce-absorbing feature.

Toasted rice powder *thinh*

Toasted rice is used to give gritty texture to dishes such as *bi*, shredded pork, and helps bind meats such as those used in sausages. *Thinh* is made by soaking rice in water, toasting, then grinding it into a powder. Either regular or glutinous rice can be used, but the latter will produce a coarser powder. You can also buy *thinh* in small plastic bags at Asian markets.

Tofu *dau hu*

Also known as bean curd, tofu is made by combining soybean milk and a coagulant such as gypsum powder. The curds are pressed together to form cakes. Tofu is delicate tasting, but it can absorb flavors and spices quite well, as in the Spicy Lemongrass Tofu (page 193). (See also page 188.)

Turmeric *bot nghe*

Ground turmeric is used extensively in Vietnamese cooking, for both flavor and color. It's a common ingredient in marinades and in rice-flour batters. In its fresh form, turmeric is like ginger, a knobby root with small fingers. It has dark-brown skin with ring-like markings. The flesh is bright orange, and when added to curries, soups, stews or rice dishes, it turns them brilliant yellow.

Vietnamese coffee *café phe sua*

A distinctively Vietnamese-French beverage, this thick, strong coffee drink is made by brewing French dark roast coffee through an individual filter. It is served with condensed milk and can be enjoyed hot or with crushed ice. See page 222. The special filters are available at Asian markets. If you can't find them, use a regular plastic filter but follow the directions carefully for Vietnamese coffee.

Water spinach *rau muong*

Also called swamp cabbage or morning glory, this leafy green vegetable has crunchy hollow stems and arrowhead-shaped leaves. In Asia, it is generally grown in swamps and ponds. The Vietnamese like to make "curls" out of the stems to use in salads and soups. *Rau muong* is used in simple stir-fries with garlic.

Wood-ear mushrooms *nam meo*

Also known as cloud ear and tree-ear mushrooms, these dried fungi don't have much flavor but are prized for their crunchy and slightly gelatinous texture. Once soaked in water, wood-ear mushrooms swell to many times their original size and become frilly clumps of rubbery tissue similar to seaweed. The two-toned larger mushrooms (black on top and tan on the bottom) can be tough and need to be sliced before using. The small black variety is better because it's tender yet still crunchy. Rinse these fungi well as they can be gritty. In Vietnam, these mushrooms are used in spring roll stuffings and in many vegetarian dishes.

Menu Suggestions

With the exception of the dinner-party menu, the following menu suggestions are designed to capture the essential spirit of *Pleasures of the Vietnamese Table:* good, wholesome Vietnamese foods served in a casual manner. These are only suggestions, so feel free to mix, match and improvise. For beverages, try serving beer, iced tea, iced pandanus tea, or water scented with sprigs of mint or lemon balm. For wine, try Viognier, Riesling, Rousanne, Gewürztraminer and Pinot Gris.

CELEBRATING PHO

Rice Paper–Wrapped Salad Rolls with Shrimp and Pork
Vietnamese Beef Noodle Soup
Iced Red Bean Pudding with Coconut Milk or
    Vietnamese Coffee

NOODLES WITH FRIENDS

Grilled Shrimp on Sugarcane
Hanoi Noodles with Grilled Pork or
    Lemongass Beef on Cool Noodles
Iced Pandanus Tea

FUN STREET FOOD FARE

Crispy Spring Rolls
Rice Rolls with Shrimp and Wood-Ear Mushrooms or Sizzling Saigon Crepes
Grandmother's Banana Stew with Tapioca Pearls

A VEGETARIAN FEAST

Salad Rolls with Jícama, Peanuts and Basil
Spicy Lemongrass Tofu
Claypot Rice with Ginger and Five Spices
Chopstick Beans with Garlic
Warm Soy Milk with Pandanus Leaf

A HOME-STYLE DINNER

Aunt Tam's Pork in Claypot
Sweet and Sour Shrimp Soup with Fresh Herbs
Table Salad
Shaking Beef
Roasted Eggplant with Scallion Oil
Steamed Rice

LOVING CRAB

Salt-and-Pepper Crab with Ginger
Chopsticks Beans with Garlic
Cucumber Salad
Steamed Rice
Lychee Sorbet

A VIETNAMESE DINNER PARTY

Mustard Leaf–Wrapped Salad Rolls
Banana Blossom Salad with Chicken
Sea Bass with Lily Buds, Mushrooms and Cellophane Noodles
Caramelized Garlic Shrimp
Water Spinach with Tofu
Steamed Rice
Crème Caramel or Fresh Fruit

Resources for Vietnamese Ingredients

Many of the ingredients in this book can be found at Asian markets, farmers markets, and the international sections of many supermarkets. If you don't live in an area where these items can be purchased, try the following mail-order sources.

For Dried and Canned Foods and Spices

Oriental Pantry
423 Great Road
Acton, MA 01720
(800) 828-0368
www.orientalpantry.com

Uwajima
519 Sixth Avenue South
Seattle, WA 98104
(800) 889-1928

La Cuisine
323 Cameron Street
Alexandria, VA 22314
(800) 521-1176

Bangkok Market
4804-6 Melrose Avenue
Los Angeles, CA 90029
(213) 264-4898

Melissa's World Variety Produce, Inc.
P.O. Box 21127
Los Angeles, CA 90021
(800) 588-0151
www.melissas.com

For soup bowls and other Asian tablewares

Utsuwa-No-Yakata
96 Linwood Plaza #358
Fort Lee, NJ 07024
(800) 269-5099
www.utsuwa.com

For Seeds and Seedlings

Nichols Garden Nursery
190 North Pacific Highway
Albany, OR 97321
(503) 928-9280
www.gardennursery.com

The Cook's Garden
P.O. Box 535
Londonderry, VT 05148
(802) 824-3400

Sandy Mush Herbs Nursery
316 Surrett Cove Road
Leicester, NC 28748
(704) 683-2014
(Can ship live lemongrass, rau ram and
other herbs.)

Lazy Susan Ranch
P.O. Box 1152
Calistoga, CA 94515
(707) 942-0120
www.lazysusanranch.com
(Specializes in supplying restaurants and gro-
cers; Web site has good information and pic-
tures of Vietnamese herbs as well as other
herbs.)

Richters Herbs
Goodwood, Ontario
L0C 1A0, Canada
(905) 640-6677
www.richters.com
(Carries extensive selection of seeds and
plants; Web site has solid information with
interesting stories and lectures.)

Index